The Vigilante Thriller

The Vigilante Thriller

Violence, Spectatorship and Identification in American Cinema, 1970–76

Cary Edwards

BLOOMSBURY ACADEMIC
NEW YORK • LONDON • OXFORD • NEW DELHI • SYDNEY

BLOOMSBURY ACADEMIC
Bloomsbury Publishing Inc
1385 Broadway, New York, NY 10018, USA
50 Bedford Square, London, WC1B 3DP, UK
29 Earlsfort Terrace, Dublin 2, Ireland

BLOOMSBURY, BLOOMSBURY ACADEMIC and the Diana logo are trademarks of Bloomsbury Publishing Plc

First published in the United States of America 2022
Paperback edition published 2024

Copyright © Cary Edwards, 2022

For legal purposes the Acknowledgements on p. viii constitute an extension of this copyright page.

Cover design: Eleanor Rose
Cover image: Clint Eastwood in *Dirty Harry*, 1971, Dir. Don Siegel © Collection Christophel / ArenaPAL www.arenapal.com

All rights reserved. No part of this publication may be reproduced or transmitted in any form or by any means, electronic or mechanical, including photocopying, recording, or any information storage or retrieval system, without prior permission in writing from the publishers.

Bloomsbury Publishing Inc does not have any control over, or responsibility for, any third-party websites referred to or in this book. All internet addresses given in this book were correct at the time of going to press. The author and publisher regret any inconvenience caused if addresses have changed or sites have ceased to exist, but can accept no responsibility for any such changes.

Library of Congress Cataloging-in-Publication Data
Names: Edwards, Cary, author.
Title: The vigilante thriller : violence, spectatorship and identification in American cinema, 1970-76 / Cary Edwards.
Description: New York : Bloomsbury Academic, 2022. | Includes bibliographical references and index. | Summary: "A critical analysis of the depiction of vigilantism in 1970s American cinema"– Provided by publisher.
Identifiers: LCCN 2021048051 (print) | LCCN 2021048052 (ebook) | ISBN 9781501364129 (hardback) | ISBN 9781501364112 (epub) | ISBN 9781501364105 (pdf)
Subjects: LCSH: Vigilantes in motion pictures. | Motion pictures–United States–History–20th century.
Classification: LCC PN1995.9.V464 E39 2022 (print) | LCC PN1995.9.V464 (ebook) | DDC 791.43/6556–dc23
LC record available at https://lccn.loc.gov/2021048051
LC ebook record available at https://lccn.loc.gov/2021048052

ISBN: HB: 978-1-5013-6412-9
PB: 978-1-5013-9173-6
ePDF: 978-1-5013-6410-5
ebook: 978-1-5013-6411-2

Typeset by Deanta Global Publishing Services, Chennai, India

To find out more about our authors and books visit www.bloomsbury.com and sign up for our newsletters.

CONTENTS

List of illustrations vi
Acknowledgements viii

Introduction 1

PART ONE The historical spectator and the Vigilante Thriller 25

1 Narrative images and critical reactions 29

2 Sociopolitical contexts 53

3 Cinematic contexts 73

PART TWO Spectatorship 121

4 Violence 127

5 Establishing the gaze and identification 154

6 Functions of the gaze and identification 163

7 Neurosis, hysteria and psychopathy 189

8 Violence, identification and the other 199

Conclusion 205

Appendix 217
Filmography 218
Bibliography 222
Index 233

ILLUSTRATIONS

Figures

1. Tzvetan Todorov's Narrative Model 119
2. Travis Bickle spectates in *Taxi Driver* (1976) 121
3. Bill Compton kills Frank: overt technique used in the murder of Frank in *Joe* (1970) 134
4. Scorpio aims at an unknown woman and the spectator in *Dirty Harry* (1971) 143
5. Scorpio's gaze in *Dirty Harry* (1971) 143
6. Bickle's selection of guns at the shooting range in *Taxi Driver* (1976) 151
7. Melissa's status as target and source of conflict/confusion is signalled in the title sequence in which she appears in the centre of the O/target in *Joe* (1970) 155
8. Melissa and dolly in *Joe* (1970) 156
9. Joe passively stares at the screen (watching a Western) in *Joe* (1970) 164
10. A privileged view of Amy in *Straw Dogs* (1971) 168
11. An act of provocation or defiance or both? *Straw Dogs* (1971) 168
12. David's gaze from inside the farmhouse, in *Straw Dogs* (1971) 170
13. David squints as he looks through the farmhouse window, signalling his poor gaze, in *Straw Dogs* (1971) 171
14. David undresses, seen from Janice and Bobby's point of view, in *Straw Dogs* (1971) 172
15. Doyle gazes in *The French Connection* (1971) 176
16. While Charnier and Nicoli dine, Doyle stands in the background of *The French Connection* (1971) 177
17. Charnier uses the mirror – he controls the gaze, in *The French Connection* (1971) 177
18. Charnier waves at Doyle, and us, expressing his power and manipulation of the gaze in *The French Connection* (1971) 178
19. Callahan spies on 'Hot' Mary in *Dirty Harry* (1971) 180
20. Callahan's point of view takes the scopic gaze during *Dirty Harry* (1971) 181

21 A powerless Paul Kersey observes the hospital in *Death Wish* (1974) 183
22 Kersey watches TV resting in a passive pose in *Death Wish* (1974) 184
23 Becoming active Kersey look out of his window in *Death Wish* (1974) 184
24 Kersey admires the Wild West show in Tucson in *Death Wish* (1974) 185
25 Kersey's powerful gaze in *Death Wish* (1974) 186
26 Scorsese, in the background as an extra, gazes at Betsy, in *Taxi Driver* (1976) 187

Tables

1 Oppositions in the Western 102
2 Variations on Western Narratives 109
3 Violence Lists 130
4 Box-Office Figures for the Vigilante Thrillers 217

ACKNOWLEDGEMENTS

Thanks first to Dr Nigel Morris, Dr Neil Jackson and Professor Ann Gray. Without their guidance, particularly that of Nigel, one doubts whether these ideas would ever have coalesced. Thanks also to Professor Paul Cobley, Professor Sarah Barrow and Dr Gregory Frame for essential feedback. Elements of the research for this book have previously formed the basis for a paper delivered at London Film and Media 2011, later published as 'The Narrative Image and Critical Reception of the 1970s Vigilante Thriller' in *The London Film & Media Reader 1* (2013). Another paper, 'Formal Radicalism vs Radical Representation in *The French Connection* (William Friedkin, 1971) and *Dirty Harry* (Don Siegel, 1971)', delivered at the American New Wave: A Retrospective at Bangor University, July 2017, has been adapted into a chapter with the same name in *New Wave, New Hollywood: Reassessment, Recovery and Legacy* (2021) edited by Professor Nathan Abrams and Dr Gregory Frame. Thanks too to Katie Gallof and Erin Duffy at Bloomsbury for answering my, no doubt, obvious questions.

Thanks as well to my wife and daughter, for giving me the space and time to tilt at windmills.

Introduction

18 December 1970:

> Arville Garland of Detroit – dubbed the 'real-life Joe' after the movie *Joe* was released – was sentenced to one count of manslaughter and three counts of second-degree murder for the murder of his daughter and three friends in their 'student-hippie' residence on May 8, 1970. *Time* magazine reported, 'Garland has received hundreds of letters of support. Said one California father of a teenage girl: "There must surely be many among us who have done in our hearts what you have done with your hands. To have those to whom we have opened our hearts and treasures say, 'Your truth is not truth, your values are without value' can be beyond bearing."' Other messages were simply congratulatory. One came with a twenty-dollar bill. None contained any criticism of the killings. (Thomas 2014: 289)

Two months after Arville Garland murdered his daughter and her friends, *Joe* was released in US cinemas. Directed by a then unknown John G. Avildsen, the film follows two men, working-class Joe Curran (Peter Boyle) and middle-class Bill Compton (Dennis Patrick), who develop an unorthodox relationship after Joe realizes that Bill has done what he can only dream of: murder a hippy. At the film's bloody denouement, Joe and Bill enter a hippy commune and, in a moment that releases Joe's pent-up anger and rage, kill those they find. In the final moments Bill shoots his own daughter Melissa (Susan Sarandon) in the back. Director Avildsen and screenwriter Norman Wexler had clearly hit on something that chimed with American audiences as the film became a surprise box-office hit and created the careers of Avildsen and Boyle. The voice of working-class Joe Curran, one filled with bile and hatred for a world changing around him, rang out clearly. His racist, homophobic and anti-youth rants were even released on a tie-in LP. Some of the audience cheered him on, while others yelled back at the screen, 'Next time we're going to shoot back, Joe' (Lev 2000: 25).

Such was the film's notoriety that during Garland's trial the judge, Joseph A. Gillis, instructed both the prosecution and defence to watch the film and carefully screened the jury to ensure they hadn't, worried of the effect it might have (*Time* 7 December 1970). When Joe Curran pronounced, 'These kids they shit on you, they shit on your life, they shit on everything you believe in, they shit on everything!', he evoked the letter quoted in *Time*, 'Your truth is not truth.' The contemporary upheaval in American society had opened clear divides;[1] it seemed as if there was one side that cheered Joe Curran on and another side deploring the film as an incitement to fascism and violence. The Vigilante Thriller was born out of these ideological confusions.

The six films of this study – *Joe*, *The French Connection* (William Friedkin, 1971), *Dirty Harry* (Don Siegel, 1971), *Straw Dogs* (Sam Peckinpah, 1971), *Death Wish* (Michael Winner, 1974) and *Taxi Driver* (Martin Scorsese, 1976) – became a focus for contemporary critics who often grouped the films together, as did later analyses, suggesting they were part of a 'right cycle' movement of films during the 1970s (perceived as appealing to a more traditional, older and right-wing audience, rather than the youth audience engaged by counterculture, left-wing, films). This binary split lends the films an ongoing sense of cultural significance particularly given the increasingly divided, and divisive, political developments of our own times. Perhaps due to their continued ability to alarm in their depiction of controversial topics they are often dismissed out of hand as right-wing texts, supposedly appealing to the audience's baser instincts. This denies, however, the films' complexities and the complexity of the spectatorship process. It also over-simplifies two central and important questions: Why did this type of film appear during the early to mid-1970s, and why were they so controversial with critics but successful with audiences? This work is also a response to two more questions inspired by the contemporary reactions: Why and how do we watch violent films? The presumption of a right-wing subject position ignores the multiple interpretations offered by these texts and follows simplistic assumptions that continue to be made when film violence and its political meanings are considered. The films examined here may be part of a greater movement towards a more explicit depiction of violence in American cinema during the New Hollywood period, but they also are a unique cycle that asks problematic questions in key areas of American identity: masculinity, violence, law and order, and justice. That these films were critically received with a mixture of alarm and opprobrium is indicative of the problems that the films, and this work, explore.

As a cycle the Vigilante Thriller started and reached its apotheosis in the 1970s. The cycle experienced high box office from its inception in 1970 with *Joe*, reaching a critical high point with *Taxi Driver*. The six films had a cumulative North American box office of over $160 million,

---

[1] Initially *Joe* was titled *The Gap*, only for the jeans company to get there first forcing a title change.

a sizeable impact, and helped cement the status of their lead actors. Other releases in this period with similar themes, and varying box-office success, include *Walking Tall* (Phil Karlson, 1973), *Billy Jack* (Tom Laughlin, 1971) and *Vigilante Force* (George Armitage, 1976) but were generally excluded from the mainstream critical discourse of the time and so are not a part of this study. However, they do attest to the growth of a cinema explicitly dealing with vigilantism. Later films that would imitate elements of the original cycle included *Rolling Thunder* (John Flynn 1977) (scripted by Paul Schrader, writer of *Taxi Driver*), *The Exterminator* (James Glickenhaus, 1980) and its 1984 sequel, *Ms .45* (Abel Ferrara, 1981) a variation with a female protagonist, and *The Star Chamber* (Peter Hyams, 1983). Each enjoyed varying levels of theatrical release and home video success, but none matched the impact of the films in this study. The fortunes of the *Death Wish* franchise illustrate a general decline in the significance and quality of the genre; beginning in 1974 with a domestic box office of $22 million, declining markedly to the final film, *Death Wish V: The Face of Death* (Allan A. Goldstein, 1994), which earned just $1,702,394. More recently, films such as *The Brave One* (Neil Jordan, 2007), starring Jodie Foster, *Law Abiding Citizen* (F. Gary Gray, 2009), *Prisoners* (Denis Villeneuve, 2013), *The Equalizer* (Antoine Fuqua, 2014) and *The Equalizer 2* (Antoine Fuqua, 2018) have been compared to the original cycle and have achieved varying levels of box-office success. A loose remake of *Death Wish* (Eli Roth) was released to minimal critical and commercial interest in 2018. None of these films has achieved the cultural significance of the original cycle.

The films considered in this work emerged as a cycle from research around their themes, context and associations made by critics (both contemporary to the films and more recent). They have in common several elements that mark them apart from other films that foreground similar issues. All are in a modern setting but deal with a clash of cultural values through protagonists whose behaviour may have seemed reasonable to a previous generation but by the 1970s had become controversial, if not outright offensive. All concern issues of law and order and justice, with characters who move outside the law to achieve their goals. All were connected by critics to a supposed decline in moral values and a shift to the political right, the decline of urban society and the role and nature of the white male in American society. Filmed at a time of great social change, these texts express and explore a contemporary anxiety – what was right and wrong in 1970s America?

Cinema is indelibly marked by its context, and so to understand these films, this study examines some of the key changes in American society that occurred during the 1960s and 1970s. In parallel to the great social changes were the concurrent, and directly related, changes in Hollywood as the last vestiges of the Studio System gave way to a new era. As Robin Wood explains,

> Although Classical Hollywood had already been dealt a series of death-blows, it might have taken a much longer time dying had it not been for the major eruptions in American culture from the mid-60s and into the 70s: overwhelmingly, of course, Vietnam but subsequently Watergate, and part counterpoint, part consequence, the growing force and cogency of racial protest and liberation movements – black militancy, feminism, gay liberation. (2003: 44)

These changes were affecting American cinema, and consequently American audiences, in profound ways. One of the most evident shifts was in censorship as the Motion Picture Production Code, long out of step with non-American cinema and what Americans could watch on TV, was finally abandoned. A new set of regulations based on age certification would be imposed in 1968 (with changes throughout the 1970s). These shifting goalposts allowed film-makers to explore ideas and themes long prohibited in mainstream Hollywood and present violence on screen in new, more explicit, ways.

As American society experienced these ideological upheavals, a new generation of film-makers, who were conversant with both domestic and international filmmaking practices, emerged freed from the confines of traditional Hollywood morality and filmmaking.[2] Significantly, however, the films of this study include filmmakers who had worked in the Old Hollywood environment, outsiders to Hollywood and those that rose to prominence as part of the Hollywood New Wave; Don Siegel's career started in the Warner Brothers Film Library in the 1930s (Siegel 1993: 36), Avidlsen got his start directing sexploitation pictures in the late 1960s (Powell and Garrett 2009: 10) and Martin Scorsese was part of the 'The Movie Brats' generation. This spread of film-makers suggests the universality of the themes with which the films deal.

It was also true that during this time the currency and power of film critics had increased, their tastes illustrating the wider generational changes, as discussed by Raymond J. Haberski Jr. in *'It's Only a Movie': Films and Critics in American Culture* (2001). Nowhere is this better illustrated than in the differing reactions to Bosley Crowther and Pauline Kael's reviews of *Bonnie and Clyde* (Arthur Penn, 1967). Crowther's condemnation of the film, in *The New York Times*, signalled the end of an illustrious career, whereas Kael's support for the film (which helped it achieve a re-release and box-office success) started her journey towards being America's pre-eminent film critic. Even just a cursory glance at the reviews of the Vigilante Thrillers shows how controversial they were with critics clearly alarmed at their supposed politics and their possible effects on the audience. When reviewing

---

[2]During the 1960s, due to a short fall in domestic production, there was a marked increase in the distribution of international films.

Straw Dogs Kael went so far as to dub it 'the first American film that is a fascist work of art' (1973: 393), and Kael was just one of many influential critics who worried about the impact of these films. The relationship between films, critics and audiences is complex and is explored in this work to build a full picture of the context in which the audience received the films. The wider social anxiety concerning crime and the critics' worry about the effect these films may have had on the audience – that they were a call to action – was part of a wider moral panic concerning the significant rise in crime in America during the 1960s and 1970s, specifically the rise in mugging rates. Nixon's election campaign in 1968 was partly run on a 'law and order' platform appealing to the 'silent majority' of Americans not caught up in the positive whirlwind of social reform. This aspect of culture, a form of Urban Paranoia, has helped define which films make a part of the study as much as the importance of the critical reaction. The contemplation of the meanings of urban life and its implied opposition to rural life are essential to this cycle, even in *Straw Dogs* which is set in rural Cornwall. In this film the nature of the urban environment is evoked and symbolized by David Sumner (Dustin Hoffman), a character trying to escape from the violence of the city, only to find it inescapable.

Among the many critical voices, connections between the Vigilante Thriller and the Western were made time and again, and this element is fully explored to establish and understand such links and to understand out of which traditions the Vigilante Thriller emerged. By the late 1960s the Western was fading from Hollywood (despite a brief revival sparked in Italy), with only some star vehicles (for Clint Eastwood and John Wayne) and revisionist films holding much sway at the box office. The mythology of the West had held a unique and vitally important place in the development of American culture, and the values expressed in the genre underpinned many of the ideological positions taken by its politicians and citizens. The decline in popularity and production of the Western signalled that the genre was no longer able to support the myths and structures of American culture in the way it had previously, tying to a more general decline in the significance of grand narratives and their organizing symbolism.[3] This decline left an ideological space into which the Vigilante Thriller stepped. Vigilante Thrillers are not, however, as some have suggested, simply relocated Westerns; the films explore the ideological positions of the Western but come to differing conclusions and representations. This is achieved through a conscious engagement with the

---

[3]Several exploitation films, such as *The Legend of Nigger Charley* (Martin Gold, 1972), offered a different examination of race in a Western context, as did the mainstream success of *Blazing Saddles* (Mel Brooks, 1974), a comedy that used humour to confront the racist undertones of the genre.

codes of the Western, codes well known to the audience, but also through the adoption and development of elements of the Thriller and the Horror genres.

Establishing a context for understanding the films and their audiences leads then to analysis of the films. It is the main purpose of this work to investigate the films from specific angles drawn from the contemporary anxieties expressed by the critics. Partly this is to test the validity of the critical responses, but also it is to open the texts and examine alternative readings and responses. Analysis using theories of spectatorship are made, with a specific emphasis on patterns of neuroses, hysteria and psychopathy (after Fuery 2004). This complicates textual understanding, relates directly to the films' protagonists and their relationship to society, and queries simplistic assumptions about identification.

The political position of the films is also considered, evaluating the possibility that they espouse fascist ideas or sympathies. The use of 'fascist' is problematic, irrespective of its application to the films. Its use is inconsistent between critics and relates directly to the ideological struggles of the times.

The final key element of this work is the concept of otherness. The othering process originates, psychologically, with the self. During this period of American history, the normative idea of the self was changing. A clear dramatization of this can be seen in a film which precedes and anticipates the Vigilante Thriller, *In the Heat of the Night* (Norman Jewison, 1967). In this film a Black, urban detective, Virgil Tibbs (Sidney Poitier), investigates a murder in a small southern town. The traditional opposition of white as normal and Black as other is consciously subverted in this film in which Tibbs is shown to be a highly moral and sophisticated figure as opposed to the ignorant, racist townspeople. Caught in the middle of this conflict is the local white police chief, Bill Gillespie (Rod Steiger), who is presented with a choice to adjust and work with Tibbs or to reject him and support the status quo (with all its inherent injustices). Gillespie's dilemma was faced by many Americans during this period – whether to adjust to a new order or to refuse it and risk becoming the alienated other. This sense of self and other becomes essential to understanding the Vigilante Thriller as they are films in which oppositions are consciously blurred, to the point that self and other become closely correlated and, in *Taxi Driver*, indistinguishable. This then impacts on ideas of identity and narrative and how the subject creates themself.

The structure of this work follows a progression that first establishes context, and then examines textual form, before moving onto theories of spectatorship and otherness. This establishes the Vigilante Thriller as a unique cycle in American cinema that dramatizes the ideological shifts in American society in which the nature of the other was being reconceptualized to reflect that which had previously been seen as the self. This dichotomy is not resolved by the films (that would happen elsewhere), but the spectator was invited to engage with the ideological shifts while simultaneously gaining pleasure from recurrent tropes and codes from the Western and other genres and engaging with many of the contemporary anxieties associated with a changing culture.

Part One of this work explores the contextual factors that informed the spectator's viewing of the films. This includes a detailed exploration of their marketing to establish the films' narrative images, to better understand how the spectator was addressed prior to entering the cinema. This continues into an analysis of the critical reactions from both the United States and the United Kingdom to gain a picture of how contemporary critics viewed the films and to explore which issues they found controversial and how this was established. Following this, an overview of the social/political context is given (with particular emphasis on law and order) and of the cinematic context in which the films were made, including discussion of the influence of the Thriller and Western genres and how genres were being transformed during the period. A formalist analysis is used to explore narrative structures and oppositions to aid understanding of the changes and developments from the Western, including their ideological similarities and divergences.

In Part Two the spectator and the process of identification become the focus. This section discusses theories of spectatorship but also examines the representation of violence and crime, giving a deeper interrogation of the issues first raised by the reviews and critiques of the films. This is then linked to ideas concerning representations of madness and how this affects identification. The concept of modality is also raised in exploring how the spectator's understanding of a text varies depending on their understanding, position and context. Otherness and the ideological crisis that the films dramatize are discussed, delineating how previous oppositions could no longer hold, and how the Vigilante Thriller wrestles with the contradictions and problems raised by a shifting society. Finally, there is a return to the political positions of the films, revisiting the question of fascism and ideological content. The developments surrounding violence in film (from a theoretical standpoint) are reviewed, as is the concept of moral panic and how culture interacts with difficult and controversial developments. Fascism as a concept has specific meanings that have shifted over time depending on where and when it has evolved, with its use in rhetoric adopted by both the right and left of American politics. Sociologist Eugen Weber discusses how Nationalism underpins fascism, defining Nationalism as using 'intellectual arguments based on . . . ideas like tradition, history, language and race; it argues a wider community and a common destiny which are not immediately perceptible' (1964: 18).

The 'common destiny' echoes the American concept of Manifest Destiny, a concept that had begun to lose its mythic place in American society during the 1960s and 1970s. Weber also goes on to delineate Nationalism as a position adoptable by both left and right. More recently, António Costa Pinto (2011) has noted the difficulty involved in defining fascism at all, seeing it more as a phenomenon that occurs in different places at different times, and therefore having shifting characteristics, with the concept of a core national myth as a foundation. It is within the context of the foundation myths of America that the Vigilante Thriller should be understood as an attempt to understand and cope with the unpicking of America's unifying myths that occurred during the 1960s and 1970s driven by the Civil Rights movement, the Vietnam War, changes to the practice of law and order and the economic privations that occurred (particularly in urban areas). Fascist movements' embracing of ethnic division mirrors the social changes of the 1960s and 1970s in which America's racial hierarchies were changing, as is the suggestion that fascism can arise as a reaction to the supposed feminization of society, in which the mass (which is, according to Gustave Le Bon and Sigmund Freud, feminine in its childishness and lack of intellect) can be corrupted and is vulnerable to 'hypnotic suggestion' from a strong leader (Passmore 2011: 125–7). The feminization of society, through civilization, is a fault line throughout the Western (in opposition to the masculine wilderness) and is evident in the films of this study. Furthermore, the concept of the masses becomes important in understanding the rhetoric employed in reviews and news articles that worried over the impact of the Vigilante Thrillers. These intersections are vital for understanding the influences in play when theorizing the spectatorship of these six films.

The methodological approaches taken in this work grew out of the films, from primary readings to contextual factors and then to the application of theoretical models to explain the impact and controversy created during their initial release. The aim was to allow the research to provide avenues for discussion and analysis, rather than beginning with a fixed expectation of answers or results. It was a clear goal from the beginning that this would be a spectatorship study; however, it was also clear that it should locate the films within a contextual framework to understand extra-textual pressures and influences that the spectator is subject to and that inform the spectating process. One limit of spectatorship studies can be their conception of the spectator as a subject isolated from external factors, something that lacks a thorough understanding of how and why spectators choose the films they watch and how they might comprehend them. Combining concepts of historical and contextual study with spectatorship theories helps to offer a complete understanding of the Vigilante Thrillers as a film-cycle. This also allows us to explore both why these films developed in the 1970s and their potential political implications.

An overview of existing research is presented here partly to explain the development of ideas in this work, how it builds from previous work and to establish the limitations of the existing research. Specific trends in the research are identified and evaluated with the clearest gap in pre-existing research concerning several contentions made during the first reviews of the films and often returned to: that they were right wing in some way (especially in the depiction of law and order), that they reinterpreted the Western, that they included a new and problematic depiction of violence and that audiences for the films may be moved to imitate their protagonists.

The context of the Vigilante Thriller

The New Hollywood period offers a wealth of material although often this work is homogeneous in its attitude to the films examined here and the industrial and social changes of the times. Peter Biskind's *Easy Riders, Raging Bulls* (1998) and Ryan Gilbey's *It Don't Worry Me* (2004) are both thorough histories that detail the changes in the industry through the journeys of several key individuals. Although not directly applicable to understanding the Vigilante Thrillers, they provide a useful sense of how Hollywood was changing. Works that are more textually concerned include Peter Lev's *American Films of the 1970s: Conflicting Visions* (2000), Linda Ruth Williams and Michael Hammond's (eds) *Contemporary American Cinema* (2006), Lester D. Friedman's (ed) *American Cinema of the 1970s: Themes and Variations* (2007), Barry Langford's *Post-Classical Hollywood: Film Industry, Style and Ideology since 1945* (2010) and Jonathan Kirschner's *Hollywood's Last Golden Age: Politics, Society, and the Seventies Film in America* (2012), all giving an overview of the period, including discussion of political developments. Lev specifically cites, in a chapter called 'Vigilantes and Cops', *Joe*, *The French Connection*, *Dirty Harry* and *Death Wish*, discussing them as 'conservative reactions' to social upheaval. Within this are ideas about how dirt operates ideologically in American culture, suggesting the deep ideological structures that are at play in the films. Indeed, this sense of a conservative or right-wing cycle of films is consistent throughout the majority of critical writings, placing the films in opposition to earlier, more youth-oriented, left-wing films such as *Bonnie and Clyde* (Arthur Penn, 1967), *The Graduate* (Mike Nichols, 1967) and *Easy Rider* (Dennis Hopper, 1969). A key aspect of all these texts is the sense that traditional ideological structures concerning gender, race and sexuality were breaking down in both the film industry and wider culture. Derek Nystrom's *Hard-Hats, Rednecks and Macho-Men: Class in American Cinema* (2009) offers a class-based analysis of this period, suggesting a split in how reviewers of the time saw the audience. Effectively, for Nystrom, the critics were looking down on a working-class audience, seen as unintellectual. Therefore, films that might have appealed to such an audience were viewed in a similarly patronizing manner.

Specific cycles during this period are discussed by Christian Keathley, in 'Trapped in the Affection Image: Hollywood's Post Traumatic Cycle (1970-1976)' (2004), including the idea of left- and right-cycle movies, citing *Death Wish* and *Dirty Harry* as 'Fascist Cop' films. He suggests a right-wing reaction to America's failure in Vietnam which further helps to contextualize the films within the contemporary ideological conflict. Peter Krämer, in *The New Hollywood: From Bonnie and Clyde to Star Wars* (2005), gives an extensive overview of changing trends through the 1960s and 1970s, highlighting a move towards more male- and youth-oriented films. Michael Ryan and Douglas Kellner's *Camera Politica* (1990) offers a political and historical reading of this time, albeit with a distinct bias; they acknowledge that they were 'disturbed by the changes in dominant cultural representations' (1990: xi) as they saw them from 1967 to the mid-1980s, in which they perceived a shift from left to right. This bias colours their work. For instance, although they identify Black criminals in *Dirty Harry*, they fail to discuss that there are also Black victims. However, they give a useful overview of the period and how developments in 1980s cinema developed from, and in some senses answered, issues and questions from the 1970s.

Ideological associations between 1970s American cinema and the social upheavals of the time are given closer analysis in Robin Wood's *From Vietnam to Reagan* (2003). Although he does not give more than passing attention to the films of this study, he does usefully discuss the 'breakdown of ideological confidence in American culture and values' (2003: 23). The picture that emerges from all these texts is that the ideological upheavals of America were reflected in the industrial and representational changes in American cinema, and that ideas of right-wing and left-wing can be transposed clearly onto films. Indeed, the view that these films are simply a right cycle and espoused a right-wing view, and were therefore enjoyed by right-wing audiences, is generally unchallenged except in some criticism of *Straw Dogs* and *Taxi Driver*, both of which are seen within the context of the director's wider careers and form part of the auteur[4] debate around their work. (*Straw Dogs* is, in particular, a film that writers have dealt with from many angles, perhaps in an attempt to rehabilitate it from the initial alarmed reaction.)

A key text concerning Peckinpah is Stephen Prince's *Savage Cinema: Sam Peckinpah and the Rise of Ultraviolence* (1998). Prince offers very detailed textual analysis of *Straw Dogs* but also sits his analysis in a wider discussion of violence in cinema and offers useful categories for discussing this topic. Other works on Peckinpah that have informed this study include Michael Bliss's *Justified Lives: Morality and Narrative in the Films of Sam Peckinpah* (1993) which highlights the sexual motifs in the film, and its depiction of violence and bigotry, David Weddle's *Sam Peckinpah: If They Move . . . Kill 'Em!* (1996) which gives a biographical account of Peckinpah's life and the making of his films, and Terence Butler's *Crucified Heroes: The Films of Sam Peckinpah* (1979) which analyses *Straw Dogs*' structure in comparison

---

[4] We could suggest the invocation of the auteur debate lifts a film from being a popular work to being something more serious, and therefore worthy of more serious study.

to the Western. The relationship between the Vigilante Thriller and the Western emerged as a suggestion by many writers, including some of the initial reviewers, and became a key theme of the research when connected to the ideological shifts of the time.

Ed Buscombe in *The BFI Companion to the Western* (1988) offers a thorough overview of the Western genre from its inception to decline. Importantly, Buscombe presents his ideas with statistical evidence (such as the decline from Westerns as 33 per cent of American films during 1952 to only 11 per cent in 1967). He sees this decline as caused by demographic shifts and the rise of the police thriller as a pseudo-replacement. David A. Cook, in *A History of Narrative Film* (1990), goes further by relating the decline of the genre to the same political events that I suggest prompted the appearance of the Vigilante Thriller. Cook sees many of the developments in the Western as direct questions of its foundation mythology. This is particularly evident in films that take the Native American's point of view, and he discusses how the traditional oppositional structures of the Western had become untenable during the 1960s. However, there is little sense of how cinema dealt with these issues outside of revisionist Westerns. The ideological issues are also explored in depth, and connected to political rhetoric, in Richard Slotkin's *Gunfighter Nation: The Myth of the Frontier in Twentieth Century America* (1992), which also discusses the importance of the Western myth to American identity, including its presentation in film. John G. Cawelti, in *The Six-Gun Mystique*, suggests 'new and conflicting attitudes toward violence, sexism and racism' (1984: 15) as contributing to the Western's decline. Links to the conflict in Vietnam are made by Yvonne Tasker in *Spectacular Bodies: Gender, Genre and the Action Cinema* (1993), who also sees Vigilante films as relocated Westerns. Rick Worland and Edward Countryman, in 'The New Western American Historiography and the Emergence of the New American Western' (1998), discuss the Western as being played out in relation to socio/political changes in American society during the 1960s and later. Several authors suggest that police and crime-based films replaced the Western in both cinema and on TV. *Coogan's Bluff* is cited by Martin Rubin, in *Thrillers* (1999), as a liminal film, part Western part modern urban thriller. Paul Cobley, in *The American Thriller: Generic Innovation and Social Change in the 1970s* (2000), and Buscombe (1988) make similar parallels. Cobley, partly working from Jerry Palmer, gives a thorough discussion of the Thriller genre's development during the 1970s, highlighting the narrative convention of conspiracy and suggesting how the structures of thrillers function ideologically, adding a structural understanding of thrillers to this work.

To investigate formal and thematic similarities between the Western and the Vigilante Thriller three works were consulted in detail: Will Wright's *Six-Guns and Society: A Structural Study of the Western* (1975), Jim Kitses's *Horizons West* (1970) and Cawelti (1984). All three offer an overview of the genre but also use a formalist approach that elucidates patterns and themes.

Comparing these elements to the Vigilante Thriller gives a clear set of points with which to discuss similarities and differences. For example, Kitses sees the Western as built on a binary opposition between the wilderness and civilization. The independence and freedom of the wilderness are set against the promise of peace and humanity offered by civilization. The Western hero 'stands at the centre, torn between two worlds' (1970: 11). This opposition, although seemingly irrelevant given the Vigilante Thriller's mostly urban setting, proves useful in relation to the behaviour of characters who align with those qualities inherent in Kitses's opposition, rather than in a literal discussion of environment and to the possibility of a metaphorical conflation of the two (into an urban wilderness, or urban jungle). Concepts of opposition in the Western support theories of otherness, which becomes relevant when considering the destruction of binary oppositions. Jane Tomkins's *West of Everything: The Inner Life of Westerns* (1992) was also consulted to further the question of gender, another concern of the Vigilante Thrillers' critics. Tomkins comprehensively shows how female characters, in Westerns, often represent civilization and therefore threaten the free and masculine world of the hero (but are also a cause to be protected and defended). A final element of research concerning the Western acknowledged developments away from Hollywood and the traditional form, including the *Dollars* Trilogy of Sergio Leone (of which Christopher Frayling's *Spaghetti Westerns: Cowboys and Europeans from Karl May to Sergio Leone* (1998) gives a thorough history and analysis) and revisionist Westerns such as *Little Big Man* (Arthur Penn, 1970) and *Soldier Blue* (Ralph Nelson, 1970) (both discussed by Cook (1990)). These films emerge during the decline of the traditional Western and the development of police thrillers and Vigilante Thrillers. Both Cobley (2000) and Cawelti, in *Mystery, Violence and Popular Culture* (2004), discuss how this period in Hollywood cinema is one of generic transformations and innovations, and Rick Altman, in *Film/Genre* (1999), offers a thorough overview of generic development and audiences' understanding. Although none specifically apply their analyses to Vigilante Thrillers, these writers show how film-makers were experimenting with form and genre during this period.

Molly Haskell's *From Reverence to Rape: The Treatment of Women in the Movies* (1974) was originally investigated in relation to the sexual politics of film, but she also suggests an evolution from the police thriller to the Vigilante Thriller. She compares *Madigan* (Don Siegel, 1968) to *Dirty Harry*, and *Bullitt* (Peter Yates, 1968) to *The French Connection*, noting that the later films eliminated women from the narratives except in 'the most marginal contexts' (1974: 363). Rubin (1999) and Robert Reiner ('Keystone to Kojak: The Hollywood Cop' (1981)) trace comparisons between early noir thrillers and later police thrillers, through films such as *In the Heat of the Night* to *Dirty Harry* and *The French Connection*. Another film that emerged as influential was *Coogan's Bluff* (Don Siegel, 1968), cited by Paul Smith in *Clint Eastwood: A Cultural Production* (1993) as a direct antecedent of *Dirty Harry*. These comparisons have proven useful as they highlight that the Vigilante Thrillers do not appear out of a vacuum but are the culmination of a set of factors (including the financial success of police thrillers).

The significance of another genre was prompted by Nigel Andrews's review of *Straw Dogs* for *Monthly Film Bulletin*, which states, 'At once harrowingly realistic and richly suggestive *Straw Dogs* promises to emerge as a classic of the horror film' (1971: 249). If not directly related to the other films in this study, this was worth investigating to shed light on the reception of *Straw Dogs* and to widen understanding of genre in this era. Several texts provide useful analysis here particularly Carol Clover's *Men, Women and Chainsaws: Gender in the Modern Horror Film* (1992) and Tony Williams's *Hearths of Darkness: The family in the American Horror Film* (1996). The former offers detail in the genre's development through the 1970s, and the focus allows for consideration of the shifting gender representation in US cinema (as illustrated particularly in the chapter on rape-revenge films) which is especially relevant when considering the role of Amy Sumner (Susan George) in *Straw Dogs*. The latter book develops analysis of how the horror genre changed in response to the same social and cultural movements described earlier. This includes the emergence of a parodic American family running through such films as *The Texas Chainsaw Massacre* (Tobe Hooper, 1974) and *The Last House on the Left* (Wes Craven, 1972), both of which demonstrate shifting values in American culture through the inversion of traditional representations.

Another key contextual cinematic issue that arose from research was the changing nature of US film censorship, including the shift from the Production Code to a rating system, comprehensively covered in Stephen Prince's *Classical Film Violence: Designing and Regulating Brutality in Hollywood Cinema 1930-1968* (2003). He extends this further, with reference to Sam Peckinpah's films, in *Savage Cinema: Sam Peckinpah and the Rise of Ultraviolence* (1998) which covers the regulation of violence in the 1970s, which highlights several influences on the changes, including shifts in the Hollywood industry's structure, the influence of European cinema and news reports coming from the Vietnam War. Michael Leech, in *I Know It When I See It: Pornography, Violence and Public Sensibility* (1975), reiterates the relationship between representation of violence on TV news and that on the cinema screen, giving a view contemporary to the Vigilante Thrillers themselves. James C. Robertson, *The Hidden Cinema: British Censorship in Action, 1913-1975* (1989), details the equivalent history in the UK where the changes were less radical, evolving through the 1960s and 1970s. An insider's view on the UK is given by John Trevelyan, writing for *Screen* in 1970. However, as this was written by the then secretary of the British Board of Film Classification (BBFC), an awareness of bias is essential. James Kendrick's *Film Violence: History, Ideology, Genre* (2010) gives further insight into the censorship and classification systems in the United States.

Analysis of the narrative image, establishing how spectators were addressed by the films, has meant researching promotional and advertising materials for each of the Vigilante Thrillers. Fortunately, modern DVD reissues contain useful elements such as theatrical trailers (often including variant forms). For example, the re-mastered *Straw Dogs* released by Freemantle Home Entertainment (2004) includes a 1971 on-location documentary, the 1971 US theatrical trailer, three 1971 US TV spots and two 1971 radio spots. This amount of publicity material is not available for all the films, but through online retailers, original US press books for all except *Joe* have been acquired. These vary in-depth and detail but offer a good source for analysing production companies' attempts to anchor the meanings of the films through specific copy and images.

The Vigilante Thrillers as film texts

Stanley Corkin gives an insightful overview of how New York was depicted in various films, including the New York-based films of this study, in *Starring New York: Filming the Grime and Glamour of the Long 1970s* (2011). Exploring various myths of New York and urban living, Corkin shows how the setting can be recast to suit different narratives. Corkin also gives very good historical detail on the financial crisis that the city underwent in the 1970s. Jake Horsley's *The Blood Poets: A Cinema of Savagery* (1999) analyses *Taxi Driver*, *Dirty Harry* and *Death Wish*, with discussion of the transposition of the Western to an urban environment. Other texts that offer differing views on *Taxi Driver* include Cynthia J Fuchs's '"All the Animals Come Out at Night": Vietnam meets *Noir* in *Taxi Driver*' (1991), *Scorsese on Scorsese* edited by David Thompson and Ian Christie (1989), Robert Philip Kolker's *A Cinema of Loneliness: Penn, Kubrick, Spielberg, Altman* (1980), Maria T. Milioria's *The Scorsese Psyche on Screen: Roots of Themes and Characters in the Films* (2004) and Leighton Grist's *The Films of Martin Scorsese, 1963-77: Authorship and Context* (2000). In relation to *Straw Dogs* Stevie Simkin's *Early Modern Tragedy and the Cinema of Violence* (2006) is perceptive concerning the role of violence in narratives, particularly the relationship between rape, power and poverty. Michael Bliss, in *Justified Lives: Morality and Narrative in the Films of Sam Peckinpah* (1993), discusses the sexual motifs of the film and how it depicts violence and bigotry. Weddle (1996) gives background information on the development of *Straw Dogs* as does Simkin in *Straw Dogs (Controversies)* (2011), which gives detail on the different cuts and the censorship issues the film provoked.

There are fewer detailed secondary sources available regarding the other films studied. However, some key texts have come to light. The production and reception of *Joe*, with background on the film-makers, are covered in

Larry Powell and Tom Garrett's *The Films of John G. Avildsen: Rocky, The Karate Kid and Other Underdogs* (2014). Analysis of *Joe* occurs in Lev (2000) and J. Hoberman's *The Dream Life: Movies, Media and the Mythology of the Sixties* (2003). For *Death Wish* key texts include Marty Gliserman's article 'Watch Out Chicago' in *Jump Cut* (1975), which analyses the opposition between Paul Kersey and the criminals he kills. Christopher Sorrento (2011) analyses political transformation throughout the film, as well as assessing the critical reactions it received in *Death Wish (Deep Focus)* (2011). Xavier Mendik discusses the 'overlap between Kersey and his prey' in *Shocking Cinema of the Seventies* (2002: 67), something overlooked by most critics. Paul Talbot follows the film's production, distribution and reception in *Bronson's Loose!: The Making of the Death Wish Films* (2006).

Regarding *The French Connection* and *Dirty Harry* most discussion takes place in texts already listed, and largely this is regarding genre developments. Despite the success and influence of the films, they have had relatively little published about them. Mia Mask's 'Macho Cops: *The French Connection* and *Dirty Harry*' (2007) discusses their differing aesthetics and the gendering of Scorpio in *Dirty Harry*. Joe Street, in *Dirty Harry's America: Clint Eastwood, Harry Callahan and the Conservative Backlash* (2015), gives a thorough analysis of the lasting political significance of *Dirty Harry*, repeating previous conclusions on the political representations, and Yvonne Tasker's *The Hollywood Action and Adventure Film* (2015) discusses its effect on the development of the action film. An extensive interview with William Friedkin for *Film Quarterly* by Michael Shedlin (1972) explores the political sensibilities of *The French Connection* and discusses the director's preparations (such as spending time with New York Police officers).

Straw Dogs, *The French Connection* and *Death Wish* all originated in literature. The former is based on Gordon Williams' 1969 novel *Siege at Trencher's Farm*, although the film differs in several ways; most notably, it removes Sumner's (called Magruder in the novel) daughter and adds the rape. *The French Connection* was a non-fiction account of crime by Robin Moore published in 1969 and is loosely adapted in the film.[5] *Death Wish* by Brian Garfield was published in 1972.[6] The film changes details, such as Paul Benjamin becoming Paul Kersey, and adds the rape scene. In the film, Kersey's attacks on criminals start earlier in the narrative than Benjamin's in the novel. Although not based on a literary source, *Dirty Harry* drew inspiration from the Zodiac killer who operated in California in the late 1960s and early 1970s (and who was never caught). Scorpio's letters imitate

---

[5] Although based on Moore's book much of *The French Connection* was the invention of Friedkin and screenwriter Ernest Tidyman. One significant change was to make the ending bleaker for the main characters and suggest that few people had been prosecuted successfully.
[6] Neither Williams nor Garfield reacted positively to the respective adaptations of their work.

those of the real killer.[7] Finally, *Taxi Driver* drew inspiration from the diaries of Arthur Bremer, who shot segregationist politician, and 1968 third party presidential candidate George Wallace in 1972.

The socio/political context of the Vigilante Thriller

Time magazine articles such as 'Street Crime: Who's Winning?' (23 October 1972) and 'The Crime Wave' (30 June 1975) show that rising crime rates were being highlighted in the press. Further research was required, however, to establish the veracity of these claims. Paul Johnson, in *A History of the American People*, gives access to crime statistics. As he states,

> US crime statistics became available in the 1960s, when the rate for crimes was revealed as under 1,900 per 100,000 population. That doubled in the 1960s and tripled in the 1970s. (1997, 987)

This statistical rise is reiterated by the aforementioned *Time* article 'The Crime Wave'. Further sources, such as Melvin Small's *The Presidency of Richard Nixon* (1999), provide background on civil unrest, including terrorist attacks and protests at university campuses. Publications such as *Newsweek* and the articles reprinted in *Takin' It to the Streets: A Sixties Reader* (edited by Alexander Bloom and Wini Breines 2003) also help evidence the rise in crime but also the rising anxiety. As rape is one of the crimes depicted in the films and one that caused much critical controversy, more specific research was done. Susan Brownmiller's *Against Our Will: Men, Women and Rape* (1975) provides a valuable contemporary insight into changing attitudes to rape and women as victims of crime, with Joanna Bourke's *Rape: A History from 1860 to the Present* (2008) detailing changes in perception and laws concerning rape throughout the twentieth century. Crime is also considered in the context of moral panic, as discussed by Stuart Hall et al. in *Policing the Crisis: Mugging, the State, and Law and Order* (1978) and Stanley Cohen in *Folk Devils and Moral Panics: Third Edition* (2002).

Returning to research more specific to film, several texts about American cinema in the 1970s have suggested further points to consider, with several key

---

[7] The Zodiac killer 'is thought to have killed at least five people and, in letters signed with a distinctive target symbol, claimed to have killed 37' (Moyer 2014) in the North California area in the late 1960s and early 1970s. Scorpio's letters in the film 'exactly imitate the Zodiac killer's' correspondence with police that was printed in the *San Francisco Chronicle* (Street 2016: 63).

crimes pinpointed as having had a direct effect on the Hollywood community. Biskind (1998) identifies the murders committed by the Manson family as a key influence. Other crimes, such as those of Richard Speck and Charles Joseph Whitman (Hoberman 2003), became causes-célèbres highlighting a new sense, or sensationalism, of violence in American society. The oft-repeated story of the murder of Kitty Genovese, supposedly ignored despite her pleas for help, suggested a new hostility between residents of New York. Friedman (2007) helps complete an overview of the context into which the films were released by detailing civil unrest caused in part by the Vietnam War and the Civil Rights movement, with wide reference to legal cases and specific political moments. Williams (1996) extensively discusses the impact of the Vietnam War on American ideological codes. An overview of the political rhetoric used at this time is given by Slotkin (1990), which is also very useful in understanding the ideological underpinnings of American culture. The use of rhetoric is elaborated on by Small, who discusses Nixon's successful election in 1968 having campaigned on a 'law and order platform' (1999: 157).

From this research came the importance of legislative changes to the American justice system, particularly those concerning the rights of the suspect versus the rights of the victim. Miranda Rights (so named after the arrest of Ernesto Miranda), whereby the police had to advise a suspect of his/her rights, were introduced in 1966. They became a thematic element of the Vigilante Thriller and of the era; *Time* ran several articles concerning the problems that Miranda was posing for the police, who objected to the introduction of these rights as hampering investigations and handing too many rights to the suspect. As the films represent acts of vigilantism, investigation into actual examples was undertaken. This uncovered several reports of real groups (Goldberger 1968), some of which were cast as patriotic reactions to civil unrest, such as so-called Hard-Hat Riots (as referenced in *Time* 25 May 1970). Lawrence Webb's *The Cinema of Urban Crisis: Seventies Films and the Reinvention of the City* (2014) links *The French Connection* and *Dirty Harry* to the urban crises of the time, showing how the films created new representations of city environments.

Historical instances of vigilantism have been explored, through Slotkin (1992), with links to the racial politics of America being developed through reference to Bourke (2008), Sara Bullard, in *The Ku Klux Klan: A History of Racism & Violence, Fifth Edition* (1997) and Sarah Churchwell's *Behold America: A History of America First and the American Dream* (2019).

Theorizing the Vigilante Thriller

Vicky Lebeau's *Psychoanalysis and Cinema: The Play of Shadows* (2001) has been very useful in its overview of the psychoanalytical approach in film and on the origin of psychoanalysis itself and its parallel development with film, giving solid background information on Sigmund Freud, Jacques Lacan and their theories. Psychoanalytic theory was approached with some caveats as some of the theories used to construct the spectatorship process, such as the Oedipal Theory, are not necessarily in clinical use. However, the close development of film and psychoanalysis and the cross-over between the arenas, as described by Lebeau, as well as the insight provided by much of the work detailed later means that psychoanalytic theories are indispensable for opening the text/spectatorship relationship.

Two key writers from the 1970s period are Christian Metz and Laura Mulvey. Metz, in 'The Imaginary Signifier',[8] outlines the complexity of the text/spectator relationship, with reference to the psychoanalytic concepts of Freud and Lacan. Particularly of interest to Metz is the tension between the reality signified in the film and the spectator's consciousness of the process of signification:

> Thus the fiction film represents both the negation of the signifier (an attempt to have it forgotten) and a certain working regime of that signifier, to be quite precise the very regime required to get it forgotten. (1975: 47)

Here Metz conceptualizes the disavowal needed for the spectator to believe in the diegesis of the film, while acknowledging the spectator needs to be able to understand the cinematic language designed to create the disavowal. Metz continues his analysis, describing how the cinema presents a dichotomy in how it engages the spectator:

> More than the other arts, or in a more unique way, the cinema involves us in the imaginary: it drums up all perception, but to switch it immediately over into its own absence, which is nonetheless the only signifier present. (1975: 47)

This tension, between engagement with the film and consciousness of its fabrication, needs engaging with, especially as many reviewers asserted the audience would be influenced by the films to act in the real world. Metz continues in his analysis of spectatorship by invoking Lacan's theory of the *mirror stage* (the point at which the child gains self-awareness and self-identification (1975: 48)) but problematizes this relationship:

> The spectator is absent from the screen: contrary to the child in the mirror, he cannot identify with himself as an object, but only with some

---

[8]Lebeau, referring to Metz, describes this 'as the "mental machinery" which comes to meet cinema, the institution "outside and inside" us' (2001: 43).

objects which are there without him. In this sense the screen is not a mirror. This time the perceived is entirely on the side of the object, and there is no longer any equivalent of the own image, of that unique mix of perceived and subject (of other and I) which was precisely the figure necessary to disengage the one from the other. At the cinema, it is always the other who is on the screen; as for me, I am there to look at him. I take no part in the perceived, on the contrary, I am all-perceiving. (1975: 51)

This dual relationship, one of self-identification and perception, highlights the tension between the spectator's role as a powerful voyeur and passive recipient. Mulvey takes up similar concerns of identification and pleasure but focusses on the role of gender in the process in 'Visual Pleasure and Narrative Cinema' (1975). Mulvey sees the cinema as offering several pleasures including active scopophilia and identification and discusses an imbalance in classical Hollywood cinema which sees that 'pleasure in looking has been split between active/male and passive/female' (1975: 11). Within this opposition there is

A tension between a mode of representation of woman in film and conventions surrounding the diegesis. Each is associated with a look: that is the spectator in direct scopophilic contact with the female form displayed for his enjoyment (connoting male phantasy) and that of the spectator fascinated with the image of his like set in an illusion of natural space, and through him gaining control and possession of the woman within the diegesis. (1975: 13)

Issues of control and gender seem particularly pertinent in any study where fascism is invoked as these concepts are central to the definition of fascism. For Mulvey the classical Hollywood narrative film presents a masculine point of view, specifically a heterosexual one. Both these theorists, however, have limits in their conception of the relationship of the spectator to the film as one that is hermetically sealed from extra-textual influences.

While Metz and Mulvey represent early theorizations of identification and spectatorship, more recent developments should also be considered. Several theorists have become useful in opening this area. Francesco Casetti discusses, in *Inside the Gaze*, several aspects of spectatorship pertinent to this study (which builds on previous work by David Bordwell). Rather than film offering a 'self-contained universe, secure in its own autonomy and absolute sovereignty' (1998: 8), the spectator engages in a more complex manner, 'for example, when he puts together all sorts of scattered elements to construct a character or place' (1998: 9). Like Metz, Casetti recognizes that the relationship between the spectator and the screen is one of identification but also separation. Casetti goes further in realizing that films presume a spectator through the act of interpellation; the spectator is hailed by the text in a certain way, invited to receive the text from a certain subject position.[9] Understanding how the Vigilante Thrillers hail their audiences is therefore essential. Casetti also turns to the question of subjective and objective views in film – where, and with whom, the spectator is asked to align. To illustrate this, a scene shot from a character's point of view suggests different readings to the same events depicted through a long shot with a wide-angle lens. The former is subjective, inviting the spectator to identify directly with the character involved, the latter allowing a distance between the events and the spectator.

This area is examined in detail also by Edward Brannigan. Brannigan discusses the possibility of intersubjectivity in *Narrative Comprehension and Film*, in which the spectator is presented with 'issues that arise when objectivity and subjectivity interact in a narrative film by being alternated, overlapped, or otherwise mixed' (1992: 161). Much of Brannigan's discussion concerns non-linear narratives, but it includes the question of focalization:

> Introducing the narratological concept of *focalization* is meant to remind us that a character's role in a narrative may change from being an actual, or potential, *focus* of a causal chain to being the *source* of our knowledge of a causal chain. (1992: 101)

Rather than the spectator being told the narrative, the focalizer experiences events from which the spectator constructs the narrative. Brannigan discusses subjectivity closely, particularly connecting it to camera techniques. This is further split into Internal and External Focalization: 'In *internal* focalization, story world and screen are meant to collapse into each other, forming a perfect identity in the name of the character' (1992: 102).

> External focalization represents a measure of character awareness but from the outside of the character. It is semi-subjective in the manner of an eye-line match: we see *what* Manny looks at, *when* he looks, but *not from* his unique special position; we must infer that we have seen what he has seen and how he has seen it. (1992: 103)

Brannigan suggests that the process of identification is more complex than simply identifying a protagonist, that the spectator has multiple positions available. With regard more specifically to the camera, Brannigan discusses how various techniques imply an objective view of events or channel the spectator through a subjective, or focalized, view.

---

[9] Subject Position is used in the sense defined by Heath (1976), as a space which the spectator comes to occupy, which is constructed through the narrative and use of film language.

Gill Branston offers more discussion and depth with regard to identification in *Cinema and Cultural Modernity* (2000). With reference to Murray Smith, Branston delineates several different levels of identification:

- *Alignment*: referring to the way in which a film gives us access to the actions, thoughts and feelings of characters (for example *The Silence of the Lambs*, or *Fight Club* may 'align' us with a character without inviting allegiance to him and his values).

- *Allegiance*: the way a film attempts to marshal our sympathies for or against various characters in the world of the fiction.

- *Keying*: the stressing of one character's experience, running a sequence to that 'key', while not making it impossible to view other perspectives (2000: 144–5).

These ideas become essential for understanding how the spectator is positioned by the Vigilante Thriller, allowing an appreciation of the different positions available.

Madness and Cinema by Patrick Fuery (2004) was discovered when researching the psychoanalytic approach and proved pertinent through his discussion of ideas of hysteria in film – both representationally and as part of the spectatorship process. Fuery's ideas help delineate how spectators can relate to films in which culturally agreed behaviours and codes are transgressed. His work also helps discussion of the protagonists of the Vigilante Thrillers, particularly in exploring how their behaviours can be interpreted as neurotic, hysteric and/or psychotic and how spectators may interpret this. This, Fuery suggests, has a root in power and feelings of power, something very much at stake in American culture during the period.

To understand the representation of violence, an overview of the debates surrounding the topic is necessary. This ties into the discourse of the original reviews but should be expanded to consider the spectator's approach to film violence. David J. Slocum's 'The "film violence" trope: New Hollywood, "the Sixties" and the politics of history' (2004), and Thomas Schatz's 'Introduction' to *New Hollywood Violence* (2004) offer a clear overview of the historical debates surrounding film violence. This is further explored by James Kendrick, in *Film Violence: History, Ideology, Genre* (2009), who connects the presentation of violence, and the censorship of it, to wider ideological concerns of society. All these authors acknowledge that the representation of violence in cinema was changing radically in the late 1960s and early 1970s, including the emergence of what Stephen Prince calls (borrowing from Anthony Burgess) 'ultraviolence'.

To connect questions of identification, spectatorship and violence, the concept of modality has proven useful. As defined by Bob Hodge and David Tripp in *Children and Television* (1986), modality 'concerns the reality attributed to a message' (1986: 104). Hodge and Tripp present their findings having extensively researched children's consumption of TV, and how they understood and responded to different programmes. The concept of modality (a term borrowed from linguistics that 'concerns the reality attributed to a message' (1986: 104)) is used to describe how the audience attributes different levels of reality to different texts. The higher the modality, the more 'real' a text is understood to be. Modality aptly describes our interpretation of texts: a 'process of judgement on the part of the receiver of the message' (1986: 116). Within this is emotional response: 'Modality does not create the emotional response, but it determines the valency and force of that response' (1986: 116). The modality is fixed partly before the film begins by the narrative image, and partly by the text itself. Prince (1998) offers a way to differentiate between acts of violence and their presentation, allowing us to discuss further the representation of violence in the texts. These two elements, the referential component and the stylistic amplitude, elucidate the difference between the action represented and the construction of film violence in the Vigilante Thrillers. During the 1970s the actions represented may not have differed significantly from those in previous decades, but the stylistic amplitude did.

Prince (1998) offers extensive analysis of the violence in *Straw Dogs*, and this provides a useful model for understanding depictions in the other films, as it considers the aesthetic and referential components shot by shot. Prince makes a convincing argument in relation to Peckinpah's films, and in particular *Straw Dogs*, that a subjective montage is used. Prince also realizes the importance of understanding scenes of violence within the context of the surrounding film, as opposed to many of the critical reactions that considered the acts of violence as separate texts in themselves. Prince's analysis also raises questions regarding the voyeuristic nature of film violence, and the complicity in the acts that may, or may not, exist in the spectator. Alan Lovell, writing in *Don Siegel: American Cinema* (1975), discusses how, within the context of Siegel's films in general and *Dirty Harry* in particular, heroes are defined by the violent acts they commit, that it is an essential component of how we define and understand them.

With regard to gender, further works complement Mulvey's analysis. John Berger, *Ways of Seeing* (1972), and Haskell (1974) provide background information on the representation of men and women, with Haskell paying attention to the development of representations of violence towards women in American cinema. Clover (1992) further expands the discussion of how men and women watch films differently, as well as discussing the representation of gender when linked to rape and revenge, with *Straw Dogs* being tied to the cycle of rape-revenge films from the late 1970s.

Barbera Creed outlines several useful concepts, particularly in relation to Julia Kristeva's use of the term 'abject', in *The Monstrous Feminine: Film, Feminism and Psychoanalysis* (1993). Creed's text is a strong use of psychoanalytic ideas in the discussion of gender representation, which connects to anxiety (particularly castration) which is particularly useful with *Straw Dogs* but has wider implications when considered in relation to the rise of feminism during the 1960s and 1970s. Finally, Steve Cohan and Ena Rae Park, in *Screening the Male: Exploring Masculinities in Hollywood Cinema* (1992), and Tasker (1993) provide background for discussing the Vigilante Thrillers against the wider context of gender representation in popular cinema.

Several more general works have also been significant when considering the role of the spectator in relation to the Vigilante Thriller; both Thomas Elsaesser, in 'The Pathos of Failure: American Films in the 1970s – Notes on the Unmotivated Hero' (2004), and Keathley (2004) give overviews of contextual cinema developments with textual analysis of the films in this study. The former deals with *Dirty Harry* and *Death Wish*, placing them in opposition to more 'liberal' films of the time. Keathley discusses a series of so-called 'Fascist Cop' films (including *Dirty Harry* and *Death Wish*) as a response to contemporary issues of distrust in civic institutions. The moniker 'Fascist Cop' clearly delineates the political position Keathley ascribes to the films. Smith (1993), within an analysis of Eastwood's career to that point, discusses his developing persona up to, and including, *Dirty Harry*, about which he considers potential political meanings of the film, including whether it is fascist.

Developing from structural oppositions of the Western, the concept of otherness emerged during research for this project as key, especially when linked to the importance of grand narrative. Grand narratives, as suggested by Jean-François Lyotard in *The Postmodern Condition: A Report on Knowledge* (1984), give a society ideological coherence but were, during the 1970s, becoming unstable. The Western, as a uniquely American grand narrative, was failing during the 1960s creating an ideological problem reflected in the social changes of the time. The structural oppositions of the Western hinge, partly, on the othering of the Native American, but by the 1970s the validity of the opposition was being disavowed and the Vigilante Thriller expresses an uncertainty about traditional structures through the paralleling and blurring of antagonists and protagonists. To explore this concept Michael Richardson's *Otherness in Hollywood Cinema* (2010) was useful, as was Kobena Mercer's *Welcome to the Jungle: New Positions in Black Cultural Studies* (1994) which discusses the simultaneous attraction and repulsion that can be embodied in some representations. John Izod, writing in *Myth, Mind and the Screen* (2001), adds a Jungian perspective on the function of grand narratives, helping us to deepen the psychological understanding of these films.

Fascism as ideology and rhetorical tool

Finally, this work returns to the concept of fascism and ideology more generally. Kevin Passmore (2002) provides an effective overview of the differing definitions of fascism and the regimes that have claimed to be, or have been defined as, fascist. This assists interrogation of the early reviews and the use of the term, assessing if it has political validity. Thorough histories (Weber 1964) and critiques of fascism (Costa Pinto 2011) have been consulted to understand how the concept evolved. Andrea Slane, *A Not So Foreign Affair: Fascism, Sexuality and the Cultural Rhetoric of American Democracy* (2001), discusses various ways in which fascism is represented in American culture and how the language of fascism is used and adapted for different political agendas, which also links to Churchwell (2019). This work will conclude by drawing together the other chapters to create a fuller picture of the development and consumption of the Vigilante Thriller, drawing together issues of effects and the question of real-world effects of film violence, referring to *Ill Effects: The Media/Violence Debate* (1997), edited by Julian Petley, for a point of view on the moral panic aspects of the discussion of film violence in the media. This is given a historical perspective, linking to ideas of group psychology, by reference to Lisa Blackman and Valerie Walkerdine's *Mass Hysteria: Critical Psychology and Media Studies* (2001).

PART ONE

The historical spectator and the Vigilante Thriller

An analysis of the contemporary critical writings and the marketing of the Vigilante Thrillers marketing establishes, in Chapter 1, how the films were understood critically and how the contemporary audience was encouraged to read them, while also establishing a rhetorical framework that has pervaded later work on the films (much of this will be challenged later in Part Two). Film texts exist within the wider culture, including the cinematic culture of the times and, as Graham Allen observes, 'texts cannot be separated from the larger cultural and social textuality out of which they are constructed. All texts, therefore, contain within them the ideological structures and struggles expressed in society through discourse' (2000: 36). To further our understanding of spectatorship in context requires an understanding of how the films were received during their release and how this relates to wider ideological and sociological concerns. Several key ideas highlighted by Allen are useful for furthering the understanding of how texts relate to each other, to society and to the spectator.[1] Alongside intertextuality, how texts refer to

---

[1] It should be made clear that spectatorship is being used in terms of a subject position; due to the age of the films and lack of data, there has been no attempt to construct an audience through empirical research methods.

one another, Allen describes paratextuality as 'those elements which lie on the threshold of the text, and which help to direct and control the reception of the text by the reader' (2000: 103). For the film spectator that threshold is described effectively by John Ellis. Defining cinema-going as a cultural event, Ellis discusses the concept of narrative image, a way to understand many of the paratexts that inform a film: 'An idea of a film is widely circulated and promoted, an idea which can be called the "narrative image" of the film, the cinema industry's anticipatory reply to the question "What is this film like?" If anything is bought at the box office that is already known by the audience, it is the narrative image' (1982: 30).

Generally speaking, and with reference only to marketing strategies available in the 1970s rather than viral alternatives available today, this information was controlled and distributed by a film's production company through several channels. These include the title of the film itself, posters, newspaper advertisements, front-of-house material, trailers and the casting of stars. Ellis suggests that a full reading of a film requires an understanding of the narrative image, and as part of this, the voices of critics are pertinent, especially as a group of influential critics emerged during the New Hollywood period who helped contribute to the Vigilante Thrillers' individual paratexts. During the 1970s writers such as Pauline Kael and Andrew Sarris helped dominate the critical discourse and helped set the agenda for the spectator's understanding. Taking this into account, the narrative image becomes a critical factor in how the spectator constructs meaning through expectation.

Building on this consideration of the socio/political contexts of the Vigilante Thriller helps to contextualize reception even further and sheds light on the critical reaction to the films, as film critics are subject to the same socio/political factors as spectators. This highlights the relationship between the films' themes and contemporary socio/political issues. Working backwards from the issues highlighted in the critical reactions, concerns about law and order are established as key. Contemporary publications, such as *Time* which ran a series of articles about the topic, help establish the seriousness of certain specific aspects of law and order that other writers, such as Lev and Friedman, build on in their overviews of how the cinema of the period responded to political issues (such as the Civil Rights movement and the Vietnam War).

The importance of legislative changes in America, particularly those concerning the rights of the suspect versus the rights of the victim, is essential to this. Miranda Rights introduced in 1966 are a key thematic element of the Vigilante Thriller and *Time*, along with other publications, ran several articles concerning the problems that Miranda was posing for the Police, who objected to these rights as hampering investigations and handing too many rights to the suspect. As the films represent acts of vigilantism, the history and continued existence of this are covered. This includes reports of real vigilante groups, some of which were cast as patriotic reactions to civil unrest such as the so-called Hard-Hat. The media's narratives of law and order are explored, such as those about the murder of Kitty Genovese, which establishes the discursive background to this topic, as is the rise of mugging as a moral panic, discussed in reference to Hall (Hall et al. 1978) and Cohen (2002), which helps explore the tensions of the time.

Alongside the socio/political context, Part One explores the changing trends in cinema that influenced, and presaged, the Vigilante Thriller. This includes changes in the industry, especially the changes in censorship and certification that occurred and some discussion of shifts in wider media that had a direct impact. The late 1960s and early 1970s was a time of great change in how films were produced in Hollywood, which allowed for developments in style and representation. It was also a time of shift and developments in genre, and the Vigilante Thriller must be understood in a generic context. This relates specifically to the rise of the police thriller (and the development of the thriller more generally during the period) and, more importantly, to the decline of the Western. The Western, as suggested by many critics, looms large over the Vigilante Thriller although this poses several questions: How was the Western itself evolving as a genre in the late 1960s early 1970s, and how does the Vigilante Thriller compare to the Western? Certainly, some critics perceived them as displaced Westerns, and several of the film-makers were connected to the Western (which may be important from an intertextual perspective). Formalist analysis is used to explore structural similarities/issues (modelled on the work of Cawelti, Kitses and Wright), giving a clear sense of where divergences occur from the narrative patterns of the Western, which leads to a consideration of the ideological implications of such divergences.

To understand why a movement in cinema occurs, it is important to place that movement within time and space. Rather than completing an eidetic reduction to an essential text removed from contextual factors, this is a study concerned with reception in context. We can, by examining publications such as *Variety* and using online resources, establish the box-office success of each film. This, on one level, helps inform an understanding of their importance; each film was a financial success, with two of them being in the top-ten lists for their respective years (box-office statistics are collated in Table 4 in the Appendix).[2] By exploring the paratexts, we can begin to understand why these films were successful and how they were watched.

---

[2]This is not to say that box-office figures necessarily indicate that an audience enjoyed or liked a film, particularly over the long term – they do, however, attest to an impact at the time.

1

Narrative images and critical reactions

The narrative image of a film is a complex phenomenon that occurs in a number of media: it is the film's circulation outside its performance in cinemas.

(ELLIS 1983: 31)

During the 1960s and early 1970s a movie culture took shape around universities, coffee houses, and art theatres showing foreign films. Out of endless conversations about directors and sleepless nights arguing over the latest landmark (probably foreign) film, thousands (perhaps millions) of young people contracted 'cinephilia', or as Susan Sontag explains, 'The love that cinema inspired'.

(HABERSKI JR 2001: 1)

Investigating the marketing for these films suggests how the producers intended to position their target audience and suggests dominant textual readings. This is also influenced by the critical writings which are discussed here to understand how they potentially set an understanding of the texts (that still holds today). The narrative image is not necessarily wholly fixed by producers; however, they offer a starting point. Beyond this we can establish key similarities between the advertising campaigns for each of the films, and then how the critics offered dominant readings of the films (and the problems with these). As with the analysis of critical response to the films, this section will concentrate on marketing campaigns within the United States and the United Kingdom. Each campaign is taken in turn to establish how the marketing positioned the spectator to focus on certain aspects of each film.

Marketing *Joe* (US Rating R, UK Certificate X)

As Powell and Garrett (2009: 20) note, the producers changed the films title from *The Gap* to *Joe*, a change reflected across the marketing which emphasized the Joe Curran character, despite his first appearance coming twenty minutes into the film. Retaining *The Gap* as the title would have placed much greater emphasis on the class and age differences presented (between Joe and Bill, between the parents and their children, and more broadly between changing cultures). However, changing the name to *Joe* firmly places the emphasis on Peter Boyle's character. The very choice of the name Joe suggests an ordinariness and regularity about the character but also places him in a white working-class environment (the use of Joe to represent an ordinary person, or 'Regular Joe' originates in the mid-nineteenth century (Oxford Dictionaries 2015)). This emphasis is reiterated in the posters for the film in which Joe, proudly holding a shotgun and a US flag, dominates. The comparison is informative, linking Joe's regularity with patriotism and the right to bear arms. Boyle himself, then an unknown (Powell and Garrett 2009: 18), is submerged into the figure of Joe. His clothing connotes the working-class status of the character, and his patriotism is augmented by a badge in his hat, and the US flag on the letter O in the title. Within the circle in which Joe stands a target is shown in which a hippy girl is featured (not one of the characters from the film), suggesting that Joe is targeting the girl. The tagline 'Keep America Beautiful' anchors the image, implying that Joe is pursuing such a goal by targeting her but is ironic as the hippy girl conforms to mainstream standards of beauty. The tagline itself is borrowed from the Keep America Beautiful organization,[1] a not-for-profit organization famed in 1970 for its Crying Indian Poster (in which a close-up of a crying Native American sits aside the message 'Get Involved Now. Pollution Hurts All Of Us'). This image is rich in intertextual meaning, with the subversion of a popular public service campaign to align the counterculture movement with pollution, and Joe with cleaning up America. However, this image is complicated by the attractiveness of the hippy girl and her look towards camera. She does not connote a threat, and so a question is implied – why is she the target? The

---

[1] www.kab.org

position of this target, over Joe's crotch from which the flag and rifle spring, introduces a sexual element to the image. A second poster released after reviews of the film had been published further focusses on the character of Joe, as well as a positive critical reaction to the film.

The theatrical trailer for the film reiterates this emphasis on Joe. It opens with an image of him on the phone, accompanied by the main theme song by Dean Michaels. As the song begins with the words 'Hey Joe, don't it make you want to go to war', the image cuts from Joe to a group of hippy teens, then back to Joe (in a new location) implying a disapproving gaze from Joe. A voice-over informs that 'The Cannon Releasing Corporation would like you to meet Joe'. This line creates a hermeneutic code[2] that runs counter to the name Joe – how regular is he? A series of quick cuts follows in which Joe is juxtaposed to various scenes of the hippy lifestyle, Bill and his wife (Audrey Caire), and his own home life. These cuts only stop to show a sequence in which Joe strips a rifle sitting in his basement. The previous associations and comparisons give way to an emphasis on Joe and his rifle; however, this gives way to a repeat of the previous structure in which scenes and dialogue from the film are intercut for often humorous meanings (much is made of Joe's inadequacy in bed, and his mispronunciation of 'orgy' with a hard 'g'). Much is made of the culture clash comedy when Joe and Bill go into the hippy community, but the violence of the film's ending is only alluded to. What is lacking completely from the trailer is the incident that drives the plot – Bill's killing of Frank (Patrick McDermott). Melissa is barely featured, and the blackmail plot between Joe and Bill is only alluded to, and then quite subtly. A definite image of the film is being given, but one that makes Joe the centre of the film and essentially ignores the drama within the Compton family. Joe is highlighted, but the violence in the film is sublimated, not shown.

Alongside the regular advertising in print and in cinemas, it is worth noticing the release of two albums connected to the film. One was a soundtrack, the other a *Joe Speaks* dialogue LP (Powell and Garrett 2009: 17). The LP cover includes the warning: 'this album contains adult dialogue taken from the soundtrack of an R rated film', the R highlighted in red. Not only does this LP re-emphasize the focus on Joe but it prompts close consideration of the character's dialogue, and by removing the dialogue from the context of the film opens a way of interpreting the character separately from the film's bleak ending. It is suggestive that the character of Joe had become larger than the film itself and existed apart from the contextualizing film narrative.

---

[2]Hermeneutic code is used to describe an enigma in the text, as defined by Roland Barthes (Barthes 1992).

Marketing *Straw Dogs* (US Rating R, UK Certificate X[3])

The central image that dominates the majority of *Straw Dogs*' marketing is Dustin Hoffman[4] staring out of the poster, one lens cracked in his glasses. This image is used in several variations, expressing the violence of the film, but also implying a transformation within the figure of Hoffman. Hoffman had come to prominence as an actor in *The Graduate* in which he played Benjamin Braddock, a young man with no direction (although Hoffman was thirty at the time). That film set a persona for Hoffman with which he had then experimented (particularly going against type as a street hustler in *Midnight Cowboy* (John Schlesinger, 1969)), although Mark Harris points out how Hoffman had become strongly identified with Braddock (2008: 394–6). This persona had none of the elements of violence implied by the *Straw Dogs* posters, and the image draws attention to itself through its incongruity. Despite Peckinpah's current critical status as an auteur, the advertising clearly stresses that *Straw Dogs* is a vehicle for Hoffman with his name appearing above and, at the same size, as the title. The depiction of Hoffman implies the change that occurs in the character; the transition of the David Sumner character is clearly suggested in the damaged glasses, the destruction of a classic signifier for intellectualism.[5] The bisecting of the face (hiding the left half) suggests the duality of the character, further hinting at change and transformation. One specific critical quotation employed in the posters explicitly suggests issues of masculinity: '"It flawlessly expresses the belief that manhood requires rites of violence" *Newsweek*.' It is an interesting choice, as the quotation is

---

[3]Simkin draws attention to the differences between an X in the United States and the United Kingdom, 'The implications of an American "X", however, were far more serious' and could limit release of a film (Simkin 2006: 30).

[4]A short note on the popularity of the actors in the films is worth including here, as it adds to the narrative image of each of the films. Quigley Publishing's annual poll of cinema owners and film buyers suggests a top-ten list of box-office performers from which we can understand which stars had sustained popularity. By far the most successful was Eastwood, appearing in every list during the 1970s, often in first or second place (including first place in 1972 after *Dirty Harry*'s release). Hoffman appeared in the first half of the decade, reaching a high of sixth in 1971. Hackman appears twice: at number three after *The French Connection* and during the release of *The Poseidon Adventure*, and in 1975 when *The French Connection II* was released. From 1973 to 1976 Bronson consistently appears, peaking at fourth in 1975, while *Death Wish* was still on release. De Niro appears once, in tenth place, in 1977, a year after the release of *Taxi Driver*. Peter Boyle does not appear. Quigley Publishing's lists suggest the impact of the films, and the potential influence the stars may have had on each film's narrative image (Quigley Publishing 2004).

[5]It also recalls the Odessa steps sequence from *Battleship Potemkin* (Sergei Eisenstein, 1925), a film in which violence is used in a montage sequence. Peckinpah's own films employ a similar method for depicting violence.

open to interpretation depending on the receiver of the text; it is not clear whether *Newsweek* is approving of the film or not, although the use of 'flawlessly' suggests the film is convincing. Whether positive or negative, the quotation connects to violence and masculinity setting a clear agenda for the audience. The other quotations used on these posters are typical of the positive excerpts one expects, praising the film and Hoffman's performance. The tagline on the UK release poster is suggestive and offers a specific way of reading the film and David Sumner's actions: 'The knock at the door meant the birth of a man and the death of seven others.' The imagery of this poster makes acute links between sex and violence, displacing Hoffman from the centre of the frame, instead making him a spectator (albeit one with a gun in his hand). The central image here is of Scutt's (Ken Hutchison) attempted rape of Amy (Susan George), overlaid onto a close-up of Amy's bra-less chest (echoing the opening shots of the film).[6] Associations between sex and violence are made, with Amy's body being foregrounded as a battleground.

The theatrical trailer repeats this imagery, emphasizing the siege and the sexual rivalry. The voice-over suggests a reading of the film, 'This is David Sumner. All his life he's been running away, turning his back on trouble, involvement and confrontation. Until now.' Here David's character is identified as having a desire to escape, to avoid (which could be an echo/ condemnation of the pacifist sentiments expressed across America at the time). The later quote, 'He found that a man can't hide forever', further prompts the subject of masculinity as a key theme of the film while simultaneously recalling sentiments of the Western. Here the producers are foregrounding the meanings of masculinity, with a female figure placed as a central motivator of conflict.

Straw Dogs' Press Book offers more detail on the preferred reading of the text giving a detailed synopsis and interpretation of the film. Showing an awareness of the hermeneutic code expressed through the title's ambiguity the film-makers offered this explanation:

[*Straw Dogs*] were sacrificial substitutes and were treated with the greatest deference before they were used as an offering, only to be discarded and trampled upon as soon as they had served their purpose. . . .

---

[6] It is possible that this is also a reference to the feminist movement and the myth of 'burning bras'. This would suggest a link between Amy's control of her own body and sexuality and the rape that subsequently occurs. This links to motivations cited by rapists in the 1970s that women were 'asking for it' based on their dress and aggressive behaviour, 'Was it any surprise that the increasing candour, if not sexual abandonment, of young women might be construed as invitations to sexual intercourse, some people asked?' (Bourke 2008: 75). In effect a patriarchal response to feminism.

David and Amy are Straw Dogs. They are directed into a situation which was none of their doing. The change which comes upon them is not wished by either. They have to be sacrificed to cover the sins of others (they witnessed the killing of the Major). Plainly and simply they are scapegoats.

Marketing *The French Connection* (US Rating R, UK Certificate X)

Far from hiding the difficult and controversial persona of Popeye Doyle (Gene Hackman) the marketing for *The French Connection* uses this as an enticement for the audience; Doyle's ambivalence is a reason to see the film. The central image used in the poster advertising is of Doyle shooting the French gangster Nicoli (Marcel Bozzuffi) in the back. In this image Nicoli is unarmed and the spectator has no frame of reference for his identity. Some posters have this image of Doyle flanked by the line 'Doyle is bad news – but a good cop.' A moral ambiguity is indicated here, as is a contradiction between definitions of good and bad.[7] The pain and fear on Nicoli's face extend this. Other posters showed variations on this, retaining Doyle's contradictory persona as the essence of the film with the tagline 'New York breeds tough cops. Jimmy Doyle is the toughest.' This poster develops the ambiguity about Doyle by repositioning Nicoli, making the audience as much a target of Doyle as Nicoli[8] (although arguably Nicoli's position in the posters with arms outstretched to his sides, reminiscent of the crucifixion pose, suggests him as a victim or sacrifice). With the casting of Hackman, Academy Award nominated for *Bonnie and Clyde* in 1967 but lacking a notable film since then, the film-makers signalled their desire for a convincing level of reality; Hackman's name is insignificant in the posters, while Doyle's persona dominates.

This view of Doyle is furthered by the US theatrical trailer, which opens with Doyle rousting the Harlem bar. The voice-over eschews the traditional deep male voice, and a male voice with a distinct New York accent is heard (one suspects this is linked to the attempt at verisimilitude made by the film-makers, grounding even the trailer in reality); 'Popeye Doyle, if he doesn't like you, he'll take you apart. And it's all perfectly legal because Doyle fights dirty and plays rough. Doyle is bad news, but a good cop.' The imagery

---

[7]This is also potentially a reference to the narrative of Western *The Man Who Shot Liberty Valance* (John Ford, 1962).
[8]This engagement of the audience as a target of a gunshot has a long history going back to *The Great Train Robbery* (Edwin S. Porter, 1903) and through to the gun-barrel opening of the James Bond films.

in the trailer places emphasis on the violence in the film but also on the procedural nature of the Police work, as reiterated in the voice-over, 'The stake-out, the pay-off, the chase, *The French Connection*'. There is a clear attempt to instil a high modality for the film.

The French Connection's press book is limited, emphasizing print advertising. The variations of the main poster develop ideas of 'The Great American Thriller' (what is meant by this remains unclear). One page, entitled 'Exploitation', makes much of the film's basis in reality and suggests exhibitors link the film to more recent drug smuggling busts and Police procedures, asking them to 'prevail upon their local press to do a special feature, interviews or even editorial work on the narcotics squad people in your area'. Robin Moore's book, from which the film was adapted, was also reissued with a tie-in cover that connected *The French Connection* to another of Moore's books, *The Green Berets* (1965). The other work had been adapted by John Wayne in 1968 into a film dramatizing US involvement in the Vietnam War; indeed, it was the only Major Studio film directly depicting the conflict made in American while the war was still happening. Seen as a right-wing fantasy that recalled Wayne's Second World War Films, which to many critics was out of time in its narrative and representations, it was still a box-office success (Wills 1997: 228–33) perhaps inflecting the spectator's reading of *The French Connection*.

Marketing *Dirty Harry* (US Rating R, UK Certificate X)

The choice of name, 'Dirty' Harry Callahan, is intriguing due to the potential cultural meanings of the word 'dirty'. In the film Callahan's nickname is explained by his attitude to others: 'Harry hates everybody: Limeys, Micks, Hebes, Fat Dagos, Niggers, Honkies, Chinks, you name it.'[9] However, this is not explained in the advertising. This leaves other potential meanings open. One, that 'dirty' means 'corrupt', casts question marks over Callahan's role in the Police. Another meaning is more subtle but underlines the duality between Callahan and Scorpio (Andrew Robinson) that also appears in the film. As Lev explains when discussing *Joe*, 'In *Joe*, and American culture generally, dirt seems to be connected with sex (as in "filthy pictures") and criminality' (Lev 2000: 26). This ambiguity about Callahan is followed up in the marketing; some posters carrying the tagline 'Detective Harry

---

[9] Given Callahan's name and profession it's reasonable to suggest that he's of Irish decent – making his inclusion of 'Micks' ironic and typical of the self-reflexivity Eastwood displays in his films.

Callahan. You don't assign him to murder cases. . . . You just turn him loose.' Alternative posters proclaimed, 'Detective Harry Callahan, he doesn't break murder cases, he smashes them.' Here, as with *Straw Dogs*, there is a clear emphasis on the star, with Eastwood firing his Magnum gun the dominant image throughout the poster art, with his name the same size as, and above, the title. This image builds on previous images of Eastwood[10] and would become iconic in its own right:

> *Dirty Harry* established Clint Eastwood as a man with a gun – an image that was reworked and reinforced in one marketing campaign after another throughout the decade. Moreover, the gun in many (if not most) of the posters is *aimed at us*. At least one prominent poster design for almost every Eastwood film during that era features this visual trope – a fascinating and paradoxical promotional strategy, which threatens the potential moviegoer while promising action from an aggressive, violent and slightly manic protagonist. (Frangioni and Schatz 2009: 66)

The concept of the 'manic protagonist' is one which connects clearly with the other films in this study. Another way in which to understand the film was offered through other marketing images that create an implicit comparison between Callahan and Scorpio, with them both firing weapons (although Scorpio is pushed into the top corner of the image, and it suggests, through eyelines, that he is aiming at Callahan). The tagline furthers the parallel between the two: 'Dirty Harry and the homicidal maniac. Harry's the one with the badge.'[11] This theme was reinforced by the trailer, with the voice-over intoning: 'This is a movie about a couple of killers. Harry Callahan and a homicidal maniac. The one with the badge is Harry.' Implicitly a confusion and elision between the two characters are made, that their actions are separated only by Callahan's status. The trailer's imagery reinforces this, cutting between two separate scenes where both Callahan and Scorpio use sniper rifles. The majority of the trailer then concentrates on Callahan as a force of action and his conflicts with his superiors but does also include the

---

[10]Although this study is concerned with understanding subject positioning, Annemone Ligensa's discussion of Eastwood's audiences is illuminating for how it subverts assumptions. Using empirical data from various sources, including audience polls, Ligensa shows how Eastwood's audience was not confined to a white male demographic. Indeed in 1997 Harris Poll data showed that Eastwood was the 'most popular white star among African Americans (closely following their favourite, who was also the overall favourite in some years, Denzel Washington)'. One survey of young African Americans from the early 1970s 'found Eastwood to have a remarkable standing with them, appearing third among the "most admired white Americans" (after John F. Kennedy and Robert Kennedy and tying with Lyndon B. Johnson and Hubert Humphrey' (2012: 234).

[11]Although by the end of the film he will have thrown the badge away, collapsing the difference.

story of his dead wife, an attempt at creating empathy and perhaps some psychological depth to the character (and widening audience appeal).

The original press book for the film includes various pre-written news articles for placement in newspapers during and prior to its release. These highlight several efforts to create a preferred reading. One particular article attempts to play down the identification of actor Eastwood with character Callahan (despite the clear elision in the posters) and discusses the violence that had become associated with Eastwood's films: 'Don't let Clint Eastwood's violent screen demeanor [sic] fool you. He's a pushover for kindness and consideration.' It reads as a peremptory refutation of the eventual criticisms of the film. However, the piece also acknowledges the impact of Sergio Leone's *Dollars Trilogy* on Eastwood's screen persona, something that would not have been lost on *Dirty Harry*'s audience: 'Eastwood's impenetrable toughness grew, naturally out of those Italian roles in such films as *A Fistful of Dollars* and *For a Few Dollars More* in which an absence of humaneness made him a disreputable but admired kind of movie hero.' It furthermore offers a specific explanation of the nickname Dirty Harry: 'the epithet indicating that Harry gets the dirty end of the stick rather than that he plies his profession in a less than admirable character.' Warner Bros had a clear awareness that the meaning of 'Dirty' needed fixing, to counter oppositional readings of the term.[12]

Marketing *Death Wish* (US Rating R, UK Certificate X)

As *Dirty Harry* extends Eastwood's existing screen persona and *Straw Dogs* creates a metatextual[13] reaction to Hoffman's previous roles, the marketing of *Death Wish* is firmly set in exploiting the existing meanings of Charles Bronson. There is a clear relationship between the posters for *Death Wish* and previous Bronson vehicles such as *The Stone Killer* (Michael Winner, 1973), but also *The French Connection*'s main image of the protagonist aiming his gun towards the audience. The high level of grain visible in the image can be read several ways. It directly relates the poster to newspaper printing (and a higher modality), as does the use of two colour in many of the print ads. It also signals the producers' desire to court controversy by recalling the artwork for *The Exorcist* (William Friedkin, 1973), which had been a box-office success

---

[12]The synopsis printed in the press book offers an alternate ending for the film, 'As police sirens approach, Harry turns and walks down the road, a solitary figure, his star in his pocket, the man they call Dirty Harry.' The cut released has Callahan throw his badge away, taking a much more anti-establishment stance than the synopsis suggests.
[13]'when a text takes up a relation of commentary to another text' (Allen 2000: 102).

a year before, but one that alarmed many critics and audience groups. This style of image is evocative of several horror films, including *Rosemary's Baby* (Roman Polanski, 1968) and Eastwood's directorial début *Play Misty for Me* (1971). The central image of Bronson, as Paul Kersey, clearly signifies the thriller genre and Bronson's star persona (with influence from *The French Connection* and *Dirty Harry*): however, the film also suggests the horror genre through evocation of a hellish city, the morality of good versus evil, and the fragility of the female body and the role of the paternal figure.

There is only one central poster image for *Death Wish*, although it appears in several colour variations. The tagline, used in almost all print advertising, reads 'Vigilante, City Style – Judge, Jury and Executioner'. Bronson is clearly placed as the protagonist and star with several explicit roles, and there is an evident desire to embrace controversy. The Paramount Press Book for the film has 'Suggested Copy for Marquees!' which includes the following: 'DO YOU GIVE THE VIGILANTE LIFE OR A MEDAL?' Clearly this is setting up a debate for audiences and critics to have. By acknowledging the controversy, the film would go on to create a positive out of potentially negative publicity. (It could equally be true that the controversy is one created by Paramount's publicity department.) The articles in the press book highlight several areas which Paramount were keen for exhibitors to focus on including current affairs and real-life crime, suggesting that *Death Wish* becomes the basis for 'Programs on how to Prevent Muggings' and that there should be 'Special Police Screenings'. Later the moral panic concerning crime that was generated during the early 1970s will be discussed; it is something the producers of *Death Wish* were aware of and were willing to capitalize on.

The film is also seen within the context of Bronson and Winner's previous films (together and apart); films such as *The Mechanic* (Winner, 1972), in which Bronson played a professional killer, and *The Stone Killer*, in which he played a cop, are mentioned. Authenticity is also prioritized in the copy, attempting to place the film in a real-world context. Bronson is given an authenticity as he used to live in New York, while much is made of Winner's use of location shooting. (Nevertheless, the other New York films in this study were also shot on location.) An interview with Winner acknowledges, and taps into, potential controversy:

> I am sure that many people will respond to this by decrying the premise as a violation of civil liberty. But others are bound to sympathize. Many people when they read of these terrible crimes in the streets say to themselves, 'My God if I only could get a gun I'd go out there and get rid of these brutal savages.' Of course, reasonably such behaviour would only increase the violence. But it does provide a controversy that is terribly true of the times we live in.

Several elements of Winner's response are worth examining here. He manages to simultaneously play up the relevance of his film, while distancing it from criticism (by invoking audience sympathies). The use of the word 'savages' is important in the way it draws an opposition between 'us' (the sympathetic people) and 'them' and recalls the Western.

Generally, the preferred reading of *Death Wish* provided by the press book emphasizes the status of Bronson and his character (who are constantly elided) as a lone protagonist. One article that highlights Vincent Gardenia (who plays Lt. Ochoa) suggests an alternative reading that will be returned to, 'The paradox of the story lies in the fact that the criminal Gardenia's pursuing, played by Bronson, is just an ordinary citizen.' The narrative is refocused to suggest that Bronson takes the role of antagonist, rather than protagonist. This would radically rewrite the film into one in which Kersey is a killer who should be stopped. However, it is a minor reference. One must also question, given his established persona, the suggestion of Bronson as an 'ordinary citizen'.

Marketing *Taxi Driver* (US Rating R, UK Certificate X)

Taxi Driver is another ambiguous title, offering a hint at the content of the film, but without specificity. It is in the nature of the figure of the taxi driver to be anonymous, someone with whom we interact on a purely functional level. It is this anonymity the marketing emphasizes. The marketing for *Taxi Driver* initially seems anomalous among this series of films. The poster campaign used two prints, with similar constructions. One isolates Travis Bickle (Robert De Niro) against a backdrop of New York highlighting the 'adult movie' theatres. In this image his body is hunched over as if he tries to ignore the world around him. Another image again isolates Bickle from the background which is kept dark other than a light on his Yellow Cab. In this image his gaze is off to the side, avoiding contact with the audience, but vigilant of the world around him. One tagline begins 'On every street . . .' echoing the real-world aesthetic of *The French Connection* (as does the black and white imagery). As in the other films a lone male protagonist dominates, but here there is no clear relationship to violence. Rather it is an image of alienation, with Bickle turning his back on the world. The tagline describes him as 'a lonely forgotten man desperate to prove that he's alive'. This clearly suggests a sympathetic reading of Bickle and doesn't hint at his violent, obsessive potential. De Niro's name appears above the title, but without the significance of Hoffman, Eastwood or Bronson.

The theatrical trailer emphasizes De Niro as an actor, rather than as a star persona, and adds an element of violence and horror in its depiction of guns and violence.[14] Similarly, to the film, the trailer opens with a dreamlike sequence, the taxi emerging from the sewer steam, then cutting to Bickle's eyes as he regards the New York streets. The voice-over highlights De Niro's prowess as an actor – 'in *Bang the Drum* slowly critics called him a brilliant new actor' – and suggests a less than sympathetic view of Bickle's character – 'a terrifying portrait of life on the edge of madness'. The image of Bickle recurs the trailer, linked to his obsession with Betsy and his preparation for violence: 'The Taxi Driver is looking for a target and getting ready. Getting organized. Preparing himself for the only moment in his life that will ever mean anything.'

Taxi Driver's press book gives an elaborate amount of production information emphasizing screenwriter Paul Schrader over De Niro and Scorsese. It covers the main themes of the film through the screenwriter,

> In Schrader's own words, 'Taxi Driver' dramatizes the all-too-human condition of loneliness, a human being who moves through the madding crowd, jostled, brushed, ignored or abused, but who is somehow utterly untouched by any of it because of his own secret world of fantasy and his inability to communicate with his fellow humans. In short, a lonely man, aching to be noticed, recognized and loved, but unable to attain it.

The violence of the film is played down, but the alienation of the main character is emphasized. Rather than foreground violence, it is kept (in the trailer) as an ever-present threat, hinted at but not seen.

* * *

Readings of the marketing for the films help to identify the similarities between these texts. They suggest the centrality of the lone male protagonist, the importance of violence and the status of men (and implicitly the status of women). This creates a sense of what attracted audiences to these films and suggests a preferred reading of each. This promotion is only one part of the narrative image. To further our understanding of reception we must also investigate the critical reactions to the films (an element of paratext), before turning to contextual issues. Haberski Jr. discusses how the wider cultural view of films was changing in America, 'By the mid-1960s, treating movies as a lesser art or merely as an amusement had vanished for good. Both Hollywood and the federal government – two institutions that had earlier dismissed suggestions that movies were anything but an industry – had at last provided formal recognition of the new perception' (2001: 173).

---

[14]The marketing does make mention of Scorsese, but De Niro is clearly prioritized, and his name is repeated several times in the trailer.

There are various factors that accounted for this, including the rise of film schools and the wider distribution of foreign films into the American market during the 1960s due to a shortfall in production in Hollywood. This change was reflected in film criticism and the regard in which film critics were held:

> Movie critics benefitted tremendously from this heightened interest in film. For the first time in American history they were respected as intellectuals. And why not? Millions of moviegoers followed them as priests who passed judgement on movies, directors and filmmaking styles. They issued cinematic doctrine. So, not only did moviegoers have a passion for cinema, they were also passionate about what others, especially critics, said about the movies. And when movies mattered to the public, then the critics, too, seemed to matter. (Haberski Jr. 2001: 2)

This rise in the esteem in critics is worth noting, as it suggests a direct effect on the habits of the cinema-going public (although this can only be supposition), although it doesn't tell us whether audiences trusted reviews or not. But as a way of gauging discussions around the films analysing the critics' views is worthwhile. Critics help shape dominant readings of texts, highlighting specific social and ideological issues. A positive review can help a film reach a wider audience (witness the quotations used on posters discussed earlier in the chapter). Kael's review of *Bonnie and Clyde* is often credited with helping that film attain a second release by Warner Bros., with the film's gross rising from $2.5 million on its original release to $19.1 million (Haberski Jr. 2001: 178). But there is also potential for a negative impact (much of the poor early gross for *Bonnie and Clyde* having been due to negative reviews).

Pauline Kael was one of several important critics during a time, as identified by Haberski Jr., and others, as one when film critics' influence had become greater than before. During this period critics were willing to engage with ideological elements they perceived in the films, setting a tone which much subsequent analysis failed to challenge. Kael's unique position, as America's pre-eminent film critic, has been enshrined in the various collections of her *New Yorker* reviews. Alongside Kael, other important voices of the time included Andrew Sarris (*The Village Voice*), Judith Crist (*New York Magazine*), Vincent Canby (*The New York Times*), Penelope Gilliat (*The New Yorker*), Richard Schickel (*Life*) and Jay Cocks (*Time*). Examining their views helps assess the impact of the films, and how they were seen in context, providing the backbone of this book. In contrast to these are the reactions of UK critics who identified different aspects of the films as concerning for them and their audiences – this helps highlight ideological areas of the American reactions and provide contrasts and similarities. For this, significant journals have included *Monthly Film Bulletin*, *Sight and Sound* and *Screen* (especially for work on contemporary issues of the representation of violence), as well as newspapers such as *The Times*, *The Guardian* and *The Daily Mail*. These works develop a clear picture of the critical reactions in the United States and the United Kingdom, as well as how contemporary writers connected these films through the shared concerns of fascist ideology, violence and audience effects. However, these criticisms generally see the films in isolation, without much sense of theoretical or evidential background. Some later articles, such as those in *Jump Cut*, offer greater analysis and challenge some of the initial assumptions, but generally a broad critical consensus is evident.

Analysing critical reactions raises several concerns and issues essential to understanding a films' reception. Although separate from the marketing, reviews form an important part of the paratext to each film, helping to set an agenda in which they are viewed and understood. Reviews also highlight important contemporary concerns, the American critics being anxious about the potential political messages of the films (their suggested fascism). From this, key political issues became clear: ideological conflict in US culture, perceptions and anxieties concerning crime and the enforcement of law and order, the representation of gender and the representation of violence. Violence was a key concern for both the US and the UK critics, particularly the relationship of the audience to screen violence and critical anxieties that spectators would be moved to imitate the films they watched. A clear semantic gap appears, however, in the lack of clarity throughout the reviews over their terminology, particularly over what the concept of fascism means. These concerns were tied to wider fears over social changes and what the success of these films meant for society and what they may, or may not, have been seen to promote.

Critical reactions

The major issue that distinguishes the American and British responses to the films is ideology; while the American works regularly make ideological readings, the British concentrate more on the violence in the films (which is also a central issue for American critics). Central to the American approach were the issues of machismo, totalitarianism and fascism. Kael, writing for *The New Yorker*, invokes ideas of fascism and variants of them repeatedly. *Straw Dogs* is 'a fascist work of art' (1973: 398) which presents the 'triumph of a superior man' (a phrase that is invoking both Nazi propaganda film *Triumph of the Will* (Leni Riefenstahl, 1935) and Nietzsche's concept of the superman). *Dirty Harry* is 'a right wing fantasy' that 'attacks liberal[15] values'

---

[15]It is worth highlighting that there is a difference in the definition of liberal between the United States and the United Kingdom, it clearly having stronger connotations in the United States

(1973: 385). *The French Connection* displays a 'right-wing, left-wing, take-your-choice cynicism' (1973: 318). Only her review of *Taxi Driver* displays a different sensibility. (Kael did not review *Joe* or *Death Wish*.) The suggestion that 'liberal values' are under attack is at the heart of much of the American critical responses to these films, an implied opposition between left and right ideologies (in the American sense) where the reader's support for the left is assumed.

This question of an ideological split is ably demonstrated in the reactions to *Joe*. In an interview with Peter Boyle, titled 'Reluctant Hero of the Hardhats', *Life* highlighted the key area that divided audiences about the film and the identification that the lead actor came to have with the character: 'He likes recognition and approval as well as the next actor. But on the other hand, he personally does *not* agree – most emphatically he does not – with everything he says as Joe Curran, blue-collar worker, in the film *Joe*. It bothers him every time somebody praises him for what Joe says' (Durham 1970: 69).

Although Joe Curran is repeatedly identified as a bigot, the film is not accused of being fascist per se, but the question of whether audiences would approve of Joe's actions and words continually arises. This is reiterated in the responses Boyle was getting on the streets, where the self-avowed liberal was being praised for delivering Joe's lines. Even though both *Variety* and Schickel criticized the film for lack of depth and characterization, its divisiveness was evident. *Jet* (1970: 60–1), a magazine targeting Black Americans, described the film as 'chilling (for blacks, liberals, long hairs)' and went on to describe Boyle as a 'gentle intellectual' but his character as 'the poisoned-minded, hard-hat, gun-collecting, beer guzzling, nigger-and-hippie hating white bigot'; it quoted him recalling how 'an old lady came up to me and said: "You said everything I wanted to say in that bar (scene), everything I wanted to say and can't. You are speaking for me, Joe."' The focus on the character of Joe reiterates the marketing for the film.

In Gareth Epps's article for *The New York Times*, 'Does Popeye Doyle Teach us to be Fascist?', the right/left division is capably illustrated. The introductory paragraph reads: 'It's been obvious for a long time that American filmmakers are unable to deal with the politics of the left in any recognizable way.' A simple rhetorical strategy is employed here: Epps makes a statement of fact, one to be agreed with despite his offering of little evidence (other than namechecking *I Was a Communist for the FBI* (Gordon Douglas, 1951), and *The Strawberry Statement* (Stuart Hagmann, 1970)). If such a fact is obvious, why does he need to tell us? Who has recognized this, and how long is a long time? We could ask more questions of Epps, particularly what is meant by 'left' in this context. Having assumed his readers' agreement, Epps then moves on to another

---

during a time of political upheaval.

statement, 'But recent American films have begun to show a frightening sophistication in at least one area of politics – the half-world of sadism and authoritarianism which is the breeding ground of fascist mentality' (1972: 5).

The association of fascism with sadism is one which is repeatedly made throughout critiques of the films; Vincent Canby discusses the 'high class butchery' of *Straw Dogs*' finale (1972: 1); Kael describes the 'sadists and bullies' (1973: 385) that make up the Police force in *Dirty Harry*. Schickel's *Time* review of *Death Wish* was simply entitled 'Mug Shooting' (1974). As none of these critics offers a definition of fascism, we can only define it through the associations and oppositions within their work. Regarding the general response to *Dirty Harry*, Smith notes 'The contrast between the big crowds at the movie theatres and the massively offended reviews (of all the major [US] reviewing organs, only *Rolling Stone* praised the film)' (1993: 95).

One of the key associations is with the nature of masculinity or, as Kael prefers, machismo, 'The story of *Straw Dogs* is machismo' (1973: 394). Her review, entitled 'Peckinpah's Obsession', at once talks about Peckinpah being an 'artist' and creating 'art', positive terms that are used several times but also create a sense of disappointment. It becomes implicit that it is worse that an artist has made this film, 'fascist' being used as an implicit condemnation, a misdirection of talent, and Kael couches her review in the terms of dogmatic statements about Peckinpah – his 'romantic perversity' for instance. It is a clear didactic strategy, allowing Kael to admire Peckinpah's technique as a filmmaker while simultaneously objecting to the content. This is further pushed by the comparisons to his previous films which are seen as 'rich and varied'. The title itself is both a statement and a question: it begs what is Peckinpah's obsession? Of course, Kael will tell us. The answer to the question is an obsession with 'machismo' ('manhood', 'unmanly' and 'superior man' are also used in the review) and how that relates to the presentation of the 'professor's hot young wife . . . who wants to be raped and sodomized'. The use of 'sodomized' is intriguing and does not accurately reflect the action in the film (although other critics have interpreted the rape similarly[16]), as there is no explicit evidence for it. Kael may be exaggerating here, to press her agenda more clearly. Issues of masculinity are discussed at first in her review, and fascism is invoked later, with their relationship made clear by terminology that first implies fascism and then the use of direct references in phrases such as 'the triumph of a superior man'. Eventually Kael comes to the point that she has been building towards: 'Sam Peckinpah,

---

[16]In an interview with *Playboy* Peckinpah discussed this issue: 'I'd like to point out to Miss Kael and these other so-called critics that rear entry does not necessarily mean sodomy. . . . I guess Kael and her friends have anal complexes' (Murray 2008: 104).

who is an artist, has, with *Straw Dogs*, made the first American film that is a fascist work of art.' In the two remaining paragraphs variations on the word 'fascist' are used three times. Having set up the ideas of machismo, rape and violence, Kael invokes fascism, investing the term with those meanings rather than a political or historical sense. Similarly, Canby describes how David Sumner 'wins title to his masculinity by killing or maiming in various ingenious ways a group of country thugs who try to invade his house' (1972: D1), furthering the view that *Straw Dogs* endorses Sumner's actions.

Epps goes further in his use of terminology, describing both *Straw Dogs* and *Dirty Harry* as 'rationale fascism' which is further linked to masculinity and machismo: 'The lesson, however [of *Straw Dogs*], is classic fascism; the quest of the meta-experience of violence as a validation of existence, along with a contempt and brutalization of women' (1971: 15). Epps states David Sumner's goals as, 'To have passed through the portals of murder into the world of manhood, and by doing so have conquered the menace of women. It is a totalitarian pastoral' (1971: 15). 'Totalitarian' here reads as a synonym for 'fascist', despite the differences between the terms. These words surface again throughout American critics' work. Ebert (1971) stated that *Dirty Harry*'s 'moral position is fascist. No doubt about it'. For Kael, the same film 'is obviously a genre movie, but this action genre has always had a fascist potential, and it has finally surfaced' (1973: 388). In discussing *The French Connection* Kael is more circumspect, praising the director: 'Friedkin has done a sensational job' (1973: 317). However, she makes an implicit statement when comparing the film to depiction of a 'fascist conspiracy' in *Z* (Costa-Gavras, 1969). For Epps, *The French Connection* 'cannot be called a fascist film'; instead, it is a celebration of authority, brutality and racism (1972: 22), begging the question of how Epps defines fascism. He goes on to accuse it of lacking a 'unifying ideology'. There is no discussion here of how it could offer a unifying ideology, but he goes on to state that *Dirty Harry* and *Death Wish* do offer an ideology without fully exploring what this means or how it is done. Epps invokes (in an echo of Kael) Nietzsche when discussing *Dirty Harry*, 'a simply told story of the Nietzschean superman and his sado-masochistic pleasure'. He then asks his readers to 'place some pressure on producers and distributors to stop offering us fascist propaganda and sado-masochistic wet dreams'. Canby goes further: 'I doubt even the genius of Leni Riefenstahl could make it artistically acceptable' (1972: 1). Riefenstahl is also referenced in Shedlin's comprehensive analysis of *The French Connection* in *Film Quarterly*, where it is described as 'a network of implications and assumptions that transmit rightist propaganda' (1972: 3). Shedlin goes on to connect *The French Connection* explicitly to contemporary concerns:

> By playing on our confused fantasies of a frightened and schizophrenic culture, the makers of *The French Connection* have built a product

that addresses itself directly to the major issues of our society – racism, corrupt power, brutality, drugs – and yet manages to subsume all social significance beneath an explosion of gaudy adventurism that ultimately reinforces the heroism of the authorities it seems to be criticising. (1972: 3)

Taxi Driver avoids such ideological criticism. Kael concentrates on the portrayal of Bickle as a psychopath, relating the film to 'real life'. Schickel, in *Time*, follows a similar theme, 'There is a certain kind of urban character who, however lightly we brush up against him, he instantly leaks the psychopathy of everyday anguish all over us.... Familiar Breed. Travis, the taxi driver, is such a creature' (1976).

In general, the reviews of *Taxi Driver* concentrate on this aspect. Writing in *The New York Times* Canby titled his review 'Scorsese's Disturbing *Taxi Driver*' (1976a: 1) describing Bickle as an 'aberration' and a 'first class psychotic'. Violence rather than ideology becomes the other dominant concern in many reviews, with the penultimate scene of *Taxi Driver* prompting Candy to write that it is 'of a violent intensity that is not easily supported (for me, anyway) by what has gone before' (1976a: 1). Writing later in the same year Canby published an article, 'Explicit Violence Overwhelms Every Other Value on the Screen' (1976b: 69). In this he re-examines *Taxi Driver* as an example of how 'the volume of screen violence is being raised to the point where you can no longer see it', giving a strong description of the final shoot-out, 'We are presented with the vividly photographed spectacle of a number of people with a high-powered gun at point-blank range so that blood, guts and bone become the medium as well as the message of the movie' (1976b: 69). At once Canby deplores the violence presented but also suggests the saturation of violence in cinema renders it invisible. In the same article he describes the violence in *Straw Dogs* 'intolerable'. For Schickel (1976) violence is not a problem in itself, but it undermines *Taxi Driver* and seems unnecessary: 'violence that seems forced and – coming after so much dreariness – ridiculously pyrotechnical.'

Whereas criticism of *Taxi Driver* concentrated on the psychotic behaviour of Travis Bickle, often reviews for the other films focused on the possible effects of the films on their spectators. Indeed, the reaction of the audience is dissected as much as the films. Inevitably this positions the reviewer apart from the audience and by implication superior to them. Notice Kael's description of the audience in her review of *The French Connection*:

Audiences for these movies in the Times Square area and the Village are highly volatile. Probably the unstable, often dazed members of the audiences are particularly susceptible to the violence and tension on the screen; maybe crowds now include a certain number of people who can't stay calm for two hours. But whether the movies bring it out in the audience or whether the particular audiences that are being attracted into the theatre, it's there in the theatre, particularly in the late shows, and you feel the violence on the screen may at any moment touch off violence in the theatre. The audience is explosively live. (Kael 1973: 315)

There is a clear distancing of Kael from the audience. They have become a unified other likely to erupt into violence (although Kael hedges her bets somewhat, using 'probably' and 'may'), described as 'unstable' and 'dazed'. What Kael doesn't feel the need to discuss is the lack of any 'explosion' recorded in real life. Similar hyperbole accompanied *Straw Dogs* which was compared, unfavourably, to events in Vietnam by Schickel, 'Even at My-Lai there were at least some individuals present to raise moral objection to the event' (1972: 14).[17] Variety was more direct in calling it 'an orgy of unparalleled violence and nastiness with undertones of sexual repression' (Variety 1969). *Joe* is reported to have inspired vocal reactions in its audience, but intriguingly these reactions were polarized. Alongside those who approached Peter Boyle to praise him for performing Joe's opinions and voiced their support during the film (Hoberman 2003: 287), others were less positive. Lev describes them, 'The young New York audience who stood up and talked back to the screen ("Next time we're going to shoot back, Joe")' (2000: 25). Klemesrud in *The New York Times* conducted an anecdotal survey of the responses to *Death Wish* in an article titled 'What Do They See in Death Wish?' (1974: 87). She discusses how she got 'caught up in the spirit if things – I found myself applauding several times too' (notice the distancing and regret in her writing). The article quotes 'random interviews' to gauge public reaction to the film. Despite their randomness, there is a clear sense of choice in the interviews; seven men to four women, three of whom are Black (two male, one female). The Black voices are balanced, one approving of the film, two disapproving (on racial grounds). Women's reactions are highlighted, suggesting that their approval of the film would be more shocking, although 'Many, but not all, of the women interviewed defended Bronson's vigilante actions more than men did' (1974: 87). The lack of clarity in 'many' is evident, as is the elision between Bronson and his character Paul Kersey, which suggests a desire to project the film into the real world. Masculinity is clearly identified in the pleasures the film offers. Adding to her 'evidence' Klemesrud then quotes 'Three mental health professionals' (all male), who repeat a similar line that the film 'plays out a "fantasy"' and that only someone with a 'mind that's in a delicate balance' would be moved to imitate the film (Kael's audience perhaps?). The ordinary filmgoer is seen in alarmist terms, with Klemesrud asking:

---

[17]The My Lai Massacre is discussed further in Chapter 2.

Does this mean, then, that 'Death Wish' is going to inspire people to pick up guns and take the law into their own hands? Will criminals become fair game in this city? Even before 'Death Wish' came out, examples of vigilantism were making headlines all over the city: 'Four Men Attack and Knife an Alleged Rapist' . . . 'Store Owner Chases and Kills Hold-Up Man' . . . 'Passersby Chase and Capture Purse Snatcher'. (1974: 87)

Klemesrud herself ignores her own contradiction here. Alarmed that *Death Wish* will inspire copycats acts, she cites pre-existing acts, suggesting that the film is a depiction of what is already happening, rather than one that incites such acts. In the same newspaper, writing in July 1974, Canby described *Death Wish* as 'a despicable movie, one that raises complex questions in order to offer bigoted, frivolous, oversimplified answers' (1974a: 27). Having reviewed and condemned the film, Canby was moved by its success to write again, in August of the same year, suggesting that 'Its message, simply put, is; KILL. TRY IT. YOU'LL LIKE IT' (1974b: 85). Canby moves on to describe the reactions of the audience, 'If you allow your wits to take flight, it's difficult not to respond with the kind of lunatic cheers that rocked Loew's Astor Plaza when I was there the other evening. At one point a man behind me shouted with delight: "That'll teach the mothers!"' (1974b: 85). For Penelope Gilliat in *The New Yorker*, the 'audience yells with glee' (1974). There is an implicit condemnation of the audience throughout these articles and what concerns about *Death Wish* is not so much the film itself, but the audience's enjoyment of the film and what this means. For Ebert 'It's propaganda for private gun ownership and a call to vigilante justice' (1974). In response to *Dirty Harry*, Canby suggests that it is 'the first kind of violent movie, designed to transform all of us into surrogate rats' (1972: 1), whatever a surrogate rat may be. Underlining all these reviews is the sense of the audience as a mass, an other, that may be directly influenced by the films.

Joe received much less press in the United Kingdom, with Andrews notably commenting (similarly to US critics) that the film offered pleasure to younger audiences with a 'last-scene martyrdom and the middle-aged the alternate consolation of brute vengeance and prurient experimentation in the hippie way of life' (1971: 76). The reaction to *Straw Dogs* was much more widespread and forceful, highlighting and condemning the 'gratuitous' elements, often in reaction to the film's Cornwall setting. A selection of headlines in UK newspapers sum up the attitude:

The Daily Mirror: YOKEL HORROR IS THE LAST STRAW (Thinkell 1971).

The Daily Express: The message that will shatter you (Christie 1971).

The Daily Mail: Hoffman Horror in our Wild West (Wilson 1971).

The Evening Standard: After this, anything goes ... (Walker 1971).

Straw Dogs became as much a talking point in the newspapers as a film. Such was the outrage within the critical community that '13 of the most eminent critics of the country' (*The Evening Standard* 1971) felt the need to voice their concerns in a letter printed in *The Times* (Cashin et al. 1971) which criticized the BBFC. They were drawn from a cross section of British newspapers (including *The Sun*, *The Guardian* and *The Evening Standard*). Their main concerns were as follows:

> we wish to underline what many of us have already indicated and condemned in our separate reviews of the film *Straw Dogs*: that in our view the use to which this film employs scenes of double rape and multiple killings by a variety of methods is dubious in its intention, excessive in its effect and likely to contribute to the concern expressed from time to time by many critics over films which exploit the very violence which they make a show of condemning. (Cashin et al. 1971)

Although ostensibly about the BBFC's policies, this letter highlights wider concerns about the impact of cinematic representations of violence. Three days after receiving the letter Stephen Murphy (then president and secretary of the BBFC) replied in *The Times* (Murphy, 1971), suggesting that the critics were out of step with public opinion, and he drew attention to reviews in the US magazines *Time* and *Newsweek* that had praised the film. It is a subject that Barr draws attention to in the summer 1972 edition of *Screen*, in which he outlines how many newspaper critics praised *A Clockwork Orange* while defending its depiction of violence, then subsequently attacked *Straw Dogs*. Barr critiques the inaccuracy and inconsistency of the critics, seeing their approval of one film and dismissal of the other as a reaction to filmmaking technique and the reputation of the films' directors. Some of the reviews condemning *Straw Dogs* seem almost to titillate with their use of language (something not lost on the film's promoters who used some of the more outrageous phrases to advertise the film). Alexander Walker's (1971) description of Susan George as a 'nymphet' and using words like 'buggered' is exploitative in itself. Tom Milne, writing in both *The Times* and *Sight and Sound*, and Andrews, in *Monthly Film Bulletin*, were able to critique the violence of the film but still praise it: 'At once harrowingly realistic and richly suggestive *Straw Dogs* promises to emerge as a classic of the horror film' (Andrews 1971). Andrews's suggestion that the film is a horror suggests that understanding of genre may have affected the critics' responses. The critical reception for *Straw Dogs* must also be understood in the differencing versions of the films watched in the United States and the United Kingdom. Simkin discusses how the film was cut to in both countries, but more heavily in the United States to achieve an R rating, not an X. This was especially evident in the double rape scene where the cutting for the censors changed the shape and potentially the meaning, as Simkin explains, 'The US edit was even more severe [than the UK one], with the censor removing around thirty seconds of the sequence between Charlie and Amy, significantly reducing the sexual activity represented, and cutting around seventy seconds of the second rape in order to achieve the required "R" rating' (2011: 108). This created questions as to whether the scene had become more or less ambiguous in its meaning but certainly curtailed its screen time. Whether this reflects in the reviews is difficult to ascertain; however, it is reasonable to say that despite the different cuts the opprobrium shown to the film was evident on both sides of the Atlantic.

Concern with violence is present in the UK reviews for *The French Connection* and *Dirty Harry* (which are often compared due to their close release dates), although the reviews are generally positive and lack the anxiety expressed in the United States. There are exceptions; 'This fantasy of carnage, with the camera gloating over the flesh wounds is, sick', wrote Cashin in *The Sun* (1972) in regard to *Dirty Harry*. Cecil Wilson in *The Daily Mail* wrote of the film's 'preoccupation with blood, beatings-up and psychotic excesses' (1972). Only Milne (1972), in *Sight and Sound*, suggested an ideological analysis, describing '*Dirty Harry*'s "Fascist" attentions', yet felt the need to couch the term in inverted commas. Concerning *The French Connection*, response seemed to accept the violence as part of a 'true and horrifying story of drug smuggling' (from Brian Freemantle's *The Daily Mail* review, December 1971). The film's basis in truth perhaps allowed reviewers to view the violence differently from *Dirty Harry*, that it had more justification to be included. David Pirie commented that the 'violent sequences are almost all presented racily and amusingly, stressing Doyle's "loveable" toughness' (1972), and Ian Christie described it as 'exciting and authentic in its detail' (1972). There is no criticism here for Doyle's shooting of a suspect in the back, the accidental shooting of a mother with a pram or the racism depicted in the film. *Death Wish* comes in for much sterner criticism. Issues are raised about the effect of the film on the audience, and there is a focus on genre. Writing in New York for *The Guardian*, Jane Rosen suggested a link between the film and a rise in gun ownership in the city: 'Two men have been shot in two days who would have been alive today if they had not carried guns to protect themselves. New Yorkers fear a new film called *Death Wish* is inspiring a resurgence of the old American tradition, encouraging people to arm themselves in this way' (1972).

John Coleman picked up on the controversy which arose around the film in New York: 'It will be interesting to see how home audiences react' (1975). John Torode provided the answer: 'To my surprise passions seem to run just as deep in London. On Sunday night I queued in the rain to see *Death Wish*. And sure enough the packed audience cheered as Bronson gunned down random muggers' (1975). For Dilys Powell the film was a sign of a worrying trend; 'more and more the cinema invites sympathy with those who reject the law' (1975). Genre classification is discussed by several critics, including Walker, for whom *Death Wish* 'is really an up-dated and transplanted Western. Part of its seductive appeal comes from the old-fashioned short-cuts it appears to offer to complex problems of urban life' (1975). The use of 'seductive', to be taken in against one's will by something attractive but corrupting, reinforces the sense that the audience is passive and likely to be influenced by the film. *The Daily Mail* went further in connecting *Death Wish* to real crime in an article suggesting that 'one of the most senior police officers in the country last night advised everyone – "police and public alike" – to see *Death Wish* as a warning of what could happen in this county' (Gilchrist 1975). In the same article Colin Woods, assistant commissioner for the Metropolitan Police, 'had a grim warning for Britain: "What we saw on that screen could happen here very soon – perhaps within three years if we are not very careful"' (Gilchrist 1975). The article suggests a causal relationship between a rise in mugging to vigilante groups forming and is suggestive of a wider moral panic. One single voice, Colin McArthur in the left-wing magazine *Tribune* (1975), responded to this outcry, and the assertion that the audience's behaviour would be affected, comparing critical response to that of *The Virgin Spring* (Ingmar Bergman, 1960). He suggested that the audience for *Death Wish* was responding to the formal aspects of the text, rather than any moral message. When compared to the other films, the reception of *Taxi Driver* is much more positive. In a similar vein to *The French Connection* the relationship to reality is used to justify the violence depicted in the film. It has a 'raw factual look', according to Gordon Gow in *Films and Filming* (1976). Derek Malcolm took an opposite view, explaining that the film 'operates first and foremost on an imaginative level' (1976). In comparison with *Death Wish* the reaction is overwhelmingly positive, and one concludes that this is as much to do with the film-makers as the film itself. Whereas Winner had become a successful filmmaker he had little respect from the critical community. Scorsese and De Niro, however, were highlighted for praise, with the artistic merits of the film justifying the presentation of crime. Tom Hutchinson in *The Sunday Telegraph* (1976) explained, 'This is an angry film that never once seems to exploit what it depicts, because it is concerned with something beyond the immediate shock of action.' Perceived artistic merit, and perhaps a sense that a different audience will be queuing for this film than for *Death Wish*, possibly explains the less alarmed reactions to *Taxi Driver*.

As the American critical reactions were more ideologically based, it is worth interrogating how the term 'fascist' functions: how the word is being employed. Writing in 1944 George Orwell discussed the problems associated with the term 'fascism' in an essay entitled 'What Is Fascism?' Having surveyed the use of the term, he concludes:

> It will be seen that, as used, the word 'Fascism' is almost entirely meaningless. In conversation, of course, it is used even more wildly than in print. I have heard it applied to farmers, shopkeepers, Social Credit, corporal punishment, fox-hunting, bull-fighting, the 1922 Committee, the 1941 Committee, Kipling, Gandhi, Chiang Kai-Shek, homosexuality, Priestley's broadcasts, Youth Hostels, astrology, women, dogs and I do not know what else. (Orwell 1944)

Thirty years later Orwell's conclusion held. In his essay 'Power and Strategies' (1980) Michel Foucault recognized a similar situation, 'The non-analysis of fascism . . . enables [it] to be used as a floating signifier, whose function is essentially that of denunciation. The procedures of every form of power are suspected of being fascist, just as the masses are in their desires' (as quoted in Slane 2001: 1).

The function of fascism as an element of rhetoric is one that offers various meanings. Smith locates this within a 1960–70s American context: 'The word *fascist* enjoyed a peculiar and even excessive usage of its own in the sixties and early seventies (being used popularly not so much to describe social phenomena that were the same as Germany's National Socialism, but rather a shorthand for excoriating the everyday workings of the repressive state apparatus of capitalist America)' (1993: 90–1). Slane (2001) explains how the accusation (and the more specific accusation of Nazism) was used by both sides of the abortion debate in the United States – that pro-abortionists are fascist in the 'holocaust' they perpetrate against children, and that anti-abortionists are fascist in their anti-choice practices. The term becomes one that can be easily applied to either side of a debate, with neither using the term specifically. This problem of definition extends to 'violence' which also requires some specific definition if it is to be used in a clear way. Certainly, there are some assumptions throughout the critical reactions: that film violence is harmful in some way to the spectator; that these films (for US critics anyway) communicate right-wing ideologies which spectators would passively absorb; and that spectators would be drawn to imitate the Vigilante Thrillers.

2

Sociopolitical contexts

Whatever legislative program the administration finally developed, the chief problem it faced in 1969 was the perception that the United States was coming apart at the seams. The nation was awash in unprecedented political and racial violence and in a perceived rise in criminality that made many Americans insecure, even in middle-class neighbourhoods and homes.

(SMALL 1999: 157)

Across the U.S., the universal fear of violent crime and vicious strangers – armed robbers, packs of muggers, addict burglars ready to trade a life for heroin – is a constant companion to the populace. It is the cold fear of dying at random in a brief spasm of senseless violence – for a few pennies. For nothing.

(*TIME* 13 JULY 1970)

Discussing the sociopolitical context of the late 1960s and early 1970s is difficult without recycling various tropes of social change, the psychological effect of the Vietnam War and distrust in government and the establishment which would reach a peak with the Watergate scandal. The purpose of this chapter is to highlight several significant issues in the sociopolitical climate that directly inform the films of this study. Key among these is law and order, which underwent radical change throughout the United States in the 1960s and 1970s. Not only was crime rising but the role of the Police and the rights of the suspect (and by implication the victim) were also changing. Vigilantism was not only being addressed in the films discussed here but it was also happening both before and after their release. Added to this was a shifting sense of the identity of the white American male, partly spawned by the Vietnam War. Where previously narrative image and paratext have predominated, this section deals more broadly with intertextual relations: how the films are informed by and then comment upon contextual sociopolitical developments.

In the United States, the 1960s was a time of great disruption with changes in civil rights directly affecting the population. Despite, or perhaps because of, the gains in terms of equality, American society was getting less content and at ease with itself. Johnson describes these changes:

> In what was called 'the demoralization of American society', a number of statistical indicators came together. In the thirty years 1960-90, while the US population rose by 41 percent, there was a 560 percent increase in violent crime, 200 percent in teenage suicide, over 400 percent rise in illegitimate births, 300 percent rise in children living in single parent homes – producing *in toto* the significant fact that children formed the fastest-growing segment of the criminal population. During this period, welfare spending had gone up in real terms by 630 percent and education by 225 percent. (1997: 987)

When Richard Nixon ran for president in 1968, law and order formed a central part of his campaign irrespective of whether his administration could do much to influence such an issue, 'When Nixon ran on a "law and order" platform, he knew there was little the federal government could do to affect local law enforcement. This was the first time that crime had been a central issue in a presidential campaign' (Small 1999: 157). Nixon's emphasis on this issue and subsequent attempts to pass legislation tackling racketeering and corruption demonstrate a shift in the issue of crime as a central element of American politics and the concerns of the American populace. Despite the stereotypes of peace and love, the 1960s were a time of staggering increases in crime in the United States, much of which appears to have been driven by drug use, 'During the 1960s, the number of heroin addicts increased from 50,000 to more than 500,000' (Small 1999: 160). The dark side of the 1960s counterculture was evident, 'US crime statistics became available in the 1960s, when the rate for crimes was revealed as under 1,900 per 100,000 population. That doubled in the 1960s and tripled in the 1970s' (Johnson 1997: 987). Nixon's stance may have been tough, but the statistics suggest it was ineffective. Analysis of statistics is always inherent with risks. Questions should be asked as to what was being counted as a crime for these measures (for instance, reports or arrests). However, such significant increases cannot be dismissed and the perception of rising crime on the American psyche cannot be ignored. More importantly the increase was being associated with violent and sexual crimes, rather than petty theft or minor offences. As *Time* reported in 1975,

> By any measurements, crime has become an ominous national problem. Since 1961 the rate for all serious crimes has more than doubled. From 1973 to 1974 it jumped 17% – the largest increase in the 44 years that national statistics have been collected. In the past 14 years, the rate of robberies has increased 255%, forcible rape[1] 143%, aggravated assault 153% and murder 106%. (30 June 1975)

Of course, it was not just through crime that traditional definitions of law and order were being challenged. Civil Rights marches had become an important mode of political expressions during the 1960s and 1970s, representing the upheavals in the political landscape and challenging what was considered right and normal: 'The seventies also witnessed a virtual revolution in personal rights advocacy. In particular, the areas of gay rights, women's rights, and disability rights gained national importance' (Friedman 2007: 13). The image of the heteronormative American (white and middle class, the 'regular Joe') was being disturbed. Towards the end of the 1960s, the campaigns and marches took on a more violent edge:

> As the Sixties turned into the Seventies, the trend was for campus demonstrations to acquire coordination and specific political purpose, and so to become correspondingly more violent and alarming to those in power. When President Nixon appeared on national TV, April 30, 1970, to announce draft-extensions on account of the trouble in Cambodia, there was an organised series of demos at campuses all over America, some of which degenerated, or were pushed, into riots. At Kent State University in Ohio, students set fire to the local army cadet building, and this act of arson led the governor of Ohio to send in 900 National Guardsmen, who occupied the campus. (Johnson 1997: 913)

The Kent State protest ended with four students being killed and nine others being wounded when the National Guard opened fire. The violence, however, was not limited to the authorities or to acts of arson, 'In 1969, there were 602 bombings or bombing attempts; in 1970, there were 1,577. Of the cataloged [sic] bombings that took place from January 1969 through April 1970 and caused forty-one deaths, 56 percent were the results of

---

[1]'Forcible rape, as defined in the FBI's Uniform Crime Reporting (UCR) Program, is the carnal knowledge of a female forcibly and against her will. Attempts or assaults to commit rape by force or threat of force are also included; however, statutory rape (without force) and other sex offenses are excluded' (fbi.gov).

campus disorders, 19 percent from black extremists, 14 percent from white extremists, and 8 percent from criminal attacks' (Small 1999: 157). Violence was not limited to students and 'extremists' however, nor was it a wholly left-wing affair. The political class was quick to take notice of the upheaval across America and the 1968 presidential election illustrated this effectively. Nixon's law and order stance was targeted at, what he dubbed, the 'silent majority' of Americans opposed to social change and violent protest. The election campaign of independent candidate George C. Wallace, governor of Alabama, appealed specifically to those against the social changes of the 1960s:

> Wallace, a right-wing populist and segregationist, railed against the establishment, the 'overeducated, ivory-tower folks with pointy-heads' who wore 'sissy britches'. He promised, 'If I ever get to be president and one of those demonstrators lay down in front of my car, it'll be the last car they ever lay down in front of.' His American Independent Party was on the ballot in all fifty states. By September [1968], he could claim 21 percent of Americans polled. (Small 1999: 26)

Although Wallace had no real chance of winning, he arguably split the vote for Hubert Humphrey, helping Nixon to win. His popularity also helped give voice to millions of Americans angry at what was happening in the country. In 1969 this voice became violent, 'On May 7 in New York a crowd of construction workers stormed City Hall and beat up students who were occupying it – the first "hard hat" demo against the New Left. This was Nixon's "silent majority" beginning to react"' (Johnson 1997: 914).

Given what was happening across the country, and in particular in New York, the popularity of *Joe* is clearly related to people's own fears and experiences. It is easy to read the actions of the hardhats as a form of vigilantism, taking the law into their own hands against those who threatened their way of life and challenged the establishment. As *Time* described them, 'a gang of 200 hardhats, equipped with U.S. flags and lengths of lead pipe, had waded into a crowd of anti-war students in Wall Street' (*Time* 25 May 1970). Although not a construction worker, Joe Curran is a hard-hatted factory worker.

Within this context of a steep rise in crime, and the increased social unrest and violence, several events stand out as important crimes that became not only socially relevant, as signs of changes in American culture but as influential on this study's films: the killings perpetrated by Richard Speck in 1966, the sniper attacks of Charles Whitman in the same year, the murder perpetrated by the Manson family in 1969, and the 1964 murder of Kitty Genovese. These are part of the backdrop of violence against which America's perception of itself changes:

Even as Chicago police exchanged gunfire with the black residents on the West Side, the city hosted the cold-blooded murder of eight student nurses by twenty-five-year-old Dallas drifter Richard Speck. It was, as *Time* put it, 'an incredible, nearly soundless orgy of mutilation and murder'. Then, only weeks later at the University of Texas in Austin, came the 'Madman in the Tower'. Another twenty-five-year-old, this one an erstwhile altar boy, former Eagle-Scout, ex-marine, and current student of architectural engineering, named Charles Joseph Whitman, purchased ammunition, as he told the clerk, 'to shoot some pigs'. After killing his mother and his pregnant wife, Whitman installed himself atop the library tower in the middle campus and began picking off victims – killing twelve and wounding another thirty one in a ninety-seven-minute 'mad orgy of violence' (*Newsweek*). (Hoberman 2003: 152)

Whitman's actions suggest a clear influence for the Scorpio character in *Dirty Harry* (having previously inspired *Targets* (Peter Bogdanovich, 1967)). Speck's drifter can be seen in the rootless characters of Scorpio and Travis Bickle. Further to these crimes were the Manson family's killings:

In the wee hours of Saturday morning, August 9, 1969, with *Easy Rider* in theatres for less than a month, Charles Manson's gang ventured forth from the Spahn Ranch and murdered Sharon Tate, eight months pregnant, in a Benedict Canyon house at 10050 Cielo Drive she and Roman Polanski had rented after it had been vacated by Candice Bergen and companion at the time, Terry Melcher. Four other people were killed as well, including the hairdresser Jay Sebring, and two friends of Polanski's. (Biskind 1998: 77–8)

The Manson killings are much written about and appear to have had a profound effect on Hollywood and the rest of America. Even the homes of the rich and famous were no longer impervious to invasion. Allied to the violence, the apparent lack of motive for the crimes, the perception and boundaries of criminal actions changed in America. Writing in the late 1990s Biskind described how this, for him, marked the spiritual end of the 1960s, 'The great irony, of course, was that the murders happened a brief two years after the Summer of Love, a week before Woodstock, the celebration of all that was supposed to be best about the '60s. It was as if, at the moment of ripeness, the dark blossoms of decay were already unfolding' (1998: 79). The image of Manson himself provides rich textual study. His appearance aligned him with the hippy counterculture, but he held far-right beliefs. His mixture of symbols (echoed in the combination of peace-symbols and military gear worn by Scorpio in *Dirty Harry*) encapsulates the symbolic upheaval of the times. The definition of his gang as a 'family' strikes at the heart of a founding institution of American society.

The murder of Kitty Genovese, in March 1964, is one which helps to explore a shift in the perception of American culture, especially in urban environments. What fascinates is not the murder itself so much as the press reaction, the use of it as an indicator of a general moral decay in the United States, especially New York. Kirshner cites the murder of Genovese as part of New York's 'descent into lawlessness', observing that

> in New York and elsewhere, even more pervasive than the crime itself was the fear of crime, the normalcy of crime, each of which had toxic effects on society. The murder of Kitty Genovese in 1964 became famous because thirty-eight of her neighbours failed to respond to her screams. But before those elements of the story became known, the murder of a young woman in a quiet residential neighborhood [sic] was barely news; it got a few paragraphs on page 26 of the *New York Times*. (2012: 120)

The reason this murder became a cause celebre, and part of a wider moral panic, was not the murder itself but the supposed indifference of thirty-eight witnesses. In *The New York Times*, under the headline 'Thirty–Eight Who Saw Murder Didn't Call the Police', Martin Gansberg reported that

> For more than half an hour 38 respectable, law abiding citizens in Queens watched a killer stalk and stab a woman in three separate attacks in Kew Gardens. Twice their chatter and the sudden glow of their bedroom lights interrupted him and frightened him off. Each time he returned, sought her out, and stabbed her again. Not one person telephoned the police during the assault; one witness called after the woman was dead. (1964: 1)

In his article Gansberg emphasizes the fact that the thirty-eight 'watched', referencing a 'shocked' police officer, baffled 'because the "good people" failed to call the Police'. Gansberg's emotive account concentrated on the witnesses' indifference, affording the perpetrator of the murder, Winston Moseley, just two short paragraphs. Subsequently Rosenthal published a book, *Thirty Eight Witnesses* (1964), and the murder helped change the psychological understanding of group behaviour, 'The events of that night in New York in 1964 paved the way for the development of one of the most robust phenomena in social psychology – Latané and Darley's (1970) *bystander effect* (the finding that individuals are more likely to help when alone than in company)' (Manning 2007: 555). This one crime not only pervaded the media but became a mainstay of psychological theory.

However, it now appears that most of the report in *The New York Times*, subsequently repeated in other media and psychology textbooks, is inaccurate. Manning, Levine and Collins re-examined the case, discovering differences between *The New York Times* version (which set a narrative subsequently repeated) and their analysis of legal documents and court transcripts from the time. They found that

> Not all of the 38 witnesses were eye witnesses (some only heard the attack); witnesses have since claimed they called immediately after the first attack; none of the eye witnesses could have watched Kitty or her attacker for the full 30 minutes because they were visible to the witnesses for only a few moments; there were two separate attacks not three . . . the second attack occurred inside part of a building where only a small number of potential witnesses could have seen it; Kitty was still alive when the police arrived at the scene. (2007: 557)

Going even further, Manning et al. dispute the number of witnesses: 'the evidence suggests there were rather fewer than the 38 eyewitnesses referred to in the textbooks, and no list of the 38 has been made available' (558). Others have subsequently claimed to have called the Police but gained a negative reaction (partly related to the area in which the crime was committed).

As Kitty Genovese's assault was not ignored in the ways Gansberg suggested, what does this reporting, and its subsequent influence, suggest about the status of crime in New York in 1964? Perhaps the answer is that New Yorkers were more than willing to believe this of each other; indeed, more than that, that professional psychologists were willing to develop these supposed events into a theory still taught today. As Manning explains, 'It provides a cautionary tale about the dangers of modern life' (2007: 559). The reporting of Genovese's murder is clearly part of the moral panic about crime in America during the 1960s and 1970s, and it points to a breakdown in trust and social cohesion. Cohen (2002) identifies the first stage of a moral panic as one of Exaggeration and Distortion, which reporting of the Genovese case applies. Further stages include Prediction (it is assumed such acts will happen again), and Symbolization in which the crime, and words related to it, acquire a symbolic power. Genovese's name acquired that power in America.

Genovese's murder illustrates the moral panic about crime in America but one event itself does not create a moral panic; others are needed to contribute. *Policing the Crisis* (1978), while primarily concerned with the UK, covers America's reaction to mugging and discusses the moral panic in America and how this was subsequently adopted in the UK. 'Mugging', a term that first appeared in America, had shifted its meaning during the 1960s:

> 'mugging' was no longer being used in the United States simply as a descriptive and identifying term for a specific kind of urban crime. It not

only dominated the whole public discussion of crime and public disorder – it had become a central *symbol* for the many tensions and problems besetting American social and political life in general. 'Mugging' achieved this status because of its ability to connote a whole complex of social themes in which the 'crisis of American society' was reflected. These themes included: the involvement of blacks and drug addicts in crime; the expansion of black ghettoes, coupled with the growth of black social and political militancy; the threatened crisis and collapse of the cities; the crime panic and the appeal to 'law and order'; the sharpening political tensions and protest movements of the 1960s leading into and out from the Nixon-Agnew mobilisation of 'the silent majority' and their presidential victory in 1968. (Hall et al. 1978: 20)

The extensive investigation into mugging in the UK, as dissected in *Policing the Crisis*, may have existed more in the media than the real world but, and in a similar sense to America, the crime became symbolic for wider social and cultural issues.

Susan Brownmiller (1975) discusses the Genovese case quoting the 'thirty-eight' witness figure without question (further indicating how the story had become accepted). She does, however, discuss an aspect that was not reported: Genovese was sexually assaulted by her attacker Winston Moseley while she lay dying. Moseley, it was revealed in court, had committed rape previously without getting caught. Genovese's rape was not part of the initial commentary about the case, and this questions the contemporary view of rape, especially pertinent as it is featured in three of the films of this study (depicted in *Straw Dogs* and *Death Wish* and occurring off-screen in *Dirty Harry*). It was also a crime more heavily reported during the 1960s and 1970s. It is, as Brownmiller explains, a crime in which the victim is much less likely to be believed or investigated:

According to the FBI itself, forcible rape is 'one of the most under-reported crimes due primarily to fear and/or embarrassment on the part of the victim,' and one in five rapes, or possibly one in twenty, may actually be reported, which skews all reportable statistics. Further a probable bias by police and juries against the word of the female victim – and particularly the word of a black female victim – drastically cuts down on the number of cases available for study. On a national average, police say that 15 per cent of all rape cases reported to them turn out on cursory investigation to be 'unfounded' – in other words they didn't believe the complainant. In reported rape cases where the police *do* believe the victim, only 51 per cent of the offenders are actually apprehended, and of these, 76 per cent are prosecuted, and of these 47 per cent are acquitted or have their case dismissed. (1975: 190)

Despite obvious issues with the statistics that can be discovered for this period, it is clear that, like other violent crimes, there was a steep rise in rape in America: 'In 1973 the FBI reported 51,000 "founded" cases of forcible rape and attempted rape, across the United States, a rise it noted, of 10 per cent over the previous year and a rise of 62 per cent over a five year period' (Brownmiller 1975: 190). Whether this rise in cases is wholly due to increased incidence or a rise in reporting is impossible to say – Brownmiller partly attributes it to more women reporting rape, spurred on by the social changes initiated by the Women's Movement. Joanna Bourke charts a similar rise in the UK, describing rape as a crime that 'soared' through the 1960s.

Bourke discusses rape, in the United States and the United Kingdom, during the 1960s and 1970s with reference to sociological perspectives during the time. This discussion highlights several key issues: the possibly causal relationship between the urban environment and crime, and the debate about who was to be blamed for rape. Underpinning this was a wider debate (also present in Brownmiller) about who rape was about – men or women? That the urban environment was a contributory factor to the rise in crime curried favour with many and connected to the wider sense of urban decay. As Bourke relates, 'By the late 1960s fears about young men raised on city streets took a new form – anxieties about "subcultures of violence". These subcultures were portrayed as teaching men aggressive "scripts", which they then enacted. . . . American commentators such as Shaw and Moore[2] tended to place the emphasis on the dangers of inner-city slums' (2008: 130). As part of this narrative of the corrupting nature of the city, and especially the slums, rape became an expression of poverty (an argument that displaces the excuse for the crime away from perpetrators to society). Urban decay is well evidenced. Focussing on New York, Kirshner states that 'Even in the robust days of the early 1960s, the city's underlying structural problems were increasingly evident. Two trends were fundamental: the secular decline of New York's manufacturing industries (and employment), and suburbanization (2012: 120). The effect was seen in the political sphere leading up to and throughout the 1970s:

> John Lindsay won a close three-way election in 1965. The young Kennedy handsome-liberal Republican ran on a 'city in crisis' theme. It was a self-evident argument: the city was losing eighteen thousand factory jobs a year in 1965, and signs of decay were everywhere: on an average day 40 per cent of its aging fleet of garbage trucks were out of service. . . . Garbage piled up on the city streets at a rate of ten thousand tons a day. (2012: 120)

This decline reached a chilling peak when, in 1975, members of the New York Police and Firefighters Unions distributed over a million copies of a

---

[2]Clifford R. Shaw and Maurice E. Moore (1968), *The Natural History of a Delinquent Career.* Greenwood Press: Chicago.

pamphlet titled *Welcome to Fear City: A Survival Guide for Visitors to the City of New York*. Partly printed in protest at cuts by then mayor Abraham Beame, prompted by the over $5 billion in short-term debt the city owed, the pamphlet's cover depicted a hooded skull, and the inside listed a series of precautions to be taken by any visitor to the city such as staying off the streets after 6.00 pm. Although perhaps an exaggeration, the pamphlet reflected the crisis and staggering growth in crime over the previous decade (Baker 2015).

If the decline in the American city is well evidenced and seen as explicitly related to crime, the rise in the feminist movement and the social changes it enacted had a surprising effect on theories surrounding rape. Discourse developed in

> which the rapist was portrayed as someone forged within a crucible created by unmarried, white and educated women. What were these women doing that could so seriously corrupt young men, spurring them to act in their sexually abusive ways? According to some commentators, these women were demanding equality with men, particularly in the workplace and education, but also in the home. They were insisting on their right to rule their own lives – to talk, dress, work and move as they chose. What came to be known as 'second-wave feminism' empowered women, and, according to this line, disempowered men and turned some to sexual violence. (Bourke 2008: 138)

Returning to Brownmiller, rape is further complicated by the reactions of the Police, who often cared little, or assumed fault in the victim, including the suggestion that many who reported rape were simply prostitutes who hadn't been paid (1975: 410). Brownmiller discusses a distinction in rape claims between those that the Police considered to be founded and those unfounded. As evidenced in a study in Pennsylvania,

> Rapes reported 'within hours' and cases involving strangers, weapons and 'positive violence' stood the highest chance of being believed. Rapes by strangers that took place in automobiles were considered more dubious than rapes by strangers that took place in the home or on the street. All dating rapes that occurred in automobiles were held unfounded by the Police in this Pennsylvania study. (1975: 410)

Going further, Brownmiller reports that the Police were more likely to believe victims who screamed or fought back. Two types of rape emerge here. The first, which the Police were more likely to believe and pursue, involves a victim attacked by a stranger. The victim then does everything she can, in terms of noise and violence, to escape the attack. The second, less likely to be believed, is a victim attacked by someone she knows in a situation she has consented to entering, such as getting into a car or going on a date. If this Pennsylvania study stands as a microcosm of general opinion, there is a clear distinction between, what I will term, 'recognized' rapes and 'unrecognized' rapes, with recognized meaning that the Police, and society, recognize the claim as legitimate. In the films of this study, the rapes shown and referred to in *Dirty Harry* and *Death Wish* are depicted as recognized – where victims are attacked by strangers. In *Death Wish* there is clear resistance and distress. The rape in *Straw Dogs*, at least in the first instance, falls clearly into the unrecognized category – Amy allows Venner (Del Henney) into the house, they have a sexual history, and she does not violently resist. The discourses surrounding rape at the time of the films' productions and releases surely then affect the reactions of the audience and critics.

The Genovese murder also raises racial questions in both the reporting and the investigation of crime. Coming from an Italian American family, Genovese's ethnicity places her apart from the dominant WASP culture of America (instead as part of a hyphenate class), as does her poverty. Joanna Bourke suggests that the racial identity of the victim had an impact on the perceived validity of the report of rape during this period. Discussing rape in America in the twentieth century, Bourke identifies a prejudice against Black women, based on myths from slavery times, that it was impossible to rape them as their bodies were overtly sexual: 'The legacy of slavery continued well into the twentieth century in the form of the myth that even free African-American women could not be raped because they were 'naturally' promiscuous' (2008: 77). Although not Black, Genovese sits apart from the dominant racial group, perhaps downgrading (in the eyes of the press and Police) the seriousness of the sexual assault against her. It is as if a hierarchy of violence exists in which different types of crime are given different levels of seriousness depending on the identity of the victim. The depiction of rape in both *Dirty Harry* and *Death Wish* certainly suggests this, particularly in the latter film in which the assault takes place in the Kersey's affluent apartment. In *Dirty Harry*, the crimes escalate towards the rape and murder of Scorpio's final victim, a teenage white girl. This final outrage is what pushes Harry to take the law into his own hands, violating the orders of his superiors. Previous murders, of an anonymous white woman viewed from afar and a Black child from a poor environment, are not depicted in such outraged fashion (the latter occurs off-screen). This hierarchy is also evident in *Taxi Driver*, in which Bickle chooses to fixate on Iris (Jodie Foster), a twelve-year-old white girl in prostitution, ignoring the plight of non-white and older women.

Miranda Rights

The introduction of Miranda Rights in 1966, in reaction to the arrest of a confessed rapist Ernesto Miranda, was a key moment in law enforcement in

America. It shifted the emphasis of policing towards the rights of the suspect, constraining and controlling the Police. The issues of suspect's rights and the powers of the Police are at the heart of *The French Connection*, *Dirty Harry* and *Death Wish*. The Miranda procedure was reported in *Time* as follows,

> Before any interrogation can take place, said the court in Miranda, police must advise a suspect in 'clear and unequivocal terms' that 1) he has the right to remain silent, 2) anything he says 'can and will' be used against him, 3) he has a right to counsel before and during questioning, and 4) if he cannot afford a lawyer, he is entitled to have one provided by the state. (1 November 1968)

This shift in the arrest procedure prompted various debates, questioning whether the Police themselves had been disempowered and whether suspects' rights had been placed before victims':

> Miranda has plunged many police into despair. Omaha's Public Safety Director Francis Lynch argues, 'If we can't get the truth, we can't solve cases. If we can't talk to the accused, whom can we talk to? The victim is often dead or missing.' Cincinnati Prosecutor Melvin Rueger complains, 'Guilt or innocence is no longer the issue. The prime issue is whether a suspect was searched, interrogated or detained.' Minneapolis Chief Calvin Hawkinson hits the 'tone' of the ruling: 'The emphasis of the court's decision is on individual rights and the public be damned, at a time when the crime rate is increasing'. (*Time* 5 August 1966)

Ironically in a culture given to stressing the rights of the individual, enshrined in the Bill of Rights, this objection was couched in social terms. The clear implication of Miranda was that the Police cannot be trusted to arrest and interrogate suspects in a legal and justified manner. This distrust was something shared across America and not limited to minority groups. In *Dirty Harry*, the district attorney (Josef Sommer) upbraids Callahan stating, 'Where the hell does it say that you've got a right to kick down doors, torture suspects, deny medical attention and legal counsel? Where have you been? Does Escobedo ring a bell? Miranda? I mean, you must have heard of the Fourth Amendment. What I'm saying is that man had rights.' In *The French Connection* the issue of Warrants is brought up several times and in *Death Wish* the Police's impotence in the face of crime is discussed, especially when Kersey's vigilante actions start having a positive impact on crime rates ('muggings from 950 a week to 470').

A year before Miranda was introduced, the Watts Riots, in Los Angeles from 11 August 1965, drew attention to the racially divisive nature of Police action when 'a confrontation between a black driver and white police officers in the Watts neighborhood [*sic*] of Los Angeles exploded into urban unrest. Six days later, 34 people were dead and property damage totalled $40 million' (Gershon 2016). Broadcast live on television Hoberman describes how the riots became 'TV interactional', with crowds drawn to the damaged and burning locations shown on television. Local radio spread inflammatory rumours such as 'Snipers were reported on the Harbor Freeway, looters said to be heading for white neighborhoods' (Hobermann 2003: 136) and even the Los Angeles Police Department (LAPD) was 'prone to fantasy. A ten-car convoy of Negroes with red armbands was hallucinated in the Ventura Freeway; another group in a yellow school bus was reported on the Golden State Freeway' (Hobermann 2003: 136). Eventually the National Guard were called in, while 'the white inhabitants of Los Angeles and Orange County frantically stocked up on rifles, knives, bows and arrows' (Hobermann 2003: 137). The riots themselves were the consequence of tensions which had developed over several years during which the Black population of Los Angeles had grown[3] and housing segregation laws continued to be enforced, while a mostly white LAPD was repeatedly accused of police brutality against the Black community.

Writing in relation to the Democratic Presidential Conference of 1968 in Chicago (the city which becomes Kersey's intended destination at the end of *Death Wish*), Norman Mailer gives a damning account of Police brutality against peaceful protesters. He recounts how bystanders became involved in various conflicts during the conference:

> A few feet away a phalanx of police charged into a group of women, reporters, and young McCarthy activists standing idle against the window of the Hilton Hotel's Haymarket Inn. The terrified people began to go down under the unexpected police charge when the plate glass window shattered, and the people tumbled back through the glass. The police then climbed through the broken window and began to beat people, some of whom had been drinking quietly in the bar. (1968: 171)

Although Mailer's view of the conflict was not universally held, he vividly describes the confluence of politics and violence at the time and demonstrates the problematized meanings of the Police. His contention that psychological studies comparing criminals and Police 'fail to detect a significant difference' (1968: 174) is not evidenced, but it ably suggests the confusion over right and wrong at the time and the continuing question over who could wield power legitimately.

---

[3] 'Between 1940 and 1965, Los Angeles' County's black population had grown from 75,000 to 650,000. Most black people in the country lived in Southeast L.A., a section of the city that was home to failing schools and little or no access to public transportation' (Queally 2015).

Vigilantism

The concept of vigilantism has a long and problematic history in American culture. (Smith suggests it is a 'social phenomenon indigenous to America' (1993: 93).) It is at once connected to the desire to be independent and to defend oneself and one's property (a link back to the frontier), and simultaneously provokes ideas of lynching and racism. Inevitably, in a time in which race relations were in flux, invocation of the term 'vigilante' would conjure differing associations for differing people. Richard Slotkin, in an extensive examination of the American myth of the frontier, suggests this about groups founded during the 1700s to 1800s:

> *Vigilantism* has been used to describe a number of local movements occurring at various times that have in common the use of extralegal force by an organisation of citizens to suppress 'criminal' threats to the civil peace of prosperity of a community. Although some of these movement[s] invoked British, Scottish, or Teutonic precedents, the vigilante phenomenon seems peculiar to 'settler-states': political communities established on the periphery of a colonizing 'metropolis' in which the forms and powers of government are initially tenuous. The simplest and earliest type of frontier vigilantism involved the application of 'lynch law' (mainly banishment and corporal punishment) against criminals and 'undesirables'. More complex (and violent) were the various forms of 'regulator' movements, in which vigilante actions against individuals were part of a larger pattern of resistance to government authority – for example, the South Carolina 'Regulators' of 1767-69, and the Whiskey Rebellion of 1794. The latter type of vigilantism was, in effect, a rudimentary exercise of the right of revolution asserted in the Declaration of Independence. But after 1865 vigilantism acquired broader significance directed against the 'dangerous classes' of the post-Frontier, urban, and industrial order. As a result, the vigilante ideology itself was transformed from an assertion of a natural and democratic right-to-violence to an assertion of class and racial privilege. (1992: 173–4)

Clearly the term was in use and was tied into the myths of expansionism on which much of American identity is founded. However, it also associates with racial politics and with sexual politics, including rape.

The scale of lynching in Southern states between the late 1880s and early 1900s is breathtaking. As Slotkin explains (with reference to James Cutler's *Lynch Law* (1904)),

> In the peak years of political struggle over disenfranchisement (1882-1903) there were 3,337 recorded lynchings in the United States, 2,585 of them in the South, of which 1,985 were of Blacks – an average of just

under two Blacks lynched in the South each week for 20 years. The trend persisted in later decades: in 1918 the NAACP[4] verified the occurrence of 63 lynchings and cited an additional 12 that had probably occurred but not been verified. (1992: 183–4)

Slotkin goes on to discuss how two forms of lynching come to exist in writing about the West, differentiating between a Western Lyncher and a Southern Lyncher:

> The western lyncher-hero represents a superior class of American Anglo-Saxon who is privileged to use violence with a freedom hitherto granted only to the Indian fighter, because the existence of civil society is imperilled by the threat of a numerous 'dangerous class'. Southern lynching fails to meet this test, because government there already privileges the superior race at the expense of the presumed dangerous class, the Blacks, and because the manner of lynching argues that those in charge belong to the worse classes. (1992: 184)

Joanna Bourke connects the proliferation of lynching in Southern states to anxieties and paranoia about Black sexuality, and the threat that Black freedom (political and social) represented to white male authority. Here lynching becomes a tool of suppression based on myths of the Black male's sexual aggression: 'The most common justification for lynching was that white women had to be protected from black men intent on corrupting their virtue' (2008: 101). Sarah Churchwell identifies how lynching was 'not always, or even primarily, a furtive outbreak of violence in the dead of night. By the turn of the [twentieth] century, in many parts of America lynching had turned into entertainment, a blood sport' (2019: 64). This extended to daytime, public, lynching with crowds, some drawn to events from outlying areas in which 'Victims were frequently tortured and mutilated first; pregnant women were burned to death in front of a peanut-crunching crowd' (2019).[5] A crowd as large as 10,000 watched the lynching of Jesse Washington in May 1916, where he was 'castrated, then his fingers were cut off, then he was raised and lowered over a bonfire for two hours, until he finally died' (2019: 65). It is not difficult to see how scenes in *Dirty Harry*, *The French Connection*, *Death Wish* and *Taxi Driver* in which the protagonists kill Black men might have invoked the spectre of lynching in the minds of the audience.

---

[4] National Association for the Advancement of Colored People.
[5] Churchwell also notes that lynching was not limited to Black Americans but also Catholics and Jews (2019: 64).

Although not all lynching was based on rape, Bourke suggests it was 'the most common excuse', tying vigilante violence explicitly to discourses around race and sexuality. Later in this work is a thorough examination of the Western film genre in which the term 'vigilante' acquired several meanings, but it is important here to understand the context of the term 'vigilante' in America, especially given the resurgence of vigilante groups during the late 1960s and early 1970s.[6]

Despite being limited in number, and short-lived, the existence of vigilante groups during that period helps express the fear and anxiety being felt throughout the country. *Time* reported that 'Vigilante groups and private security agencies are flourishing. Half the nation's 60 million households contain at least one gun' (*Time* 13 July 1970). By 1975 the same magazine was reporting:

> As a further means of protection, Americans are forming vigilante groups. In many residential neighbourhoods of major cities, men come home from the office, hurry through dinner and then go out to take their turns patrolling nearby streets. Usually they are armed with nothing more than clubs and whistles. In Chicago's Woodlawn, a secret organization composed of 22 blacks, half of whom are Vietnam veterans, has sworn to eradicate crimes in the ghetto by fair means or foul. (*Time* 30 June 1975)

The inclusion of Vietnam veterans suggests a relationship to the violent actions and situations that occurred in Vietnam. It, of course, creates a textual link to *Taxi Driver* and Bickle's explanation of his past. Focussing on one specific example of vigilantism, led by Tony Imperiale in New Jersey, suggests how organized some groups were:

> Imperiale is the organizer of Newark's North Ward Citizen's Committee, which claims a dues-paying membership of 200 and thousands of enthusiastic followers. In their leader's view, they are 'defenders of law and order,' banded together in the wake of last summer's Newark riots to stand up to Communist-inspired racial pressures. In the view of Gov. Richard J. Hughes, they are 'vigilantes'. (Goldberger 1968: 313)

Making use of guns and karate training from Imperiale, this group would patrol part of Newark in 'radio-equipped cars'. This is just one instance of a group being established in the late 1960s to respond to the growing feeling of embattlement by some of the rise in crime and changes in society; Goldberger

---

[6]San Francisco was also home for 'the largest vigilante movement in American history' during the 1850s, an image at odds with the assumed left-wing sympathies of the 1960s (Street 2016: 57).

ascribes this to a strong racist motivation in Imperiale's group: '[Imperiale] was hailed as a saviour by hundreds of white residents who are convinced that the Negro is taking away everything the white man has earned' (1968: 313).

Vietnam

The effect of America's war in Vietnam is extensively documented and will not be repeated here. Instead, emphasis on a specific issue that emerges from the conflict that has a strong impact on the Vigilante Thriller is made: how the Vietnam War affected the representation of American masculinity. Tony Williams outlines this change, 'During the 1960s and 1970s, ample evidence appeared documenting American atrocities against the Vietnamese people. Ideologic codes were thrown into crisis. The average American farm boy soldier was no longer Audie Murphy but a cold-blooded killer' (1996: 130). Although writing specifically about the horror genre, Williams points to a general shift in the meaning of the archetypal white American male away from the traditional frontiersman. Indeed, this depiction was made impossible by the My Lai massacre (in which the US Army killed between 347 and 504 unarmed Vietnamese men, women and children, and raped 20 women and girls, on 16 March 1968 (Levesque 2018)), and other atrocities. Unrest at home and the increase in crime further problematized how America viewed its men. Williams sees this as part of an existing culture of repression: 'Vietnam has not made monsters but provided a cataclysmic environment for male violence that is repressed within military and family institutions' (1996: 130). Here Vietnam is a catalyst, exposing violence that already existed. What American masculinity meant was in crisis.

The figure of Scorpio, in *Dirty Harry*, suggests this in his mixture of far-right and far-left iconography, 'The peace movement was by no means peaceful in its demonstrations, its CND locket worn by violent activists as well as Scorpio' (Williams 1996: 138). This is something *Dirty Harry*'s director acknowledged:

> The first time the audience fully sees Scorpio, hiding on a roof, he is wearing highly polished parachute shoes with white laces going up the sides. He is rubbing first one shoe, then the other, against his dirty, tan dungaree pants. On his belt is a large, lopsided peace symbol. No verbal exposition is ever given, but to those who might have questioned this strange attire, it is possible that in his tilted fashion he could have returned from Vietnam bearing a crazy grudge. (Siegel 1993: 370)

The ideological crisis that Williams suggests is evident in the confusion of signifiers that predominate in the Vigilante Thriller and the blurred lines between left and right, right and wrong. *Joe* shows how traditional models of American masculinity, white working-class males and veterans of the Second World War could move to be antagonistic and murderous in a shifting society. *Taxi Driver* offers a self-proclaimed Vietnam veteran, whose view of justice and morality exists outside of normal codes. In *Death Wish* the protagonist abandons his pacifist leanings and turns to older forms of morality in the wake of violent intrusion into the home. *The French Connection* represents a character who walks along a fault line of violence (especially regarding race). *Straw Dogs* adds to this: David Sumner flees violence and conflict in America but is unable to escape or repress these forces. Certainly, there is evidence that the My Lai massacre affected Sam Peckinpah, 'On April 4, 1971, while in England working on *Straw Dogs*, Peckinpah sent a telegram to President Nixon urging him to press for a full investigation of the My Lai incident' (Prince 1998: 35). In *Straw Dogs*, Vietnam becomes conspicuous through its absence, part of the troubles that Sumner is running from, the televised violence the locals tease him about.

The Vigilante Thriller channels the confusion over the meaning of the American white male, attempting to deal with the ideological shifts and different positions emerging. No longer capable of sustaining the myths of the frontier, of the cowboy, the American white male takes on degrees of violence previously unthinkable. The defeats in Vietnam also attacked a fundamental element of the American psyche: 'America had always celebrated war and the warrior. Our long unbroken record of military victories has been crucially important both to the national identity and the personal identity of many Americans – particularly men.... The result was a massive disjunction in American culture, a crisis of self-image: If Americans were no longer winners, then who were they?' (Gibson 1994: 11).

Problematizing the other

Law and order, the Police, victim's and suspect's rights and the very meaning of the traditional moral figure of society were in debate in the political consciousness throughout the late 1960s and 1970s and influenced the creation of the Vigilante Thrillers. As Keathley suggests,

> The Fascist Cop films were those right cycle films that most explicitly staged the ideological conflict in American Culture at this time. Like the left cycle films of this period, *Death Wish* and *Dirty Harry* diagnosed American society as diseased and corrupt, but saw radical liberalism as the problem. What is foregrounded in these films is not a system that is controlled capriciously by a powerful, privileged few, but one

that is undone by the legal restrictions placed on law enforcement to protect society, thus rendering the police impotent and the criminals empowered. . . . These films can also be read as Vietnam allegories, for they portray the political right's exasperation at a military involvement marked at every turn by rules and regulations of engagement which implicitly restrict the possibility of success. (2004: 304)

The sociopolitical context also colours the understanding of the critical responses discussed earlier. A picture is built of a culture in ideological flux, where the symbols that had predominated for much of the twentieth century were no longer capable of bearing their own ideological weight. They were becoming exposed as society shifted, with changes to the nature of race relations, gender relations, government's authority over its citizens and the legitimacy of the dominant strata of society to rule. It is a change felt not just in the Vigilante Thriller but also evident in the wider cinematic culture. These shifts had particular relevance for the white male, previously the dominant force and dominant positive representation in society:

This disruption of cultural identity was amplified by other social transformations. During the 1960s, the civil rights and ethnic pride movements won many victories in their challenges to racial oppression. Also, during the 1970s and 1980s, the Unites States experienced massive waves of immigration from Mexico, Central America, Vietnam, Cambodia, Korea and Taiwan. Whites no longer secure in their power abroad, also lost their unquestionable dominance at home; for the first time, many began to feel that they too were just another hyphenated ethnic group, the Anglo-Americans. (Gibson 1994: 11)

The combination of social and political changes undermined many of the certainties previously held. The Vigilante Thriller draws on many of these.

The ideological shifts in American society during the 1960s and 1970s deeply affected the meaning of the 'other'. Previously this concept had been based on the image/idea of the Native American and the wilderness, a myth fundamental to the foundation of the state as Richardson explains:

Nature was domesticated; but it remained present precisely as 'other', and where it remained untamed it had to be excluded, consigned to the wilderness that lay beyond what was conceptualized as 'American'. In this confrontation, the native population was conflated with the otherness of nature and was likewise expected to be tamed or, if it could not be tamed, to be exterminated. (2010: 12)

This boundary, between the same and other, is explicitly based on the frontier. By the 1970s, however, that border had long ceased to exist and attempts to forge a New Frontier (through space exploration, or further West in Vietnam) had not succeeded, particularly in ideological terms.

* * *

The role of the other in society is fundamental to the definition of the normal self, even though it remains a site of ambiguity, 'The self is always implicated in the other and indeed it may be said that the *I* can never know the *other* precisely because it is nothing but a projection of the self. It is, in fact, an essential element of self-awareness: there can be no self without an "Other" against which to measure itself' (Richardson 2010: 12).

During this period, and dramatized by the Vigilante Thriller, the definition of the self was in crisis, with the ideological codes underpinning American values and self-image shifting with changes in society. These changes then necessitate a shift in the other, the projection of the self. During the Vietnam War the use of terminology drawn from the Western for the Vietcong suggests an attempt to preserve pre-existing concepts of the other. However, the failure of the War is partly a failure of this rhetoric; the Vietcong were clearly not Native Americans, nor did the war in Vietnam map neatly onto the ideological structures of Manifest Destiny and Westward expansion. Indeed, by the late 1960s revisionist Westerns had begun to transform the image of the Native American so that they no longer bore the meanings from the previously held structure (an idea also present in the *Keep America Beautiful* campaign referenced in posters for *Joe*). Other groups such as Black Americans and homosexuals were becoming part of the mainstream culture, gaining rights once reserved for straight white men. Several successful films from the 1960s had already interrogated the changes in otherness; *The Graduate* (Mike Nichols, 1967) demonstrates hidden otherness tied to sexual desire and alienation; *In the Heat of the Night* uses the signifiers of otherness (sexual depravity, violent group behaviour, poor intelligence) to depict the white men in the film, in contrast to the urbane Virgil Tibbs. This confusion impacts the Vigilante Thrillers directly and helps us understand their confused political positions and the strong critical reactions to them. In Part Two we shall see how the films cope with this.

3

Cinematic contexts

The years from 1965 to 1970 were an exceptionally intense period of change in American cinema, during which the old studio system, now commonly referred to as 'Classical Hollywood', was finally swept away by a tide of social and industrial changes whose combined power was arguably the most traumatic experience that Hollywood had ever encountered.

(SHIEL 2006: 12)

Lee Harvey Oswald fired two long bullets through President John F. Kennedy's head on November 22. Almost every one of us watched it on television. And watched it again and again. And watched Jack Ruby split open Oswald's guts with a handgun. Again and again. Television became reality. We saw that murder is messy and that death carries pain to those who survive. It was a nationwide exercise in mourning and voyeurism. From that moment on, slowly but surely, the movies added a new element to screen violence. It was no longer enough for a character to be shot and fall down dead like kids playing soldiers in an empty lot. Now we had to see the blood, the bits of the brain, the pain, the agony, the flies on the corpse.

(LEECH 1975: 76)

Just as American society was undergoing fundamental shifts, so the film industry was changing in the period of the late 1960s and early 1970s.

These shifts were textual (in the technical and thematic content of the films), audience-related (through shifting demographics) and institutional (in the final breakdown of the Studio System). As in other parts of this work, the goal here is not to offer a comprehensive history but to highlight specific elements that deepen our understanding of the Vigilante Thrillers. A consistent rhetorical trope concerning Hollywood in the 1960s and 1970s is of a rise in left-leaning countercultural cinema, led by youth-oriented films such as *Bonnie and Clyde* and *Easy Rider*, made possible by changes in American cinema censorship and the influence of non-Hollywood films. In these the audience is openly invited to identify with countercultural figures who directly reflected the changing landscape of America, the 'breakdown of ideological confidence in American culture and values' (Wood 2003: 23). However, this trope ignores the success of more conservative films throughout the 1960s. Films such as *The Sound of Music* (Robert Wise, 1965) and *Guess Who's Coming to Dinner* (Stanley Kramer, 1967) suggest a more traditional audience still existed, one that wanted more traditional messages and morals. For every X rated *Midnight Cowboy* (John Schlesinger, 1969), there is a *Love Story* (Arthur Hiller, 1970). Christian Keathley identifies a 'Post-Traumatic Cycle' of films, running from 1970 to 1976, that further dramatizes the ideological crisis that was represented by *Bonnie and Clyde* and *Easy Rider* at the end of the 1960s: 'An important characteristic of these films is that their heroes exist in the middle position between the "official hero" and "outlaw hero" favoured by classical cinema. . . . The protagonists of the post-traumatic cycle films are usually marginal establishment figures' (2004: 299). Films such as *McCabe and Mrs Miller* (Robert Altman, 1971), *Five Easy Pieces* (Bob Rafelson, 1970) and *The Parallax View* (Alan J. Pakula, 1974) embody this movement, which builds on earlier counterculture cinema as a 'second movement of left-oriented films' (2004: 303) but expands into the trauma created by American involvement in Vietnam. Keathley sees *Death Wish* and *Dirty Harry*, dubbed Fascist Cop movies, as reacting to similar ideological problems but offering different solutions: 'As the inverse of the counter-cultural cycle of films, the Fascist Cop movies, too, suggest that the only position of agency available is one outside of existing institutions' (2004: 303). Out of the same ideological conflicts emerges a distorted mirror image, embracing anti-authoritarian figures, but who deal with the cultural changes in very different ways.

Developments in censorship and the presentation of violence

As violence was posited as the main concern in critical reactions to the Vigilante Thrillers, a consideration of shifts in censorship and the presentation of violence is pertinent. The rise in violence and crime in American society is reflected in a change in how violence is depicted in many Hollywood films, made possible by a breakdown in the efficacy of Hollywood's self-censorship and regulation system. The Motion Picture Production Code, also known as the Hays Code, was formulated in the 1930s and administered by the Motion Picture Association of America (MPAA) into the 1960s. However, the influence of films made outside America, therefore outside the Code, but distributed throughout America due to a shortfall in film production in Hollywood was one factor that helped make the Code irrelevant. Stephen Prince identifies key shifts in censorship that helped Hollywood develop a new creative freedom. These included 'The revision in September 1966 of Hollywood's thirty-six-year-old Motion Picture Production Code and the creation two years later of the Code and Ratings Administration (CARA) with its G-M-R-X classification scheme' (2003: 197). The end of the Production Code was made inevitable by changes in TV where Jack Ruby's shooting of Lee Harvey Oswald was repeated ad nauseam, and TV programmes (not subject to the Code's rules) were becoming more violent. News reports from Vietnam and America's own streets added to this, with depictions of real-life violence becoming more explicit than that shown in cinemas. In 1967 United Artists released all three of Sergio Leone's *Dollars* films into US cinemas (*A Fistful of Dollars* (1964), *For A Few Dollars More* (1965) and *The Good, The Bad and The Ugly* (1966)). Although not an isolated case of European cinema succeeding in the US market, these films are highlighted here due to their relevance. Made outside of the auspices of the Production Code, in Italy and Spain, these films helped usher in a new depiction of violence in its explicitness and shifting moral context (Prince 1998: 18).

Without the moral framework of the traditional Hollywood Western, Leone exposed a hollowness to the myth of the West, by stripping the genre of its moral pretensions. Leone's films would be followed in Hollywood by Peckinpah's, and others', and helped form Eastwood's screen persona (one which contributes to the audience's understanding of *Dirty Harry*). Earlier in the decade the James Bond films, beginning with *Dr. No* (Terence Young, 1962), showcased violence in a more flippant way (including a scene in which Bond (Sean Connery) kills another man coldly by shooting him several times in the back). Within Hollywood, cracks had begun to appear in the 1950s, with films such as *The Man with the Golden Arm* (Otto Preminger, 1955) being made outside the code. Outside of mainstream Hollywood, independent producers had regularly ignored such strictures to exploit issues such as sex, violence and drugs. Although these films were mainly distributed through drive-in and regional theatres, they demonstrate a demand for the subjects that the MPAA designated as taboo, no doubt exacerbated by changes in the film industry and wider culture in the 1950s when 'studios had lost control of their first-run theatres, government censor boards were under attack by the courts, and, in 1952, the Supreme Court finally granted films the same First Amendment protections that media like newspapers and magazines had long enjoyed' (Prince 1998: 12).

The move towards a classification system and not an approval system did not, however, halt the close relationship between producers and the MPAA which had been evident before the late 1960s. Articles in both *Harper's Bazaar* and *The Los Angeles Times* (throughout 1971–2) discussed 'that scripts were routinely submitted and sent back with strong recommendations on deletions and editing' (Simkin 2011: 32). *Straw Dogs* became a key text in this debate, particularly concerning the role of the head of CARA, Dr Aaron Stern, and whether the cuts to *Straw Dogs* had made it a better or worse film (Simkin 2011: 31–4). This also attests to the ongoing debate towards media violence and its supposed potential to corrupt the audience in an era when the president had been elected partly on a 'decency' manifesto (Simkin 2011: 27).[1] Despite this controversy, the films themselves evince the overwhelming trend was towards a liberalization of censorship laws. *Straw Dogs* was directly affected in several ways, particularly the rape scene, and the cuts demanded by CARA may have shifted the understanding of American critics and audiences (the cuts demanded by the BBFC were less significant). As Simkin explains,

> The US edit was more severe, with the censor removing around thirty seconds of the sequence between Charles and Amy, significantly reducing the sexual activity represented, and cutting around seventy seconds of the second rape in order to achieve the required 'R' rating. The sequence the US audiences saw had only a glimpse of Scutt unbuttoning his trousers, Amy screaming as she realises what is happening, and Charlie staring at Scutt, before the scene cut to David returning from the moor. (2011: 108)

Ironically, these edits may reduce the amount of on-screen violence but also created some confusion about how the second rape occurred and how exactly Amy reacted to it as 'shots of Amy, clearly in pain and distress' have been removed (2011: 108).

In the UK, classification and censorship were also going through a series of changes, although there was more of a transition than an overhaul. James C. Robertson (1989) discusses these in detail, establishing how successive secretaries of the BBFC (then British Board of Film Censors, not classification as it is today), John Trevelyan and Stephen Murphy, oversaw a move from restrictive practices designed to preserve moral values, to ones which more

---

[1] Much of this reaction was also linked to the rise of the so-called Porno-Chic in the early 1970s, during which films such as *Deep Throat* (Jerry Gerard, 1972) became successful and threatened to make pornography a mainstream entertainment.

closely reflected shifts in the British public's views. Trevelyan himself wrote about these at the time:

> While in the last ten years we have greatly liberalized in the field of sex, we have not adopted a similar policy when dealing with scenes of violence, which we believe to be more harmful, both personally and socially, and we have been restrictive when dealing with films which might encourage drug taking.
> As far as our 'X' category is concerned we do not regard ourselves as guardians of public morality, and we base our decisions on an assessment of public acceptability at the time; in this way we act as a kind of barometer of public taste for the industry. (1970: 26)

In the same edition of *Screen*, Vicki Eves wrote extensively about the debates surrounding the effects of violence that were current. She suggests that several figures dominated in the United States and the United Kingdom:

> In the United States, Dr. Frederick [sic] Wertham, whose original observations had been against comic books as a 'new kind of harm, a new kind of bacillus that the present-day child is exposed to', later turned his attention to television, which he considers has a cumulative effect on children, and functions as a mediator between the child and his environment. Arthur Schlesinger, the American historian, also believes that television teaches children 'the morality of violence' and gives us his impression of the 'children of the electronic age' who sit 'hypnotised by the parade of killings, beatings, gunfights, knifings, maimings, brawls which flash incessantly across the tiny screens'. In Britain, Mrs. Mary Whitehouse, one of the most constant critics of television violence, speaks of the 'sub-Christian concept of living' that television is propagating and points to the widespread effects that television is having on crime. (1970: 31–2)

Eves does not take these criticisms at face value, nor limit her investigation to TV. By looking at the sociological research, she realizes that 'there is no definitive case presented by research data to show that the media is an important reinforcing agent. Neither is there adequate evidence to prove that violence in the media renders people more likely to commit violent acts' (1970: 41). However, she acknowledges that the dominant discourse at this time, at least in the popular press, drew direct links to watching violence on TV and in cinema, and acting out violent acts. The growth of groups such as Whitehouse's Nationwide Festival of Light, which in 1971 had a rally in Trafalgar Square which 35,000 people attended (Whipple 2010: 319), exerted influence on policymakers and film-makers, although it is difficult to measure how much, and some producers may have courted the controversy her campaigns brought. It is fair to say, however, that many people were motivated to join such groups and vocally objected to changing censorship and classification.

It would be easy to dismiss such protests as moral panics. However, the rise in violence in society and the increased representation of violent events do correlate, something explored by the psychologist Albert Bandura in the early 1960s. According to Bandura,

> film and television violence has four chief effects upon the viewer, none of which is cathartic. It teaches aggressive styles of behaviour, weakens personal restraints over acting aggressively, desensitizes and habituates people to violence, and influences the pictures of reality (e.g., beliefs about the likelihood of personally encountering violence or about the incidence of violence at large in society) that people carry them in everyday life and on which they base much of their behaviour. (Prince 1998: 117)

This, however, creates a self-repeating structure in which those who are against the representation of violence in the media may develop an unrealistic view of violence in society due to media representations of violence.

Generic transformation

Both Cobley (2000) and Cawelti (2004) see the period during the transition to New Hollywood as one in which traditional Hollywood genres went through a period of innovation (Cobley) and transformation (Cawelti). Genre remains a key element of the spectator's understanding of a film within which variations of the genre, which Altman describes as a 'generic crossroads' (2004: 165), are sought. The dawn of the New Hollywood saw an increase in the production of films that created a self-conscious dialogue with the spectator about generic expectations, allowing for countercultural pleasures to be integrated into familiar generic structures. Thus, as Cawelti explains, film noir is engaged with and then diverged from in *Chinatown* (Roman Polanski, 1974), as is the gangster film in *Bonnie and Clyde*. He also points out that the 1970s was a decade in which pastiche and burlesque were notably popular, such as the films of Mel Brooks, and in which the major genres of American film were 'demythologized': 'Instead of simply reversing the meanings conventionally ascribed to the opposing forces of criminal and society in the gangster genre, *Bonnie and Clyde* expressed a complex and dark awareness that this basic opposition was itself a mythical simplification' (2004: 165, 206).

Within this an exhaustion of mainstream genres such as the Western was occurring, simultaneous with the decline of the mythology underpinning the genres and a 'growing historical awareness of modern popular culture'

(2004: 165, 208). Engaging with the subject of genre then is pertinent in understanding how the Vigilante Thrillers arose (and out of which genres), and how they were consumed (this also evokes many of the reviews that suggested the films as evocative of the Western). The two genres most relevant in this discussion are the Thriller and the Western. Both were undergoing innovations during the period, and elements of both have been seen by critics (contemporary and later) as informing the Vigilante Thrillers as texts. Cawelti sees both the Western and the hard-boiled detective thriller as indelibly connected; they are specifically American and have protagonists that have 'similar characteristics' (2004: 180), such as a 'readiness for violence', but only when forced into situations when such action is demanded. Both heroes have 'personal codes of morality that transcend the written law and the conventional morality of society' (2004: 181). Both 'are contemporary versions of a myth of the isolated hero in a pervasively corrupt society and have welled up out of a strain of pessimism and despair in the American tradition ... doubts about the American dream' (2004: 191).

Webb discusses the impact of this on style, suggesting that the 'induced documentary' style of *The French Connection* was a response to 'postmodern fragmentation and depthlessness' going further to explain that 'The apparent exhaustion of classical film genres in the 1970s therefore produced two primary responses: a tendency towards self-reflexivity, genre deconstruction, and pastiche on the one hand, and the turn to docufiction and realist aesthetics on the other' (2014: 111). These elements become evident throughout the Vigilante Thriller: in how the Western and thriller genres are reconceived; in elements that self-consciously discuss their own meanings (such as Callahan's reasons for being 'Dirty', the representation of the media in *Death Wish* or Bickle's voice-over in *Taxi Driver*); and in the use of differing filming techniques, such as Peckinpah's employment of telephoto lenses and Friedkin's instructions to his camera operator, Enrique Bravo, to 'follow the action without knowing where the actors would move next' (Webb 2014: 111).

Thrillers

Thrillers have their own morality. It is a morality which has little in common with the ethics that are publicly admitted to regulate men's lives in our society: it has no respect for equality, privacy, due process of law or the impartiality of authority. It is a morality of unequivocal self-assertion tempered only by an entirely personal sense of decency.

(PALMER 1978: 5)

Palmer (1978) endeavours to give a comprehensive overview of the literary thriller genre. His work gives a basis on which to consider another generic influence on the Vigilante Thriller, one that offers a counterpoint to the Western in several ways and informs the analysis of the Vigilante Thrillers themselves. Palmer considers how the thriller had developed from the literary to cinematic form and provides a breakdown of formal aspects of the genre, placing the work within a sociological perspective that proves useful in understanding the place of the Vigilante Thriller among this oeuvre. Further to that Paul Cobley (2000) and Peter Lev (2000) conduct specific analysis of the developments of the genre contemporaneous to the Vigilante texts and in relation to them in some cases.

As Lev and Cobley discuss, there was a rise in conspiracy and paranoid thrillers during the 1970s, many of which dealt with the political fallout from the period through narratives that detailed an individual, or in some cases a duo, uncovering a plot in which the once reliable elements of American social structures (government, military and/or business) are seen to be secretly undermining the society they claim to defend and uphold. The success of films such as *Chinatown*, *The Parallax View*, *Three Days of the Condor* (Sydney Pollack, 1975) and *All the President's Men* (Alan J. Pakula, 1976)[2] suggests a willingness for contemporary audiences to engage directly with political issues and the possibility that, as evidenced through Watergate's dramatization in *All the President's Men*, for Hollywood to openly exploit audience anxiety about real-world situations. This indicates not only the willingness of producers to exploit contemporary politics but also suggests an audience interested in seeing these themes and problems played out on the cinema screen, whether the conclusion offered a victory against the conspiracy (*All the President's Men*), ambiguity (*The Parallax View*, *Three Days of the Condor*) or showed the conspiracy triumphing (*Chinatown*). Different from the Vigilante Thriller, however, is the fact that the conspiracy often includes the mechanisms of law and order (such as the CIA and the Police), whereas the Vigilante Thriller depicts these organizations as hampered at best in *Dirty Harry* and *The French Connection* (due to misplaced values), as largely absent in *Joe*, *Death Wish* and *Taxi Driver*, or as small minded and incompetent, as in *Straw Dogs*. This difference suggests a development from the concerns of the earlier Vigilante Thrillers to the conspiracy/paranoia thrillers, in which the state becomes a more sinister force.

Returning to Palmer's analysis, he opens with a discussion of the differences between Heroes and Villains in the Thriller, and he identifies three essential character types: 'The Amateur, the Professional and the Bureaucrat'. Although not intended to delineate specifically between the

---

[2] It should be noted that Don Siegel directed one of the earliest paranoia thrillers, *Invaders of the Body Snatchers* (1956), which was itself remade in 1978 directed by Philip Kaufman. Siegel's film, however, represents the threat as from another planet, rather than from within the institutions of the United States.

hero and villain per se, these types 'demarcate the zone where heroism can occur: the hero can neither be an Amateur or a Bureaucrat' (Palmer 1978: 14). The Professional is an isolated figure that operates in a self-reliant manner and is often placed in a 'situation where he is effectively deprived of support' (ibid.: 15). This is in opposition to the Amateur, usually a female character who is passive, lacks knowledge and doesn't belong, or the Bureaucrat, a figure of process and rigidity who can be, but is not necessarily, related to evil. Palmer cites Micky Spillane's Mike Hammer series in which 'Bureaucratic law-enforcement procedures fail' (ibid.: 13), a theme which is particularly pertinent to the Vigilante Thriller in which official processes are depicted as ineffective and mired in red tape (with the added contemporary debates around Miranda procedures and the rights of the suspect). These roles map problematically onto the Vigilante Thrillers. For *The French Connection* and *Dirty Harry* the similarities seem evident – both films follow professional law men who feel constrained by Bureaucrats, although neither provides a figure of the Amateur (which is often a female character to be rescued). Indeed, an element that clearly distinguishes these films from previous police thrillers, such as *Bullitt* or *Coogan's Bluff*, is the lack of a love interest for the protagonists (something that Haskell identifies as the erasure of women from narratives except as victims (1974: 363)). In terms of *Joe*, *Straw Dogs*, *Death Wish* and *Taxi Driver* these components are more problematic. The bureaucracy is evident in all four films, whether explicitly, as in *Death Wish* during the scenes in which Kersey struggles to get the Police to take his wife's death and daughter's assault seriously and in his superior effect in reducing crime, or implicitly, as in *Taxi Driver*, where the state of New York streets relates to the poor efficacy of the Police. However, the professionalism aspect is questionable and represents a movement away from traditional thriller aspects: Joe Curran has military experience, but Bill Compton does not; David Sumner has none that we know of; Paul Kersey was a conscientious objector during the Korean War but shows a talent for shooting; Travis Bickle claims to have served in Vietnam, although his methods make this questionable, as does his voice-over that suggests a delusional view of the world. The absence of professionalism does not preclude the Vigilante films having elements of the thriller in them. Rather, it suggests innovations and transformations around existing conventions, and perhaps a movement towards the cynicism that exists in the conspiracy/paranoia thriller in which all employees of government/business are implicated leaving only the ordinary man outside to try to uncover and deal with the conspiracy.

In differentiating between Heroes and Villains in the Thriller, Palmer discusses the use of violence, an aspect of the genre particularly pertinent to this work,

> The distinction between the two uses of violence is, fundamentally, that the villain is indifferent towards people to whom he applies it, whereas

the hero has to be moved to violence, and cannot be indifferent towards his victims. To the villain, victims are peripheral objects, a nuisance to be dealt with; to the hero they may be hateful (and usually deserve it), but they are still people. (1978: 21)

This is a key difference between the Vigilante Thriller and the literary thriller; I would contend that the protagonists of the Vigilante Thriller show little or no regard to their victims and in that respect more closely mirror their antagonists than was previously evident in the thriller genre. For Palmer, the personality of the villain matters less than the conspiracy they inspire; 'The conspiracy . . . is an absolute structural necessity for it is the conspiracy that drives the plot into action' (1978: 23).

This concept is something that Cobley builds on with specific reference to American cinema of the 1970s. He suggests that the definition of conspiracy 'is so wide and accommodating that it enables an expansive range of diverse texts' (2000: 3) to be considered as part of the thriller genre. For Cobley this diversity is a sign of the genre's high popularity throughout the decade in which the Vigilante Thriller sits and can be explained by developments in contemporary political events: 'The 1970s were a time when the material of thrillers – conspiracy, espionage, secrecy, crime and so forth – was a prominent part of other discourses in the social formation of America' (2000: 6). This work has already discussed some of these sociopolitical issues, but it is worth restating the centrality of law and order as an issue that had currency in political circles and the mainstream media.[3] Cobley connects the rise in crime during the 1960s–70s to corruption in government, and a more general 'crisis of authority' (2000: 91), which connects with Palmer's views on the Bureaucratic but also suggests a wider sense of the limits of the conspiracy. Within this context, Cobley cites *Dirty Harry*, *Death Wish* and *Taxi Driver* as texts concerned with vengeance, which he qualifies: 'In reading the revenge narrative of the seventies, then, it is important of consider the manifold nature of the impetus and objects of revenge' (2000: 168). Cobley also discusses the concept of generic innovation, similar to what Cawelti calls generic transformation, to explore the mutability of the thriller genre, and the limitations of seeing genre as a set of criteria rather than an evolving form. He suggests the text as a place of interaction with the spectator, rather than a fixed entity with 'meanings', and that genre is a contributor to this – that the spectator draws from this knowledge of genre to construct readings.

---

[3]In reference to Watts and Free (1974) Cobley cites a poll that measured 'The Degree of Public Concern About Major National Issues' in which Violence in America and Crime were priorities 2 and 3, Corruption of Officials was 4th, whereas Watergate was 19th. The number 1 priority was 'The rise in prices and the cost of living' (2000: 90).

In his analysis of *Dirty Harry*, Cobley distances the film from the dominant discourse of fascism that emerged from the contemporary reviews. He suggests that Callahan's attitudes to race are 'self-conscious' and that 'his anger stems from the fact that he is a white American seemingly endowed with all the privileges of his 'race' yet ultimately without power in a civic role which actually hinders him in preventing carnage' (2000: 171). This complexity is compounded by the parallels between Callahan and Scorpio, who both represent a threat to society. Regarding *Death Wish*, Cobley suggests that the text is 'knowingly anti-liberal' (2000: 176) and, in its depiction of the media reaction to crime, shows society's failure to cope with rises in crime, especially mugging. For both films, the concept of the outsider, a sense of otherness, is defining and returns in *Taxi Driver*. Callahan, Scorpio and Kersey are all outside society, both through their attitudes and their behaviours (especially their violence). So is Travis Bickle, who describes himself as apart from the dirty world he observes from his taxi. For Cobley this is built on a contradiction, that the military training that Bickle is supposed to have had and which was endorsed by society, becomes the source of othering when the US Military's actions include atrocities such as My Lai – this more directly dramatizes an opposition between inside (training in the United States) and outside (actions in Vietnam) that is present in all the films. This engagement is a distinct generic innovation in the Thriller:

> The protagonist often treads a path and takes action which places him 'outside' contemporary American society as it is understood at that moment in time; alternatively, the protagonist is stigmatized as an 'outsider' but enacts proceedings which are popularly received as appropriate 'inside' responses to the current social world. The divergent ways in which some commentators and many audiences attempted to negotiate the tension of 'inside'/'outside' which characterized revenge texts suggests that such is a focal point for the social investments which constitute generic innovation. (Cobley 2000: 186)

Palmer discusses several sociological aspects of the thriller that relate to the Vigilante Thrillers and connect back to the Western. One aspect of these is what Palmer terms 'Competitive Individualism', a concept that emerges out of the industrial revolution and explains why the thriller hero emerges, at first, during the nineteenth century. The emphasis on competition and respectability during this period demands a hero who acts individually and competitively but also represents the existing social order. The thriller fulfils a specific ideological function, in which the hero opposes 'a pathological disruption of an otherwise ordered world' (1978: 203). The thriller also resolves issues inherent in the individualism of the hero and his defence of society, a communal desire. If the purpose of the thriller is to unify the competitive individual with society, through the defeat of a conspiracy that threatens that society, then the endings of the Vigilante Thrillers reinforce Cobley's suggestion of generic innovation, as the protagonists remain apart from that society and suggest that the problem has not, or cannot, be resolved. As Lev notes,

> Movies such as *Joe*, *The French Connection* and *Dirty Harry* . . . are surprisingly ambiguous in their populist sentiments, responding to the complexity of the turmoil of the period. *Joe* is an antihippie movie, but it concludes by criticizing the older generation. *The French Connection* is a police-centred action film which includes a terrifying final scene of Popeye stalking anything that moves. *Dirty Harry* is another police-centred action film, but it focusses on fractures between the rank-and-file police, the city bureaucracy, and the law. (2000: 39)

Lev's analysis of these three films suggests that within what seems to be a simplistic thriller narrative of right-wing identification, ambiguities are presented that undermine such simplistic readings. Rather than responding to these issues, however, the Vigilante Thrillers are part of the complex turmoil that defines the issues and the era. Lev asserts that *Death Wish* lacks ambiguity. However, this is challenged by the unstable mind of Paul Kersey, his past as a conscientious objector, and his potential movement from protagonist to antagonist in the text (also identified by Mendik (2002) and discussed in more detail later). Discussion of *Straw Dogs* can also be added here, a film in which a literal outsider to a society uncovers various corruptions and conspiracies which he subsequently resolves, but only in problematic ways (both thematically and narratively). Just as the ending of *Taxi Driver* creates a discourse over whether Bickle's actions have or have not been heroic, Sumner's final abandonment of his home and wife Amy undermines the preceding action of the film.

The threat of conspiracy is a structural necessity of the thriller, identified by Palmer and reiterated by Cobley as the genre's 'prime mover' (Palmer 1978: 3), a notion wide enough to account for the diversity of texts in the genre, but essential nonetheless. Conspiracy is a 'threat to equilibrium' (Palmer 1978: 3) which must be defeated to head off threats to capitalist hegemonic structures. What then of conspiracies in the Vigilante Thriller? *Joe* can be seen from several different perspectives, but all embrace a threat to existing society: Joe himself feels that social changes are emasculating him, changes that he projects onto the hippies; Bill Compton sees the hippy culture in a similar way, degrading his authority over his daughter; finally, Melissa sees the unwillingness of the patriarchal figures to change as a conspiracy against her freedom. (We could also include Frank as a corrupting figure to the innocent Melissa.) In *Straw Dogs* the local village conspires first to hide Henry Niles's (David Warner) crimes, then conspires to punish him for the death of Janice (Sally Thomsett), against the wishes of the Major (T. P. McKenna), the village's figure of law and order. *The French Connection* has a foreign conspiracy bringing drugs into America but also suggests a failure of law and order. This implies a liberal conspiracy against Police officers and the victims of crime which is reiterated in *Dirty Harry*. *Dirty Harry* also places Scorpio as a direct threat to the running of a smooth society, and, ironically in a film read as right wing, his targets are those who represent the social changes happening at the time. (He suggests that he'll target 'a Catholic Priest or a Nigger' in his letter to Police.) In *Death Wish* the conspiracy threat has become existential. Kersey fights for the ability to live in a safe city, rather than against a specific antagonist. Depending how the film is read, a second conspiracy led by the Police to prevent Kersey also occurs, or Kersey himself becomes the destabilizing force. *Taxi Driver* echoes this in which Bickle can either be the solution to the problems of society (embodied by the politician Charles Palantine (Leonard Harris), who offers only soundbites rather than solutions) or he is the problem. Cobley discusses Bickle's status as a Vietnam-Vet (something that is only suggested by Bickle himself) as representing an 'internalised threat' (2000: 178) to social order (reflected in Scorpio as well). It can be established that the Vigilante Thriller draws from the wider thriller genre in several ways. As such, the Vigilante Thriller is, like many films of this period, self-consciously using genre in a referential manner, engaging an audience aware of the codes and conventions being employed.

Returning to Palmer's quote from the beginning of this section, the question of the protagonists' 'entirely personal sense of decency' should be addressed and informs wider questions of this work. During a time of social change, the very definition of decency was in question. Throughout the Vigilante Thrillers the protagonists display their own individual moral codes which sit at odds with the collectivist ideas of social reform and the Civil Rights movement; the reinstatement of the status quo is problematized when society cannot agree what the status quo should be. Alienation and othering occur here due to the upheaval, the confusion over moral standards pushing out those who differ to a developing consensus.

Gender roles also stand as an important element of generic development during this period. Haskell discusses the shift in gender representation in Hollywood during the 1960s, noting a reaction to films in which male roles had become less active:

This response to the passive hero, and to women's liberation as well, shows up towards the end of the decade (1960s) in violent machismo films like *Straw Dogs*, *A Clockwork Orange* and *The Godfather*, and neo-machismo films (that is, getting the kicks but feigning mockery) like *High Plains Drifter* and *Dillinger*. The sudden public obsessions with books and films about the Mafia and the Nazis, both celebrating

> male power and male authority figures at their most violent and sexist, suggest a backlash in which middle-class men, fearful of their eroding masculinity, take refuse in the supermale fantasies of Don Corleone and Dr. Goebbels. (1974: 361)

Haskell suggests a growing reaction to changes in American society towards male-oriented topics. A crisis in masculinity, or the discussion of a possible crisis, forms the thematic basis of many films from the late 1960s into the 1970s. Films such as Sam Peckinpah's *The Wild Bunch* and John Boorman's *Deliverance* (1972) questioned the roles of men in different societies and environments. A sense of transition exists in these films, of a type of masculinity under threat and disappearing. This, as Haskell points out, is reflected in several police thrillers that emerge in the late 1970s and presage the Vigilante Thriller:

> Thus, the difference between Don Siegel's *Madigan* (1968) and his *Dirty Harry* (1971), of producer Phil D'Antoni's *Bullitt* (1968) and *The French Connection* (1971) is that the earlier films have token women and the latter ones exclude them (except in the most marginal contexts), thereby confirming what was latent in earlier genre films – that all feelings and rapport are between men, between a cop and his superior, a cop and his sidekick, of a cop and his nemesis, the criminal. (1974: 363)

The development between these earlier films and the Vigilante Thriller is pertinent as it shows how the latter cycle develops from existing films with proven box-office success. These can also be related to the decline of the Western (as follows). The police thrillers from the 1960s themselves are not a sudden development but build upon previous films, which Martin Rubin calls a 'Flawed-Cop Cycle', 'Merging elements of film noir and semidocumentary, the police thrillers of the early 1950s combined the organisational heroes of the latter with the social and spiritual malaise of the former' (1999: 102). This earlier cycle of films includes those that detail, as an extension of film noirs, the downfall of a corrupt cop. More pertinent to this study are Rubin's details of 'A smaller but more significant group of 1950s police thrillers [that] deal with cops whose failings spring not from moral weakness but from rigidity and excessive zeal' (1999: 102). *Where the Sidewalk Ends* (Otto Preminger, 1950) has a brutal cop accidentally killing a suspect then attempting to pin the crime on a gangster. The cop's character described by advertising as 'half-cop and half-killer' is an early example of the line between justice and crime being blurred. *The Big Heat* (Fritz Lang, 1953) sees Glenn Ford's happily married Policeman take on a 'revenge-obsessed crusade against the criminal syndicate' (Rubin 1999: 104) after his wife is murdered. Similar issues of right and wrong are essayed further in *Touch of Evil* (Orson Welles, 1958) in the conflict between

Charlton Heston's honest drug-enforcement agent and Orson Welles's corrupt cop. For Rubin, these films are 'intensified by tortured McCarthy-era liberalism, expressive late-noir stylistics, and post-war Hollywood's obsessive preoccupation with masculine vulnerability' (1999: 102). Robert Reiner makes similar conclusions, discussing a 'mini-cycle of movies in the early 1950s concerned with probing the psyche of the policeman' (1981: 205): 'Outstanding examples of the disturbed/brutal/corrupt cop cycle were [William] Wyler's *Detective Story* (1951), Lang's *The Big Heat* (1953), and Welles's *Touch of Evil* (1958). The central issue in these films is the perennial police dilemma in a democratic society of how to maintain order without violating the rules of due process in law' (1981: 205). There is, however, a significant difference between this 1950s cycle of films and the later police thrillers, although they share the central concern of law versus order: 'Unlike the rogue cop movies of the 1950s, it is the loner with whom we are meant to sympathise' (Reiner 1981: 208).

In analysing the influence of *In the Heat of the Night*, both Rubin and Reiner suggest that Gillespie is an influence on later thrillers such as *Dirty Harry* and *The French Connection*. Despite the liberal anti-vigilantism theme of the film, embodied in Sidney Poitier's Virgil Tibbs, it is Gillespie that has the greater influence on film culture: 'the Steiger character, not averse to using racial epithets or strong-arm methods, helped pave the way for such urban rednecks as Dirty Harry and Popeye Doyle' (Rubin 1999: 137). Of the significant police thrillers of the late 1960s cited by each writer, only one other shows a liberal bias similar to *In the Heat of the Night*: *The Detective* (Gordon Douglas, 1968), starring Frank Sinatra as 'the ideal, liberal policeman that all the Presidential Commissions of the 1960s sought to produce by a combination of organizational reforms and college education' (Reiner 1981: 210). Both Rubin and Reiner see three films as directly leading to the production and success of both *Dirty Harry* and *The French Connection*; these are *Madigan*, *Bullitt* and *Coogan's Bluff*.

Madigan concerns the tension between street cop Sergeant Dan Madigan (Richard Widmark) and his seemingly saintly superior Commissioner Anthony Russell (Henry Fonda). The casting of Widmark and Fonda suggests a confluence of film noir and Western, Widmark being closely associated with the former with roles in films such as *Kiss of Death* (Henry Hathaway, 1947), and Fonda appearing in several important Westerns such as *My Darling Clementine* (John Ford, 1946). Sharing several elements with *Dirty Harry*, including director, star and composer, *Coogan's Bluff* shows a nascent form of the themes of the latter film, but is, in many ways, more conservative in form and message. Within this, however, there is an ambivalent view of the main character: it is an arrogant mistake by Coogan (Clint Eastwood) that prompts the central plot of the film, and its conclusion sees him finally adopt the procedures he had initially dismissed as unnecessary. *Coogan's Bluff* articulates the relocation of the Old West and the American wilderness to an Urban Centre more obviously than any of the later Vigilante Thrillers, although they echo it. *Bullitt* precedes the Vigilante Thriller in several ways but, unlike *Madigan* and *Coogan's Bluff*, it was not directed by Don Siegel (although it does have music by Lalo Schifrin who scored *Coogan's Bluff* and *Dirty Harry* and shares a producer, Philip D'Antoni, with *The French Connection*). It focusses on the main character (played by Steve McQueen) and as such offers more of a character portrait than the other films. *Bullitt* also more strongly presents the antagonism between the cop on the street and higher authority, represented by Robert Vaughan's D.A. Chalmers (although Bullitt's immediate superior is consistently supportive). *Bullitt* paints Chalmers, the figure of authority, as much of an antagonist as the mobsters who threaten Bullitt's life. The ending, in which the witness Pete Ross (Victor Tayback) is killed by Bullitt, thus rendering his previous investigation void, brings a negative ending that foreshadows *The French Connection*. All the films contain repeated acts of violence, but *Bullitt* is more detailed, the camera focussing on blood and gunshot wounds.

All three films show a shift from traditional heroic narratives. Distrust of authority and procedure is becoming evident. The protagonists are less tethered by relationships, emerging as more complicated, ambivalent figures. Their conflicts are as much with systems as with antagonists. As Haskell suggested, the films became more interested in their heroes, with women being pushed to the margins. Peter Krämer gives an extensive overview of the changing dynamics of the American cinema audience in the 1960s and 1970s. This includes a shift in the late 1960s from female-oriented to male-oriented films:

> It is likely that the enormous success of *The Graduate* encouraged both audience and filmmakers to shift their attention away from the female protagonists as well as mostly past and foreign settings so dominant in mid-1960s superhits (most notably in *Cleopatra* (Joseph L. Mankiewicz, 1963), *My Fair Lady* (George Cukor, 1964), and *The Sound of Music*) towards male protagonists and the contemporary American scene. (2005: 14)

This was also a period when films were moving away from a family audience towards a more youth-oriented audience, with a predominately male make-up (this period includes a decline in overall attendance): 'While the taboo-breaking films were particularly attractive to some audiences, notably male youth, they alienated large numbers of Americans (in particular older people and women, and possibly those with little education), many more of whom stopped going to the movies' (Krämer 2005: 66). These developments helped precipitate changes in distribution and signal shifts in the cinema culture.

Horror

Considering Nigel Andrews's review of *Straw Dogs* in *Monthly Film Bulletin* (1971), it seems pertinent to examine developments in the horror film during this period, investigating correlations between changes in the horror genre and the Vigilante Thriller. Andrews's designation of *Straw Dogs* as a horror film underlines the inexactness of genre categorizations but also emphasizes that a film may be read differently when taken from a different genre standpoint. This is particularly relevant as during this period many of the concerns of the Vigilante Thriller are seen in horror films: the nature of family, the safety of the home, links between sexuality and violence.

Tony Williams (1996) investigates the impact of the Vietnam War on the horror genre and on depictions of the family and identifies 'connections between Western frontier imagery and contemporary descriptions of the war situation' (1996: 129). A relationship is drawn to the Puritan Captivity Narrative (that highlighted and exploited the plights of European settlers captured by Native Americans) in the descriptions of South Vietnam versus the 'marauding, demonic, Indian like' forces of the Viet Cong. Williams relates this narrative to films such as *The Texas Chainsaw Massacre* (Tobe Hooper, 1974): 'A common motif in all these films is a state of siege where the family unit struggles against outside forces. These forces represent distorted embodiments of repressed tensions' (1996: 129). Immediately this is evident in *Straw Dogs* in which the repressed sexual tensions of the Sumner household, and the local village, culminate in the final siege. Williams also investigates the moral questions raised by the Vietnam War: 'Several contemporary horror films use Vietnam's traumatic effect on American society, making relevant metaphoric connections, explicitly (*The Night Walker*) and implicitly (the vast majority of representations). Homeland protection means defense [*sic*] of the family from violation. The enemy is a demonized "other". Certain contemporary horror films suggest violence as the inevitable outcome of socially conditioned repression' (1996: 130).

Because of Sumner's violence at the end of *Straw Dogs*, and the violent content of all the Vigilante Thrillers, the concept of 'socially conditioned repression' is useful as it suggests a wider social explanation for the rise in crime and social disorder during the 1960s–70s. For Williams, implicit representations of Vietnam in horror show the war as an outlet for the violence incubated within the structures of American society, especially within the family (1996: 133). This suggests a much wider potential for violence within American society, one that can be released given the right circumstances. The use of phrases such as 'Urban Jungle' and 'Concrete Jungle' during the 1970s reinforces an elision with the jungles of Vietnam and the collapse of oppositions between wilderness and civilization. Slotkin notes the similarities between violence at home and abroad: 'In Newark and Detroit they reached a level of violence which begged comparison with Vietnam. . . . These two "war" stories developed simultaneously and were reported in parallel on nightly television news programs' (1992: 550).

Much American horror of the late 1960s and the 1970s is concerned with home invasion and the family. Films such as *Night of the Living Dead* (George A. Romero, 1968), *The Texas Chainsaw Massacre* and *The Hills Have Eyes* (Wes Craven, 1977) depict horrific, grotesque, families who, in their violence and cannibalism, parody the family turning the home into a site of trauma. In *The Last House on the Left* (Wes Craven, 1971)[4] two families are contrasted: the middle-class Collingwoods and the poor Stilos (which includes the drug-addicted Junior, hooked on drugs by his father and his pseudo-mother, the violent lesbian Sadie). When the Stilos unwittingly take refuge in the Collingwood's house, having previously raped and killed the Collingwood's daughter and her friend, the Stilos themselves are murdered by their hosts. Both families commit acts of violence, and the home becomes a killing ground. Neither family is redeemed in the film, with the middle-class home shown as being capable of violence when given the right motivation. The film demonstrates some of the questions about family and home, part of Williams's 'crisis of ideologic codes' in America. *Death Wish* and *Straw Dogs* both demonstrate the violation of the home. In *Joe*, the main character's gun collection and the Second World War memorabilia in his basement literally suggest that underneath the appearance of a normal home life violence lurks. The protagonists of *The French Connection*, *Dirty Harry* and *Taxi Driver* live in bare, sparse surroundings, without spouses. Travis Bickle, who describes himself as a Vietnam veteran, directly connects the Vigilante Thrillers to the violence in Vietnam and its effect on the ideologic codes in the United States: 'the war returns home in the figure of a wounded son or other metaphorical guises such as zombies' (Williams 1996: 131).

Taking concepts of the home further, Barbara Creed offers a definition of the *unheimlich* (the uncanny) which provides insight into the very meaning of home:

> Freud refers to those things which are frequently called uncanny: they fall into three main categories.
>
> i. Those things which relate to the notion of a double: a cyborg; twin; doppelganger; a multiplied object; a ghost or spirit; an involuntary repetition of an act.
>
> ii. Castration anxieties expressed as a fear of the female genitals or of dismembered limbs, a severed head or hand, loss of the eyes, fear of going blind.

---

[4]Loosely adapted from *The Virgin Spring* (Ingmar Bergman, 1960).

iii. A feeling associated with a familiar/unfamiliar place, losing one's way, womb phantasies, a haunted house.

All of these fears are explored in the horror film. The horror presented within each category can be defined in relation to a loss of clear boundaries. (1993: 54)

The idea of a loss of boundaries is pertinent, especially considering the social reforms and the transformation of urban areas during the period in question. For Creed, the house represents the womb, 'a place that is familiar and unfamiliar [which] is acted out in the horror film through the presentation of monstrous acts which are only half glimpsed or initially hidden from sight until revealed in their full horror' (1993: 53). This space is also key in the formation of the self: 'Almost always the origin of these deeds takes us back to the individual's quest for her or his own origins which are linked to three primal scenes – conception, sexual difference, desire. The house becomes the symbolic space – the place of beginnings, the womb – where the three dramas are played out' (1993: 53). As we shall see later, the nature of looking and seeing (and knowing) is essential to the Vigilante Thriller therefore invoking the concept of the primal scene and illicitness of looking. Looking can become a traumatic act in Creed's analysis, especially looking into the home. This querying of the formation of self connects strongly with the ambiguity surrounding the other developing in this time – the origins of the self, the home, and by analogy American society, were being contested.

Carol Clover (1992) draws together ideas of rape, revenge and the opposition between town and country. Clover uses the rape-revenge film *I Spit on Your Grave* (Meir Zarchi, 1977) to explore this and oppositions between male and female. For Clover, the main character in *I Spit on Your Grave*, Jennifer, becomes a victim of gang rape not simply because she is a woman but because 'she is a woman from the city, and from the city is to be, at least in the eyes of the country, rich' (1992: 120). A fear is defined: urbanoia, a fear of the country, 'People from the city are people like us. People from the country (as I shall hereafter refer to those people horror construes as the threatening rural "other") are people not like us' (1992: 124). Clover continues,

Just *how* they are not like us is of some interest. In horror, country dwellers are disproportionately represented by adult males with no ascertainable family attachments. . . . These men do no discernible work, are commonly shown lying about the home farm in the middle of a workday. . . . When we do see country families, something is always terribly wrong with them. (1992: 125)

An equivalence with the Venner family in *Straw Dogs* is obvious here, given the films' rural location. Indeed, the Reverend Hood (Colin Welland) states,

'You've never worked a day in your life, Tom' to the head of the Heddon family (Peter Vaughan). However, it also suggests a wider malaise concerning the family, which was once considered the foundation of society. Some correspondence to the representations of criminals in the other films can also be seen, especially in *Death Wish*. Although they are urban characters, the group of young men who attack Kersey's family demonstrate a similar disregard of work – filling their time with theft and graffiti. The degeneracy of the country, as seen in horror, also appears in the mainly urban setting of the Vigilante Thriller. This also relates to the effect of an urban, middle-class lifestyle on masculinity, something that is clearly represented in *Deliverance* (John Boorman, 1972). Clover makes the following point, 'City man may be rich, but he is also soft; and he is soft *because* he is rich' (Clover 1992: 132). Clover's discussion of town and country as an opposition also invokes class and financial status, 'One of the obvious things at stake in the city/country split of horror film, in short, is social class – the confrontation between the haves and have-nots, or even more directly between exploiters and their victims' and 'The city not only has money, it uses its money to humiliate country people' (Clover 1992: 126). The Vigilante Thriller shows that this division is not limited to the split between urban and country environments, but that there are extreme contrasts within the city itself in class issues (in *Joe*, *Death Wish* and *Taxi Driver*) and racial issues (*The French Connection*, *Dirty Harry* and *Taxi Driver*) shown through use of location and oppositions of characters. For Clover, like Williams, society is built on repressed violence, 'civilization sits lightly on even the best-bred among us; turn push to shove and we revert to savagery' (Clover 1992: 132). Clover's conclusion in relation to the urbanoia film has clear relevance to this study:

> The collision between state and country is also a collision between a state of mentality (in which citizens can submit their grievances to an executive function) and statelessness (in which citizens can rely on vigilantism). Much of the ambient horror of these films resides in the fact the statelessness – our collective past – is not dead and buried but is just a car ride away. (Clover 1992: 132–3)

The opposition Clover describes between town and country is present within the urban environments of the Vigilante Thriller; the disorder of the countryside and Vietnam (as suggested by Williams) has moved into the decaying urban environments.

In *Death Wish*, Clover's opposition between town and country is reversed. Paul Kersey finds (contrary to Williams's suggestions) that the spaces of Tucson are an idealized form of America from before the civil upheavals of the 1960s. This is explicitly contrasted to the chaos and disorder of New York. The scenes in Tucson, in which Kersey watches a staged Western gunfight, specifically recall the Western myth. Clover herself discussed this myth in relation to rape-revenge films, comparing them to 'nineteenth century representations of Indian atrocities' (1992: 136), a link that recalls Williams's invocation of the Puritan Captivity Narratives, and the threat of rape in Westerns: 'What 1940s Hollywood knew is that the implication of rape makes the deed all the more avengeable. And what the 1970s horror realized is that one's own rape is the most avengeable deed of all' (1992: 136). In *Straw Dogs* we can see a different journey, where David Sumner moves to the countryside to escape. However, the disorder of the urban space is invoked as Amy accuses David of moving to Cornwall 'because there's no place else to hide' and when Chris Cawsey (Jim Norton) and Norman Scutt tease David, asking if he was involved in the 'Bombing, rioting, sniping, shooting the blacks' in America. One of the central ironies of *Straw Dogs* is the implosion of the division between urban and country – the violence exists in both places.

This discussion of the horror film in the 1970s is by no means exhaustive. However, it highlights several areas pertinent to the understanding of the Vigilante Thriller and the wider cinematic context: that the nature of the white American male was subject to redefinition in reaction to reports from Vietnam; that representations of the home and family were increasingly problematizing those concepts, suggesting acts of repression would lead to acts of violence; and that the status of the urban environment, and what it represented, was shifting, indicating (for the middle classes at least) a softening of masculinity, linked to the growth of an urban jungle in which the horrors of urbanoia come to the city. This movement suggests a development in how the other was to be represented, with elements of the opposition between town and country being elided. It also shows the potential for reversal, the acknowledgement that otherness is seen from both sides; indeed, it shows that the concept of 'normal' was in itself in debate.

The Western

Then in the 1960s the city became the frontier, and the savages – the muggers and the rapists – were already inside the gates. Don Siegel's Coogan's Bluff, made in 1968, made this shift explicit, as an Arizona sheriff pursues his quarry through the streets of New York. The casting of Clint Eastwood, the last great totem pole of the Western, in the contemporary role appeared to authenticate the transference of the Western's traditional themes to the crime film, and Eastwood's subsequent career as the Policeman Dirty Harry confirmed it.

(BUSCOMBE 1988: 53)

You speakin' to me?

(ALAN LADD IN *SHANE*, PARAMOUNT PICTURES, 1953)

You talkin' to me?

(ROBERT DE NIRO IN *TAXI DRIVER*, COLUMBIA PICTURES, 1976)

The place of the Western and, as Richard Slotkin describes it, the 'Frontier Myth' in the psyche of the United States throughout the twentieth century, was essential. Slotkin discusses how 'Myth expresses ideology in a narrative, rather than discursive or argumentative, structure' (1992: 6), which creates a sense that myth arises naturally through 'identification with venerable tradition' (1992: 6). This myth was consistently used in the media and politics as a shorthand way of discussing the American concept of Manifest Destiny, a moral justification of the expansion into the west of America and 'The vision of the westward settlements as a refuge from tyranny and corruption, a safety valve for metropolitan discontents, a land of golden opportunity for enterprising individualists, and an inexhaustible reservoir of natural wealth on which a future of limitless prosperity could be based' (1992: 30). Slotkin also discusses how moments of 'cognitive dissonance' (1992: 30) disrupt and revise the myth. The changes in American society, covered earlier, are an extreme form of this cognitive dissonance in which the fundaments of the Frontier Myth, and by proxy the Western genre, were tested and displaced. Slotkin notes that 'historical events (like the defeat in Vietnam) always call into question the validity of "the guiding myth"' (1992: 626). The language of the Frontier Myth was used by diverse sources in the political and cultural landscape including John F. Kennedy in his invocation of 'the New Frontier'. This language was deeply embedded into American culture, and in particular American white male culture. As James William Gibson observes, 'During the Vietnam War, "Indian Country" showed up time and time again in the everyday language of the troops' (1994: 71), suggesting that the Vietcong were seen within this context. Given the fundamental nature of the Western myth to American identity, the ideological crisis precipitated by the 1960s created an ideological vacuum that the Vigilante Thriller attempted to fill.

The connective tissue between the Vigilante Thriller and the Western was explicitly drawn by both popular and academic critics, both at the time of the films' releases and through subsequent writing. The films themselves make specific textual allusions that invoke the Western and suggest a continuum of sorts. This is also reflected in the personnel who worked on and acted in the films. The analysis of Westerns that follows is twofold – an examination of the structural and generic ties, but also an examination of how the mythic and ideological structures of the Western are reflected and examined by the Vigilante Thrillers. The role of the Vigilante in fiction is tied to narrative and ideological structures. As Smith suggests, 'The individual vigilante of the movies becomes, as it were, the ideal father who will protect and serve the community. In that paternal, not to say patronizing role, the individual vigilante in fact suggests that any need for collective agitation can be obviated' (1993: 93). Of all the films of this study *Taxi Driver* has had the most specific and rigorous comparison with the Western due to its similarities with *The Searchers*. However, all the films reference or imitate the Western in various ways and several share key personnel that had worked in the genre prior to making the Vigilante Thrillers. To fully appreciate these links, an overview of the Western genre and its structures and oppositions is given later in the chapter, to illuminate the hypothesis that the Vigilante Thriller engages and reconceptualizes elements from the Western. *The Searchers* (John Ford, 1956) and two other archetypal Westerns, *High Noon* (Fred Zinneman, 1952) and *Shane* (George Stevens, 1953), will be looked at in some detail. Their status as archetypal of the genre, being filmed during a high point in production for the genre, offers a useful textual comparison point and allows for a clear examination of the claim that the Vigilante Thrillers simply remake the Western in a modern environment. To help with understanding the structural and formal elements of the genre, three key writers have been consulted: John G. Cawelti, Jim Kitses and Will Wright. All three provide extensive structural analysis, although each makes slightly different conclusions in their formalist approaches. Jane Tomkins's work further explores thematic elements, particularly in considering the impact of the genre on the American collective consciousness and the role of gender. Further to this, a short consideration of the impact of the Spaghetti Western is pertinent due to the effect on the American box-office, the genre in general, the representation of violence, how it represented key stars (Eastwood and Bronson) and reconceptualized moral and aesthetic elements.

During the 1960s the Western's cinematic prevalence was in severe decline. Yearly production of Westerns (in the United States) fell continuously from 108 in 1952 to just 20 in 1967, for both major studios and independents. Although it is true that overall feature film production fell during this period, from 324 features per year to 178, the fall in Westerns is disproportionate: in 1952, 33 per cent of all US feature films were Westerns; by 1967, it was 11 per cent. During the early 1970s there was a small increase, a high point of twenty-five features produced in 1972, but this was not sustained. This is mirrored in the consumption of Western shows on TV: their highpoint of forty-eight shows on air in 1959, declined to twelve in 1969, and to four by 1975 (Buscombe 1988).

The reasons behind this decline are debated. Buscombe suggests demographic shifts in the American cinema-going public, including towards a younger audience. The ageing stars of the Western and the genre's emphasis on maturity therefore lacked appeal (1988: 53). David A. Cook builds on this, connecting the decline to contemporary political events and shifts in attitudes towards the Western's idealized representation of America's past; something reflected in the emergence of parodic works and revisionist films released in the late 1960s and into the 1970s. Cook observes how the shifting representations of Native Americans helped undermine the moral centre of the Western, 'The hostile savages of the thirties, forties, and most of the fifties, were suddenly represented as a race of gentle, intelligent people upon whom the U.S. Military establishment had committed genocide' (1990: 513). Films such as *Soldier Blue* (Ralph Nelson, 1970) and *Little Big Man* (Arthur Penn, 1970) included analogies with the Vietnam War in their depictions of military actions on Native American communities. This idea is taken up by Cawelti in his Second Edition of *The Six-Gun Mystique* (published in 1984, thirteen years after the original). Cawelti cites three changes in American culture that affected the popularity of the Western: the disappearance of the frontier way of life (demystifying the idea of the West); the genre itself being over-produced and creatively played out; and 'new and conflicting attitudes towards violence, sexism and racism as aspects of American culture' (1984: 15). The mythology that underpinned the genre was no longer connecting to a changing population; indeed, it had become deeply problematic. Some film-makers directly examined these changes, developing the genre to reflect the shifting feelings about America's past. Peckinpah's *The Wild Bunch* (1969) unified a new stylistic representation of violence with a meditation on the passing of the Western age. Films such as *The Man Who Shot Liberty Valance* (John Ford, 1962) examined and exposed the myths of the West, while comedies such as *Support Your Local Sheriff!* (Burt Kennedy, 1969) poked fun at the well-known conventions of the genre. By 1974 *Blazing Saddles* (Mel Brooks) would directly confront the implicit racism in the genre, as well as parodying its codes and conventions. The movement towards parody and deconstruction of the genre is supported by Christian Metz's classic-parody-contestation-critique model (as cited in Altman 1999: 21) that genres eventually turn in on themselves. Jeanine Basinger gives a simpler answer to the decline: 'Vietnam killed them' (as quoted in Tasker 1993: 68). Building on this Tasker suggests:

> The western series which had dominated the television schedules of the 1950s had been replaced by the 1970s largely with crime series and, in America, the ongoing televisual saga of the Vietnam War. The associations of the western lay with an older, parent culture which was to be debunked along with everything else. The old western stars were fading, to be replaced by the nihilism of the Eastwood persona or the light-hearted jocularity of male stars like James Garner and Burt Reynolds. The western hero comes increasingly to seem anachronistic. (1998: 68)

This analysis is taken further by Worland and Countryman, with the suggestion that the Western offered an uncomfortable counterpart to Vietnam, developed through a shift in view of Native Americans who were no longer accepted as a necessary, or justified, casualty of American expansionism, 'The growing equation of the Vietnamese with Indians, particularly after My Lai, compounded anguish over the decade's political assassinations, and violent racial and anti-war protests and riots, had the subsidiary effect of tainting the Western, where most issues are settled by gun-play, as both symptom and cause of a uniquely violent strain endemic to American culture' (1998: 187). The decline in the popularity of the Western during the 1960s left an ideological space in American cinema. Although the Western may have seemed incapable of continuing through the shifts in audience and representations of the time, it does not mean that some of the values of the genre cease to be important or desired. As Slotkin states, myth has an ideological function, and for America the Western/Frontier Myth is part of the underpinning ideological structure.

As noted before, the generic innovations of the late 1960s and early 1970s American film were not limited to the development of the Vigilante Thriller. Indeed, the iconography of the Western would appear in other contexts; however, in these instances they are used as a commentary on the shift in American culture, rather than on the moral framework that the Western presented. The road movie was one such offshoot, the most influential example being *Easy Rider* (Dennis Hopper, 1969) in which characters named Billy (as in the Kid) and Wyatt (as in Earp), played by Hopper and Peter Fonda, embark on a quest to find America. As the tagline described it, 'they couldn't find it anywhere'. The famous quotation 'We blew it' runs as a commentary on the whole concept of the American nation as much as a reaction to the events of the film. During their picaresque adventures across Western America (and New Orleans), Billy and Wyatt encounter hostility to their counterculture lifestyle from the locals who embody the shifting representation of South-Western America seen in horror. *Easy Rider* was followed by several films, such as *Two-Lane Blacktop* (Monte Hellman, 1971) and *Electra Glide in Blue* (James William Guercio, 1973), which used the Western landscape to reconceptualize the concept of frontier to one which was internal rather than external, heading back East rather than going West. *Electra Glide in Blue* can be read as a direct riposte to *Easy Rider*, in which the main character, a Police Officer played by Robert Blake, is killed by a hippy and in which one character practices shooting with pictures of Ford and Hopper as targets. However, none of the later films had the same impact as *Easy Rider*. Audiences in the early 1970s would surely have been familiar with this reworking, as they would have been familiar with the Western from its cinematic and televisual incarnations, recognizing and understanding the similarities and differences.

During the Western's decline a rise in Police dramas occurred. Both Cobley (2000: 109) and Rubin discuss this, with Rubin noting, 'the police thriller was about to displace the western as the most essential form of the American action film' (1999: 140). For Rubin, *Coogan's Bluff* is a transitional film that openly suggested the development between genres:

Although subsequent police thrillers rarely make their connection to the western so explicit, the connotations are always present in more or less implicit form. The gunslinger is supplanted by the plain clothes policeman, the frontiers by the urban jungle, the six shooter by the .44 Magnum, and the horse by the motorcycle or automobile. In thrilleresque fashion, the grandly adventurous dimensions of these traditional elements are problematically transposed into a diminished, modern, lo-mimetic context. (1999: 140–1)[5]

Further to this, Buscombe suggests that 'The Western had always offered violence as the solution to the threat of lawlessness, but in a ritualized form, removed from everyday reality by the distance of time and place. Now the crime film shifted its premise and invaded the Western's territory' (1988: 53). For both Rubin and Buscombe, a fundamental difference between the Western and the Vigilante Thriller that impacts directly on the spectator's reading of the texts is the relocation of the violence into a modern urban setting. This movement is key to understanding how the two genres generate different meanings and to understanding how the narrative codes of the Western break when removed from their traditional settings (both time and place). To further understand the structure of the Western genre and to be able to discuss how the Vigilante Thriller comments on it and disrupts it, an overview of the fundamentals of the genre is necessary.

In terms of creative talent, three of the films (*Straw Dogs*, *Dirty Harry* and *Death Wish*) have obvious ties to the Western. Sam Peckinpah had previous success in the genre, both in film and in TV, and *The Wild Bunch* is a key revisionist text. The change of the novel's title from *Siege at Trencher's Farm* to *Straw Dogs* was an attempt to gain distance from the Westerns that Peckinpah was known for (Weddle 1996: 402): Peckinpah had directed the Westerns *The Deadly Companions* (1961), *Guns in the Afternoon* (1962), *Major Dundee* (1965) and *The Ballad of Cable Hogue* (1970), as well as *The Wild Bunch*, and had worked on several Western shows including *The Westerner* which he helped create.[6] Terence Butler investigates the possibility of *Straw Dogs* being a relocated Western, an attempt to 'examine the preoccupations of the Western in a non-generic context' (1979: 69) and that '*Straw Dogs*' English village is more a western township than a Cornish village' (1979: 69) in its displaced versions of the priest (the Reverend Hood) and lawman (Major Scott) as 'custodians of order'. The casting of Dustin Hoffman a year after *Little Big Man* (Arthur Penn, 1970)

---

[5]Mimetic is meant here in the sense that it was used by Northrop Frye (1957) in *Anatomy of Criticism*: texts of low-mimetic quality emphasize the theme of individuality.
[6]A further relation that should be acknowledged; Peckinpah started his career as an assistant on Don Siegel's film *Riot in Cell Block 11* (1954) (Siegel 1993: 163) and worked on several other Sigel films, including *Invasion of the Body Snatchers*.

creates an intertextual link to the revisionist Westerns that relocated the role and nature of the American Indian and recast members of the expanding American civilization (such as the Cavalry) as villains. Eastwood remains to this day intimately linked to the Western. This originates in his role as Rowdy Yates in the popular series *Rawhide* which ran for eight seasons on CBS between 1959 and 1965, but his cinematic persona was created in Sergio Leone's *Dollars* films. This persona, dubbed 'The Man with No Name' by American advertisers, serves as a prototype for Harry Callahan and other Eastwood roles, defining a 'laconic and even animal aura' (Smith 1993: 12). Eastwood's continual appearance in Westerns, during and after their decline, saw him become a figurehead for the genre, taking over from ageing stars such as John Wayne. Eastwood's form of Western hero greatly differed from what went before and helped lay the ground for the complex morality of the Vigilante Thriller. *Dirty Harry*'s director, Don Siegel, had previously directed Eastwood in *Two Mules for Sister Sara* (1970), as well as *Coogan's Bluff*. Like Peckinpah, Siegel had worked in Westerns in both film and TV. This looking back to the Western is made evident in the opening scene of *Dirty Harry* in which the camera pans over a memorial board to San Francisco Police Officers that dates back to 1878 (a date towards the end of the Old West); the final scene in which Callahan throws his badge away evokes the ending of *High Noon*. Buscombe suggests that Eastwood's appearances in *Coogan's Bluff* and *Dirty Harry* 'appeared to authenticate the transference of the Western's traditional themes to the crime film' (1988: 53).

Charles Bronson had seen success in several Westerns, including *The Magnificent Seven* (John Sturges, 1960) and Leone's *Once Upon a Time in the West* (1968). Winner had directed two Westerns, including *Chato's Land* (Michael Winner, 1972) that starred Bronson.[7] *Death Wish* makes explicit textual links to the Western genre, most evidently in Paul Kersey's visit to Tucson during which he witnesses a Wild West show. Further to this, details of dialogue, such as Kersey asking a mugger to 'Fill your hand', and mise en scène (including a magazine cover featuring a noose), directly reference the conventions of the Western. An early draft of the film's script included Kersey watching *High Noon* before setting out into the New York night (Talbot 2006: 9). The other films contain links which are less obvious, but no less pertinent, and the above are only the most superficial. In *Joe*, the narrative structure imitates the Puritan Captivity Narrative in several ways, displaying anxieties about losing a female character to an alien/other culture, and in elements

---

[7]In which Bronson played a Native American. Indeed, Bronson's own ethnic heritage – his original surname was Buchinsky and his family originated in Lithuania – is indicative of Hollywood's willingness to cast actors across racial divisions (sensitively or not); in *The Magnificent Seven* Bronson's character is Mexican, in *The Great Escape* Polish.

of iconography (especially around Frank). Structural parallels between *The Searchers* and *Taxi Driver* have been noted by several writers, with the former being cited as an influence on the latter, something that has been confirmed by screenwriter Paul Schrader (Byron 1979: 46). *The French Connection* lacks superficial links, but as we shall see later, there are structural connections, and it is notable that Friedkin's inspiration to make the film was in part the advice of Howard Hawks, a director noted in the genre (Mask 2007: 65).

To further understand the correlation between the Western and the Vigilante Thriller, a formalist discussion of the two genres is required. Formalism allows for a structural comparison but also explores the audience's expectations and understanding. Although the Vigilante Thriller replicates some elements of the Western, the structural differences, especially in their endings, subvert the suggestion that these films are simply relocated Westerns. Indeed, the relocation and recasting of these stories make such a thing impossible. A key formal aspect of the Western is a binary opposition between civilization and wilderness, the latter being an embodiment of the other. The defeat of the other forms the crux of the Western narrative. Formal analysis reveals how this breaks down in the Vigilante Thriller – the nature of the protagonists and antagonists expressing confusions about the nature of the other, confusions that remain unresolved by their endings. In relation to the shifting nature of otherness during the 1960s and 1970s, the protagonists of the Vigilante Thrillers come to be both self and other – a nexus for the cultural conflict. This is not to say that a more traditional form of othering does not take place; rather, that it is complicated by how the Vigilantes are presented in a way that confuses the delineations of self and other clearly defined in the Western.

In reference to Tzvetan Todorov, Hill explains the basic story structure as one which ends in solutions, 'In the case of the detective story or film, a crime is committed (the disequilibrium), requiring a force directed in the opposite direction (the investigation) resulting in a new equilibrium (the capture of the culprit). Implicit in this requirement of the new equilibrium is the idea of a narrative solution' (1986: 55). This sense of solution not only functions to complete the narrative but has an implicit ideological component, 'There is a presumption built into the very structure of conventional narrative, that "problems" can be overcome, can, indeed, be resolved' (1986: 55). Conventional narrative offers reassurance in which the audience is shown an ordered representation of life at the narrative's resolution. As we shall see for the traditional Western this holds. The endings of the Vigilante Thrillers, however, subvert this structure through openings that question the existence of a state of equilibrium and in endings that fail to resolve the problems.

To explore this further, the writings of several influential critics on the Western are relevant; all take a formalist approach but differ somewhat in their analysis. These critics's works, Jim Kitses' *Horizons West* (1970), Will Wright's *Sixguns and Society* (1970), and John G. Cawelti's *The Six-Gun*

Mystique (1975) were written contemporaneously with the Vigilante Thriller, and were among the first works to attempt a serious and comprehensive examination of the Western genre. Their work creates an overall sense of structure, both narrative and thematic, for the Western. Elements of each critic are examined later and discussed closely in relation to the Vigilante Thriller. Kitses combines both an overview of the genre and work on several key film-makers associated with the genre. Most important for this study is Kitses's analysis of the Western as built on a binary opposition between wilderness and civilization: 'central to the form we have a philosophical dialectic, ambiguous cluster or meaning and attitudes that provide the traditional thematic structure of the genre' (1970: 11). The ground between wilderness and civilization is occupied by the hero who will ultimately defend civilization, his choices and dilemmas dramatizing the ideological tensions. In reference to the film of Anthony Mann, Kitses states: 'The hero stands at the centre torn between the two worlds' (1970: 66). Kitses's oppositions are outlined in Table 1.

Death Wish most directly embodies Kitses's oppositions. Paul Kersey travels West from New York (the industrialized, institutional centre) to Tucson (which embodies the frontier despite its aeroplanes and cars – albeit ones with bull's horns on the bonnet). Here Kersey is introduced to Western values by his Tucson client Ames Jainchill (Stuart Margolin) and a live Western show in which a Sherriff heroically defeats bandits. Jainchill's insistence that people require open land (an example of agrarian values) to live is at first resisted by Kersey who has an industrialized view of maximizing space. Kersey's reliance (at least initially) on the institutions of New York to deal with his wife and daughter's attack further signals this opposition, whereas Jainchill advocates personal defence. (He also wears a gun on his hip.) On his return to New York, Kersey has seemingly adopted Jainchill's values, including the gun given to him as a parting gift. However, Kersey's actions are then framed in a context that alienates him from New York society, despite some claims that he is a hero. His behaviour begins to resemble psychosis, as when he asks young urban men to 'draw' their weapons and 'fill your hand'. The finale does not see Kersey rejecting civilization or conforming to its values; rather, he moves west to Chicago, another urban centre noted for its crime rate.

Joe suggests an opposition that imitates this to some extent but reframes it as one between the counterculture (as embodied by the hippies) and the more conservative values of the blue- and white-collar workers. However, the film lacks a protagonist caught in the middle, such as Kitses's hero, placing Melissa there instead. The final scenes show that the so-called civilized side of the opposition is as capable of savagery as the other (perhaps a commentary on America's actions in Vietnam). In *Dirty Harry* Callahan acts as an individual opposing the restrictions of the institutions of

TABLE 1 *Oppositions in the Western*

The Wilderness	Civilization
The Individual	The Community
Freedom	Restriction
Honour	Institutions
Self-Knowledge	Illusion
Integrity	Compromise
Self-Interest	Social Responsibility
Solipsism	Democracy
Nature	Culture
Purity	Corruption
Experience	Knowledge
Empiricism	Legalism
Pragmatism	Refinement
Savagery	Humanity
The West	The East
America	Europe
The Frontier	America
Equality	Class
Agrarianism	Industrialism
Tradition	Change
The Past	The Future

Source: Kitses, Jim (1970) *Horizons West*. Indiana: Indiana University Press.

civilization, particularly those that uphold the rights of the suspect (referring to the debates around Miranda). Callahan displays a solipsistic nature, a brutal and pragmatic approach, and has one foot set in the world of the wild and brutal Scorpio (both men's voyeurism is repeatedly compared through the film). The San Francisco setting is important (originally the film was to be set in New York and star Frank Sinatra. When Eastwood came on board, the location was changed to avoid similarities to *Coogan's Bluff* (Siegel 1993: 358)) as it is in the westernmost part of the United States, beyond the original frontier (and a well-known centre for countercultural activity, particularly hippy culture). However, the ambiguity of the final moments, when Callahan throws away his police badge, signifier of his loyalty to civilization, calls into question his support for the institutions that have employed him and by proxy the nature of modern civilization itself. Popeye Doyle's pragmatic brutality places him firmly on the wilderness side of the opposition, but he functions within New York, a key Eastern city, again suggesting an imitation of the hero caught between two worlds. However, his clear opposition to Alain Charnier (Fernando Rey), the French drugs importer, polarizes his figure. Charnier is seen as urbane and sophisticated, as opposed to Doyle's roughness, aptly demonstrated in the scene that cuts between Charnier dining in a fine restaurant and Doyle watching from outside attempting to eat a piece of limp greasy pizza. New York, however, is not the wilderness, or even in the West, suggesting firmly that the disruption exists inside the right hand of Kitses's opposition, in which the binary oppositions have become confused. Civilization has already been achieved but brutality persists within it. Doyle's expulsion from the Police, as disclosed in an epilogue, indicates society's refusal to sanction his actions, but equally Charnier (as representative of Europe) is as dangerous, if only by proxy (through his assistant Nicoli and the drugs themselves). *Straw Dogs* is unique among these films as it is set within a wilderness; however, this Wilderness is to the East of America, not in its West. This reversal is also evident in the character of David Sumner, someone who leaves the civilization of America (for undisclosed reasons, but allusions to violence and perhaps the draft are made) but fails to integrate into their new surroundings. Indeed, much of Sumner's actions (asking in the local pub for 'American cigarettes' for instance) alienate the society into which he has moved. The ending may on first watching endorse a view of the film in which Sumner reverts to a wilderness figure, embracing his inner violence to defend his territory (both house and wife). His abandonment of both in the final scene, casting off the role of protector of women, undermines this view however, and once again exposes an inability for the tensions inherent in the oppositions to be resolved. *Taxi Driver* goes further than all the films by presenting the opposition almost entirely from the point of view of its protagonist Travis Bickle. His voice-over suggests a simultaneous existence in New York of Civilization and the Wilderness, but also the hollowness of both. The parallel couples he obsesses over, Betsy (Cybil Shepherd)/Palantine and Iris/Sport (Harvey Keitel), are both revealed to be unwitting projections of Bickle's own anxieties and desires. His rescue of Iris evokes elements of the Puritan Captivity Narrative, but Iris's desire to be rescued is something Bickle himself has created. Bickle's own costume at the end of the film, mixing the Mohawk haircut with the Six-Shooter,[8] expresses the ideological confusion of the character but also of the wider society that will eventually claim Bickle as a hero.

A key to understanding this breakdown in Kitses's opposition is the concept that civilization represents the future. By the Vigilante Thriller it has become the present and values have shifted accordingly, in some cases becoming corrupted. Within this new urban environment, a new wilderness has grown. Watch as Callahan follows Scorpio through San Francisco, a city in which playgrounds sit closely to strip bars, where public spaces such as Kezar Stadium become locations of unauthorized violence. The opening scenes of *Taxi Driver* suggest New York has a hellish quality, implied from Bickle's voice-over, the cinematography and the steam venting from the sewer grates. *Death Wish* draws an explicit comparison between the idyllic Hawaii of its prologue and the grim, dark streets of New York (a point emphasized emphatically on the non-diegetic soundtrack through the discordant sounds that accompany the Kersey's return to the city). The West of the past was a territory that promised that it could be tamed, for civilization to take over and bring order, but here the order itself is unravelling.

In analysing the Westerns of Anthony Mann, Kitses gives close attention to the character types of the films: 'Characteristically, the Mann hero is a revenge hero' (1970: 33). Revenge does not have to be a main motivating factor; however, it can be hidden in the past. Both Sumner and Kersey suggest this, although Kersey's motivation is clear and Sumner's possibly sublimated. (It is never suggested that he knows Amy has been raped; however, he has certainly been embarrassed by the local men.) In *Joe*, both Joe Curran and Bill Compton use Melissa's disappearance as a justification to visit the East Village in New York. Their dialogue demonstrates a resentment over the life they see there, one in which they cannot participate (and fail at when they try). Their humiliation and fear of exposure motivate the final shooting of the film. With Harry Callahan we are given hints at his past, the death of his wife being a possible motivation. Travis Bickle has his (self-proclaimed) history in Vietnam as a possible motivator, and his rejection by Betsy. Doyle remains without a clear revenge motive; his use of violence, however, reveals a masochistic streak which links well with Mann's heroes: 'In general, all of Mann's heroes behave as if driven by a vengeance they must inflict upon themselves for having once been human, trusting, and therefore vulnerable. Hence the schizophrenic style of the hero, the violent explosions of passion alternating with precarious moments of quiet reflection' (1970: 33), and that they are 'Dark, extreme men trapped in an impossible dilemma, a neurotic attempt to escape themselves and rise above a past of pain and

---

[8] Sport's costume is also a clash of cultural symbols, the white vest suggesting urban blue-collar life, an aristocratic but also carnivalesque top hat and Native American connoting feather.

violence' (1970: 35). These descriptions could easily be used for any of the protagonists of the Vigilante Thriller, excepting one facet – their desire to 'rise above a past of pain and violence' has become a descent into it.

Kitses's description of Mann's villains, and their relationships to the heroes, bears a close resemblance to that between Callahan and Scorpio and within the figure of Travis Bickle himself: 'In general, hero and villain are extreme men, the villain a more or less imbalanced version of the hero, and the action of the film is a cancelling out, a neutralising movement towards moderation, compromise and control' (1970: 44). The sequence where Bickle confronts himself in a mirror ably demonstrates this duality and the ending, if it is to be believed, presents us with a neutralized, calm Bickle accepted even by Betsy, to whom he gives a taxi ride. Kitses further describes how the Mann hero, 'His sanity at stake, enters the world of ordinary mortals only through a kind of metaphysical suicide, destroying the mirror of his magic, the incarnation of his pride and ambition. The villain finds release only through madness and death' (1970: 58–9). *Taxi Driver*'s finale demonstrates this 'metaphysical suicide' through Bickle's play-acting of shooting his own head with his fingers; some readings suggest Bickle dies in this sequence and the final scenes are a death bed imagining, a final release. With both readings available we can see how Bickle inhabits both hero (rescuing Iris and being acclaimed) and villain (a dead psychotic). The foregrounding of madness film bears greater analysis and will be returned to in Part Two.

Kitses's view of Budd Boetticher's Westerns is most relevant when discussing *Dirty Harry* and its protagonist. Callahan is recognizable in the 'cool' figures often portrayed by Randolph Scott, professionals for whom self-control is essential to their success and linked to their professionalism: 'This equilibrium, an essential expansion of the hero's integrity, springs from his complete knowledge of the world through which he moves' (1970: 98). Similarly, the opposition of Callahan and Scorpio echoes Boetticher's films, the villains having 'a comparatively flamboyant style' (1970: 104). More important is Kitses's observation that 'The moral of Boetticher's films is thus a simple one: everyone loses. Life defeats charm, innocence is blasted. The world is finally a sad and funny place, life a tough, amusing game which can never be won but must be played' (1970: 109). Kitses's analysis of Peckinpah's films makes a key observation regarding *Straw Dogs* but also gives insight into *Death Wish* and *Taxi Driver* as 'Peckinpah's characters suffer from not knowing who they are' (1970: 141). This is further linked to an inward conflict for the protagonist, 'a tortured struggle to achieve mastery over self-annihilating and *savage* impulses' (1970: 141). However, this formula is subverted by David Sumner who, although he may not know who he is, fails to achieve mastery over his 'savage impulses'. The climax of *Straw Dogs* shows him unleashing his pent-up violence to a level that surprises even himself, saying, 'Jesus, I got 'em all!' Paul Kersey begins *Death Wish* as a pacifist liberal who, after the home invasion and visit to Tucson, engages with his savage side; however (and similarly to Sumner), he fails to gain mastery over it, with his actions coming to resemble psychosis. In Kitses's observations about Peckinpah's Western women another break is notable. Kitses explains, 'Women are important to Peckinpah: where they know who *they* are and what their role is they can positively assist in men's search for understanding and equilibrium' (1970: 144). Amy Sumner offers a sense of provocation and resistance to her husband, her own identity called into question throughout the film.

Cawelti organizes his investigation by separating the Western genre into three aspects: Setting; Complex of Characters; Types of Situations and Patterns of Action. Each offers a point of comparison for the Vigilante Thriller. Cawelti explains that setting means more than geography, 'Tentatively we might say that the Western setting is a matter of geography and costume; that is, a Western is a story that takes place somewhere in the western United States in which the characters wear certain distinctive styles of clothing' (1984: 62). The Western, therefore, is a dramatization of the frontier, of the conflict between advancing civilization and receding 'savagery'. For Cawelti 'the social and historical aspects of setting are perhaps even more important in defining the Western formula than geography' (1984: 65). It is the clash between civilization and chaos (often represented by Native Americans) which defines the genre. The threat of chaos is clear in the Vigilante Thriller: the counterculture in *Joe*, the home-invading villagers in *Straw Dogs*, the drugs trade in *The French Connection*, Scorpio in *Dirty Harry*, the muggers in *Death Wish* and the 'whores, skunk pussies, buggers, queens, fairies, dopers, junkies' of *Taxi Driver*; but there is a reversal, in which savagery advances into civilization and the protagonists themselves are chaotic forces. Like Kitses, Cawelti notes, in reference to Complex of Characters, that 'There are three central roles in the Western: the townspeople or agents of civilization, the savages or outlaws who threaten this first group, and the heroes who are, above all "men in the middle", that is they possess many qualities and skills of the savages but are fundamentally committed to the townspeople' (1984: 73). Going further he presents three variations on these relationships. First the hero protects townspeople from the savages, 'using his own savage skills against denizens of the wilderness' (1984: 74). The second variation 'shows the hero initially indifferent to the plight of the townspeople and more inclined to identify himself with the savages. However, in the course of the story his position changes and he becomes an ally of the townspeople' (1984: 74). The third variation 'Has the hero in the middle between the townspeople's need for his savage skills and their rejection of his way of life. The third variation, common in recent Westerns, often ends in the destruction of the hero ... or his voluntary exile' (1984: 74). Each variation hinges on the hero existing between the wilderness and civilization. Callahan and Doyle are both rejected/alienated through their methods. Sumner and Kersey shift their actions/positions based on their situations and the narrative developments. All four are exiled. Bickle fully inhabits this liminality, potentially being destroyed, or integrated depending on how the ending is read. Only *Joe* rejects this formation, with both Joe Curran and Bill Compton being placed clearly on one side of an opposition (although in class terms they also oppose each other. The larger opposition/attraction to the counterculture unites them).

Female characters in Westerns are 'primary symbols of civilisation' (1984: 75), and the Vigilante Thrillers similarly sees women as representative of the home/civilized society. As Cawelti continues, 'implicit in their presence is the sexual fascination and fear associated with the rape of white women by savages' (1984: 75). The ownership of women's bodies and the threat of rape are present in each of the films. In *Joe* it is the adoption of Melissa into the counterculture (sex implied by her relationship to Frank and the Hippy lifestyle). Amy Sumner is raped and fought over, the final sequence of *Straw Dogs* suggesting a direct link with her and the farmhouse. In *The French Connection* women are the victims in several scenes, including one where Nicoli mistakenly kills a white mother pushing a pram. In *Dirty Harry*, a hierarchy of victims is created, culminating in the rape and murder of a white girl (which, with her lifeless body glimpsed from afar, is given a greater level of pathos than Scorpio's other victims). *Death Wish* connects the home and women explicitly in the rape scene, in which Kersey's wife and daughter are attacked in the living room of the Kersey apartment. Finally, Bickle's idealization of Betsy and Iris (both white) but his simultaneous sexual threat (shown most obviously in taking Betsy to a pornographic film) show his own 'sexual fascination and fear'. Once again, however, the films differ from their Western antecedents. In the Western it is the threat of rape that predominates, an implicit act that threatens the female currency on which society will be based. In the Vigilante Thriller this threshold has been passed. Melissa has already 'gone native'; Amy is raped; Doyle can only pursue the mother's killer, not prevent her death; the girl is raped and killed by Scorpio; Kersey's home and family are violated in his absence; Iris has become a child prostitute and it's unclear if she wants rescuing. Once again, we return to the prototypical Western, the Puritan Captivity Narrative, where sexual violation of white women by Native Americans formed the central threat (allied to the anxiety that the women may be absorbed into the society, much as Melissa is in *Joe*).

Cawelti's analysis of situation and patterns of action is less involved than other aspects. However, he offers a summary of the basic situation of Western plots,

> the epic moment when the disciplines of American society stand balanced against savage wilderness. The situation must involve a hero who possesses some of the urges toward violence as well as the skills, heroism and personal honor [*sic*] ascribed to the wilderness way of life, and it must place this hero in a position where he becomes involved with or committed to the action and values of civilisation. (93–4)

Vigilantes share the violent impulses (although they may be latent within them) of their antagonists; however, it is debatable whether they remain 'committed to the action of values of civilisation'. This is because those very values are a point of debate and discussion within the films. The endings of *Straw Dogs*, *Dirty Harry* and *Death Wish* demonstrate a willingness towards self-exile rather than integration. Within this basic structure Cawelti also notes a 'built-in structural emphasis on the chase' (1984: 94) and both *The French Connection* and *Dirty Harry* have chase sequences and cat-and-mouse narratives. The endings of *Joe* and *Death Wish* also imitate this. However, their endings further question the moral authority of the protagonists as they fail to become integrated into society or committed to its values.

Wright's work is more purely structuralist than either Kitses's or Cawelti's and offers an ability to make direct formal comparisons. As do the others, he notes core oppositions inherent in the Western: 'inside society/outside society, good/bad, strong/weak, wilderness/civilisation' (1975: 59), but Wright also characterizes three main Western narratives: the Classical Plot, the Vengeance Variation and the Professional Plot (to which he adds ideas on the Transition Theme) illustrated in Table 2.

There are clear commonalities between *Death Wish* and the Vengeance Variation, but once again we see how the Vigilante Thriller fails to cohere to Western resolutions as Kersey, having been asked, leaves New York, failing to give up his special status as an avenger or to leave society in total – rather he moves to another, possibly worse, urban centre. The vengeance in *Death Wish* is also problematized as Kersey fails to apprehend, or even attempt to, the men who attacked his family. Rather his actions are aimed at any person he finds committing a crime throughout the city – a group that he actively courts by visiting parks and subways during the night. *Taxi Driver* also shows imitations of this structure taking Bickle, who was a member of society (1), into conflict with villains that society is not punishing (3). His special status is conferred to himself, by himself, through his voice-over that indicates his superior understanding of the city and what is needed to solve it (a difference is recognized between Bickle and Palantine who stands in for civil society (7)). The ending suggests a re-entry to society (13), if we read the epilogue as occurring outside Bickle's own imagination. This, though, suggests its own problems as society has misunderstood Bickle's acts to be those of a hero rather than an obsessive, violent, loner. *Dirty Harry* also fits into this formula: however, caveats remain about the ending – Callahan rejects his position in the Police, rather than joining society.

The French Connection has similarities with the Professional Plot, in which Doyle works with his partner 'Cloudy' Russo (Roy Scheider) against Charnier and his associates. However, the ending (11 and 12) is subverted as Charnier escapes and Doyle and Russo are removed from the Police force. In some ways

TABLE 2 *Variations on Western Narratives*

The Classical Plot	The Vengeance Variation	The Professional Plot
1 The hero enters a social group	1 The hero is or was a member of society	1 The heroes are professionals
2 The hero is unknown by society	2 The villains do harm to the hero and society	2 The heroes undertake a job for money
3 The hero is revealed to have an exceptional ability	3 The society is unable to punish the villains	3 The villains are very strong
4 The society recognizes a difference between themselves and the hero; the hero is given a special status	4 The hero seeks vengeance	4 The society is ineffective, incapable of defending itself
5 The society does not completely accept the hero	5 The hero goes outside of society	5 The job involves the heroes in a fight
6 There is a conflict of interests between villains and society	6 The hero is revealed to have a special ability	6 The heroes have special abilities and a special status
7 The villains are stronger than the society; the society is weak	7 The society recognizes a difference between themselves and the hero; the hero is given special status	7 The heroes form a group for the job
8 There is a strong friendship or respect between the hero and the villain	8 A representative of society asks the hero to give up his revenge	8 The heroes as a group share respect, affection and loyalty
9 The villains threaten society	9 The hero gives up his revenge	9 The heroes as a group are independent of society
10 The hero avoids involvement in the conflict	10 The hero fights the villains	10 The heroes fight the villain

(Continued)

TABLE 2 (Continued)

11	The villains endanger a friend of the hero	11	The hero defeats the villain	11	The heroes defeat the villains
12	The hero fights the villain	12	The hero gives up his special status	12	The heroes stay (or die) together
13	The hero defeats the villain	13	The hero enters society		
14	The society is safe				
15	The society accepts the hero				
16	The hero loses or gives up his special status				

Source: Wright, Will (1975) *Sixguns & Society: A Structural Study of the Western.* Berkeley: University of California Press.

Joe imitates this plot as well; however, Joe Curran[9] and Bill Compton are not professionals. (There is a consistent absence of professional law enforcement in *Joe.*) Their actions betray their amateurishness and the finale, in which Compton shoots Melissa, demonstrates the lack of effect. As some of the contemporary audiences read Joe as the villain, the finale can be interpreted as showing a complete reversal, one in which the villain succeeds. *Straw Dogs* most closely imitates the Classical Plot, Sumner being the unknown who enters society (1, 2) and is recognized as different through nationality (4), which leads to him not being accepted (5). The society, led by the Major, is weak in its toleration of Niles and the Venner family. Sumner avoids conflict (10) failing to confront the workmen over the cat's death and only fighting when Niles is threatened (although he could hardly be called a 'friend'). However, the ending subverts this structure as Sumner refuses to give up his newly acquired status and take up a place in society (with his wife Amy, the signifier of society). Rather Sumner leaves, proclaiming not to know the way home.

Wright's Transition Theme helps to illuminate these endings, discussing how later Westerns began to disrupt the earlier formulae:

> In many respects, this transition theme is almost a direct inversion of the classical plot. The hero is inside society at the start and outside at the end.

---

[9]Joe Curran has, however, served in the military during the Second World War.

He still has exceptional strength and special status; but the society, which was weak and vulnerable in the classical story, is now firmly established and, because of its size, is stronger than the hero and the villains. Rather than being forced into fighting against the villains for the society, the hero is forced to fight against society, which is virtually identified with the villains of the classical story. (1975: 74–5)

The conflicts between Callahan and his superiors (including the mayor), Doyle and the FBI agent Mulderig (Bill Hickman), and Kersey and the New York Police imitate elements of this, the mechanics of society hampering the hero. In *Straw Dogs* the villains are most of what we see of society, signalling a general corruption.

In completing this formalist analysis several specific conclusions can be made. The Vigilante Thriller in some ways imitates and follows the Western; however, the differences delineated here are significant in their subversions of the underpinning ideology of the narratives. The Western narrative offers solutions to the problems that threaten society, returning to a *new equilibrium*. In the Vigilante Thriller the relocation of time and place, and the loss of the frontier both as a narrative device and an ideological concept, cause a turning inwards in which the institutions of American society are shown to be ineffective and inept. The culture that has grown has turned children away from parents (*Joe*), allowing them to take a position opposed to those that built the society. Heroes can no longer enter the society they protect; indeed, they may refuse to do so. Often the society is deeply opposed to the actions of the Vigilantes, even those that serve to protect it. Finally, the clarity of action has disappeared, in which the binary oppositions of the Western have been dissolved. One central opposition, that of 'us versus them', or of the normal versus the other, had been undermined so totally in American society that it remained an untenable structural element.

Masculinity is central to the Western; the protagonists are, in the vast majority, male and women's roles tend to be passive. Tomkins provides a comprehensive account of the gender preoccupations of the Western and what she describes as the genre's 'preoccupation with death' (1992: 30). Tomkins, in explaining the rise of the Western in both literature and cinema, sees it as an extension of the pre-existing popularity of novels that had Christian Heroism as the central theme (such as Charles M. Sheldon's *In His Steps* (1896), Lew Wallace's *Ben Hur* (1880) and Hendryk Sienkeiwitcz's *Quo Vadis* (1895)). The Western novel arises, in part, from a rejection of Christian ideals: 'The Western plot therefore turns not on struggles to conquer sin but on external conflicts in which men prove their courage to themselves and to the world by facing their own annihilation' (1992: 31). Further to this, Tomkins contrasts the Western novel to the 'sentimental novel' in which a 'woman is always the main character', 'the action takes place in private spaces, at home, in-doors, in kitchens, parlors and upstairs chambers', and 'most of it concerns the interior struggles of the heroine to live up to an ideal of Christian virtue – usually involving uncomplaining submission to difficult and painful circumstances' (1992: 38). This type of novel, celebrating domesticity and placing 'women at the centre of the world's most important work (saving souls)' (1992: 38) provides a form which the Western then comes to oppose: 'The Western *answers* the domestic novel. It is the antithesis of the cult of domesticity that dominated American Victorian culture' (1992: 39). Thus, the emphasis on the lone male hero in the Western is a reaction against the celebration of the domestic female culture that preceded it. As Tomkins explains, 'just as women's novels that captured the literary marketplace at mid-[nineteenth] century had privileged the female realm of spiritual power, inward struggle, homosociality, and sacramental household ritual, Westerns, in a reaction that looks very much like literary gender war, privilege the male realm of public power, physical ordeal, homosociality and the rituals of the duel' (1992: 42). This reaction is taken further when Tomkins considers the influence of historical and cultural changes 'The post-Civil War era saw massive movement of women out of the home and into public life' (1992: 42). This movement outside the home and into 'socially improving activities' (1992: 43) developed into the Women's Suffrage movement in the 1900s. Against this the Western is seen as a specific male fantasy, owing its popularity 'and essential culture to the dominance of women's culture in the nineteenth century and to women's invasion of the public sphere between 1880 and 1920' (1992: 44). In establishing this, Tomkins points to two parts of the social structure that had been designated as female that are largely absent from the Western: the church and the home. Indeed, women themselves are absent or less significant:

> Given the pervasiveness and the power of women's discourse in the nineteenth century I think it is no accident that men gravitated in the imagination towards a womenless milieu, a set of rituals featuring physical combat and physical endurance, and a social setting that branded most features of civilized existence as feminine and corrupt, banishing them in favor of the three main targets of women's reform: whiskey, gambling and prostitution. Given the enormous publicity and fervor of the Women's Christian Temperance Union crusade, can it be an accident that the characteristic indoor setting for Westerns is the saloon? (1992: 44)[10]

Tomkins also acknowledges the rise of a newly industrialized and urbanized population that yearned romantically for the wide-open spaces of the Western

---

[10]The opening scene of Peckinpah's *Wild Bunch* deals directly with this as the violence between two groups of men (robbers and lawmen) disrupts a Temperance March with many of the campaigners being killed or used as hostages.

as another factor in its emergence, but the issue of gender remains central to understanding the genre. It's pertinent to note the comparison between the origins of the Western and the emergence of the Vigilante Thriller in which similar social changes were occurring; for the women's movements during the Western's creation, we can parallel second wave feminism, in which women further moved into public life and the workplace, and the Civil Rights Movement. The failure of the masculine ideal during the Vietnam War (in which it is exposed as sadistic and violent), combined with racial and political changes, similarly displaces the roles of men. However, this latter period sees Western in decline, a genre no longer able to offer escape from the sociopolitical shifts.

To explore the structural and ideological similarities and differences further, we turn to a short discussion of three classic Westerns *Shane*, *High Noon* and *The Searchers*, providing some specific equivalence and divergence between Westerns and Vigilante Thrillers. The films have been chosen in part for their canonical status, but also as examples from the 1950s, when the genre reached an artistic peak before its rapid decline in the 1960s. Each also demonstrates a variation on the classic generic theme, as Wright points out, that the protagonists fail to enter society at the end of the films. Shane (Alan Ladd) rides away from the homesteaders unable to take his place with Marian Starrett (Jean Arthur), a woman who is already married to a man who will better fit into civilized society (some readings suggest that the injured Shane is riding to his death). *High Noon* opens with Will Kane (Gary Cooper) taking back his Marshall's Star and ends the film by throwing it away, inverting the movement towards society and order. Ethan Edwards (John Wayne), in *The Searchers*, remains on the cusp of society, symbolized in the famous shot where he is held in shadow in a doorway. He can look in, but not join his settled relatives. The externality to society pre-figures the Vigilante Thriller and the rejection of society that each protagonist demonstrates. (This is most obvious in *Dirty Harry* when Callahan throws away his Police badge, a deliberate echo of *High Noon*.[11] However, a difference is also clear. As Kane leaves with his wife, Amy (Grace Kelly), a hope that a new start can happen remains; it is only the town of Hadleyville that is corrupt. Callahan is isolated and left with nowhere to go, singled out, walking nowhere, in the final frame of the film.)

In establishing a shift in the Western genre in the 1950s, Andre Bazin describes the rise of the 'the superwestern', 'a western that would be ashamed to just be itself and looks for some additional interest to justify

---

[11]Peter Biskind has suggested that *Dirty Harry* remakes *High Noon*. However, as Philip Drummond suggests, 'this overlooks the widely differing political articulations of the two films' (1997: 72).

its existence – an aesthetic, sociological, moral, psychological, political or erotic interest, in short some quality extrinsic to the genre which is supposed to enrich it' (1976: 152). Bazin cites both *High Noon* and *Shane* as best illustrating this movement (he was writing before *The Searchers* was made), in which the genre shows 'an awareness it has gained of itself and its limits' (1976: 153). For Bazin, the genre had moved from simply representing the myth structures of the West, to actively discussing and commenting on them. This self-reflexivity carries over into later (1960 and 1970s) examples of the genre and into the Vigilante Thriller itself. Questions over the nature of masculinity and heroism were asked, within the context of the socially liminal states of the protagonists. In all three Westerns this is evident, with *The Searchers* also discussing race and ethnicity (particularly in the character of Martin Pawley, one eighth Cherokee, played by the Irish American Jeffrey Hunter). *The Searchers* has become associated with *Taxi Driver* due to analysis linking the two films by several theorists. Stuart Byron notes its influence on a generation of Hollywood film-makers, 'In one way or another *The Searchers* relates not only to [Paul] Schrader but to John Milius,[12] Martin Scorsese, Steven Spielberg, George Lucas, and Michael Cimino, not only to *Hardcore*, but to *Taxi Driver*, *Close Encounters of the Third Kind*, *Dillinger*, *Mean Streets*, *Big Wednesday*, *The Deer Hunter*, *The Wind and the Lion*, *Ulanza's Raid* and *Star Wars*' (1979: 45), several of whom have affirmed their love of *The Searchers*. He identifies the appeal of the film as the complexity of the protagonist Ethan Edwards, 'the quintessential pioneer, clearing the path for white civilization but totally unable to live in it. He hates Indians, but it is a tribal hatred: in truth he is as nomadic in spirit as any Indian and has a deep knowledge of language and lore' (1979: 46). Byron sees the duality of Edwards as one that runs through society at large, a series of compromises between wilderness and civilization, and suggests that *The Searchers*' growth in popularity, during the 1960s, was linked to the war in Vietnam, especially in the issues of racism, violence and the fear of the other. Edwards displays a complicated set of motivations and neuroses, particularly in relation to his family; he desires his own sister-in-law and wants not to rescue the abducted Debbie (Natalie Wood) from Comanche Chief Scar (Henry Brandon) but to kill her and remove all trace of her 'tainted' life post abduction as Buscombe explains:

> It will be the story of Ethan's mission, to avenge the rape and murder of Martha, and to rescue Debbie. But as time passes Ethan realises that Debbie will be changed by her experience. In the event, we learn almost nothing of life in captivity. All we know is what is festering in Ethan's

---

[12]Milius also contributed to the script of *Dirty Harry* and wrote the first sequel *Magnum Force*.

mind; what obsesses him is not the general process of transculturation she must be undergoing, it is the thought of her having sex with Indians that eats away at him. (2000: 20)

Buscombe also notes the link between *The Searchers* and the Puritan Captivity Narrative, a narrative that was invoked by both J. F. Kennedy and Lyndon B. Johnson in their rhetoric concerning the Vietnam War (Slotkin 1992: 495). The duality of the protagonist and the role of sexual jealousy have clear echoes in the Vigilante Thrillers. Buscombe suggests that Travis Bickle is a collapsed version of both Edwards and Scar (and that these characters are mirror images of each other – something that becomes literally true when Bickle confronts himself in the mirror).

Henderson (1985) discusses the importance of the character Martha (Dorothy Jordan) as an incarnation of 'Ideal Law', the suppression of libido (violated by Scar). This sense of the untouchable is seen in Betsy in *Taxi Driver* introduced in his voice-over with the words 'They cannot touch her.' The theme of purity and violation occurs also in *Death Wish*, with the assault on Kersey's wife and daughter. The final crime committed by Scorpio in *Dirty Harry*, which motivates Callahan to kill him, is the rape of a teenage girl. The 'violation' of Melissa, her entry into the alien culture, leads Bill Compton and Joe to the East Village and finally to the shooting at the end of *Joe*. Dirt and purity are also suggested in the living conditions of Frank and Melissa and the dirt they display on their feet, despite bathing. In *The Searchers*, denial, repression and violence are all linked – a set of issues that also occur in *Shane*. Marian in *Shane* occupies a similar symbolic role to Martha (both have names with clear biblical echoes). Marian also symbolizes a perfect society into which the protagonist cannot enter, but which is also his motivation. To defend the settlers is to defend her. *High Noon* includes a different, but equally telling, representation of women through its opposition of Amy, the protagonist's new wife married to him in the opening sequence, and Helen Ramirez (Katy Jurado), who owns the local saloon and has an implied history with Marshall Kane. Amy, a white virginal schoolteacher, contrasts to the widowed Helen, a saloon keeper, who is older than Kane and 'half Mexican, and thus neither acceptable to the "pure" American women of the region, nor eligible for a "good marriage"' who has been previously involved with Kane (Drummond 1997: 54).

High Noon shows new pressures being placed upon the protagonist, as Kane is 'ageing; cannot make reliable male alliances; is surrounded by a gallery of men who are either venal, self-interested, or washed-out; cannot keep his wife; and eventually breaks down after accepting the inevitability of his own death' (Drummond 1997: 75). The male figure is problematized here, but in a way different from *The Searchers*. Kane is acutely aware of his own mortality and is faced with an ineffective/corrupt social structure (which we also see in *Straw Dogs*, *Dirty Harry*, *The French Connection*, *Death Wish* and *Taxi Driver*. In *Joe* it is implied to be ineffective through its absence).

All three of these Westerns show the structural opposition between wilderness and civilization, with them linked expressly through the female characters in *The Searchers*. Female characters are generally introduced and depicted indoors, with their relationships being drawn through family. The protagonists exist outside the home with one exception: Helen Ramirez. However, Helen is drawn in opposition to the virginal and white Amy; Helen's Hispanic ethnicity places her on the edges of the civilized society (effectively othered) and therefore allows her more freedom. This, however, also rules her out from being with Kane himself. All three of these Westerns demonstrate an interest in the mechanics and meaning of watching, and the effect of the watching. Much of *Shane* is seen through the eyes of Marian's son Joey (Brandon deWilde) who idolizes Shane. Often the film cuts to his reaction and his view of the action. *The Searchers* operates differently, denying us a view when the homestead is raided at the beginning of the film. Later Edwards prevents Martin Pawley from looking at Lucy's dead body; instead, the film shows us Edwards's own anger and disgust. This emphasizes the emotion of the watcher again, rather than the subject of their gaze. The absence of the subject also suggests that some things may be too horrible to be seen/shown. *High Noon* explores how people are willing to ignore action and events, with the townsfolk represented as avoiding Kane and his confrontation with Frank Miller (Ian MacDonald). However, in allowing the audience access to the action, the film aligns us firmly with the protagonist, alienating us from the refusal to look of the townsfolk.

By briefly investigating these three Westerns from the 1950s, we can see some of the specific correlations between the Western and the Vigilante Thriller. However, the differences also become evident. During the 1960s several developments occurred in the Western that would usher in an ability to view the morality and structures of the genre in different ways. Although given little or no analysis by Cawelti, Wright and Kitses, the so-called Spaghetti Westerns produced during the 1960s are another important factor in the development of the Vigilante Thriller due to their success (against the prevailing trends) and their reconfiguration of the genre's traditional moral framework. Clearly the *Dollars Trilogy* (Sergio Leone, 1964–6) had an impact on Eastwood's career (taking him from TV star to film star), but the impact was not limited to this, or to those three films. Sergio Corbucci's *Django* (1966) is an example of another with a large impact, especially in its depiction of violence. These films, produced by Italian film-makers but filmed as much in Spain as Italy, changed many of the genre's key signifiers, allowing it to develop in different ways from the American forebears (this is, perhaps, because they were made outside

America). This, though, has led some to question the legitimacy of the films as Westerns, as Smith explains,

> The spaghetti westerns stretch the limits of what Steve Neale calls 'generic verisimilitude' (1990: 47). That is, their relation to the texts that together are commonly understood to constitute the genre of westerns is a relation of resistance and in a way dissent: they *are* westerns, but unexpected ones, and to judge by their critical reception . . . they are ones that are unwanted in some respects. (1993: 19)

It was the problems that Leone's films presented from a genre point of view that alienated US critics; they broke conventions too much for those raised on the traditional form. This partly explains their belated release in America (all in 1967). Frayling suggests one of the main critiques of the *Dollars* films, from US critics, was 'for their destructive view of the West, for the detachment with which Leone treats brutality, and for their excessively rich 'visual style' – an overdose of formalism' (1998: 180). The critical distance that the Spaghetti Western often achieves serves to re-present the genre, heightening the formal elements such as gun fights while simultaneously playing down, if not eliminating, the traditional moral framework: 'Traditional icons . . . are all shown to be empty symbols of authority, rendered almost irrelevant by the brutality of the social context' (Frayling 1998: 187). Leone, however, also shows a sincere love of the genre, despite the ideological critique, evident in his recreation of elements from many classic films (particularly in *Once Upon a Time in the West*). The detachment of the formal elements of the Western from the traditional moral code, a conscious de-mythologizing, came to suggest a greater freedom and flexibility that was then incorporated into US-made Westerns. The change in the depiction of violence was also seminal, one of the factors that led to the changes in US censorship in the late 1960s (discussed in detail by Frayling). However, this was not as clear-cut as to suggest that Leone's films simply showed more violence. Prince explains that

> Leone's Westerns did not feature much spurting blood or squib work, but they piled up a huge number of bodies on screen and cut Western violence loose from the moralizing that has always accompanied it in the pre-Leone Hollywood period. In Leone's West, violent death was quick, plentiful, and was viewed dispassionately, stripped of the ritualizing codes that had surrounded it in Hollywood Westerns. Leone's violence impressed audiences, and alarmed social watchdogs, not because it was graphic (it generally wasn't) but because it was so abundant and so incredibly cold-blooded. (1998: 18)

The representation of Hispanic communities in Leone's films, and other Spaghetti Westerns, opened new ethical and ethnic views of the Western, another example of a new flexibility in the genre. The Native American was significant through his absence in these films, and in general the wilderness is less of a concern. Rather the emphasis is on the corruption within the flourishing societies. In remaking *Yojimbo* (Akira Kurosawa, 1961) as *A Fistful of Dollars*, Leone remade the opposition as one between two rival gangs within one town; each gang is corrupt as the other, with the town's Sheriff belonging to one.

The development of Eastwood's persona in the Spaghetti Westerns is also significant in that it represents a shift away from traditional ideas of Western heroes:

> It can be said that the function of this presence [Eastwood] is to articulate itself to the dominance of the white protagonist over the 'native' surroundings and characters, while at the same time rarely allowing that white dominance to lay claim to the moral superiority that it accrues in other westerns. Here the brooding and tutelary presence of Eastwood's white protagonist is offered as a threatening kind of armoury of physical and mental acumen to be unleashed on any target. (Smith 1993: 13)

Engaging with the Western in such detail in this chapter has been essential as its existence and predominance pre-1960s set a formal and ideological template that defined much of American Action Cinema. Further to that the moral framework was one that underpinned much of American ideology and belief. The decline of the Western suggests several genres and films as inheritors,

> The geographical frontier of America is now closed and is rapidly receding into the past. It seems to have been replaced in the public imagination by two new landscapes which possess some of the mythic power which was once associated with the Western frontier: the city and outer space. It was a critical cliché that movies like *Taxi Driver* and *Star Wars* are urban and science-fiction Westerns. (Cawelti 1984: 11–12)

However, this transition is far from simply a relocation. Fundamentally a shift in structure and ideology has occurred, despite the inheritance of formal and moral concerns. To conclude we return to the nature of narrative itself as defined in classical narrative analysis. Figure 1 shows Nigel Morris's diagramattical version of Todorov's narrative model.

Morris explains:

> Narratives begin with equilibrium or plenitude. This is disrupted. An opposing force emerges to counter the disruption. Resultant conflict,

precondition for any drama, is followed by triumph of either the disruptive or opposing force, inaugurating new equilibrium or plenitude. The end differs from the start – the process is linear, not circular – but pleasure depends on closure to restore the fictional world to acceptable normality. Episodes in which one then the other force dominates typically extend conflict, increasing involvement by means of suspense and exploring themes or testing character. (2007: 91)

This structure works well for the Classic Western but fails to work with the Vigilante Thriller, due to the lack of a state of equilibrium, either at the beginning or end of the films. Instead, a personal conflict arises within an already existing disequilibrium. This personal conflict is between the disruptive elements (antagonists) and the opposing forces (protagonists) and is seen against a background of wider, continuing conflict. The ending of the films may have resolved the personal conflict but not the wider disequilibrium. This works against the ideological thrust of classical narrative theory in which the plot of the film offers closure to the story (both narrative and ideological). Slotkin's analysis of the journey of the Western hero shows how he, despite displaying ambivalence towards the structural oppositions of the genre, eventually comes to reconcile them:

The American must cross the border into 'Indian country' and experience a 'regression' to a more primitive and natural condition of life so that the false values of the 'metropolis' can be purged and a new, purified social contract enacted. Although the Indian and the Wilderness are the settler's enemy, they also provide him with the new consciousness through which he will transform the world. (1992: 14)

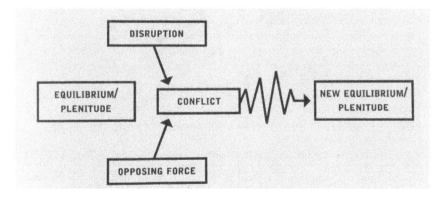

FIGURE 1 *Tzvetan Todorov's Narrative Model. Source: Morris, Nigel (2007) The Cinema of Steven Spielberg: Empire of Light. London: Wallflower.*

The otherness of the Native American creates a 'primitive' counterpoint, one that must be to some extent embraced but subsequently shed for 'civilized' society to flourish. This depends on a clarity of what the other is, drawn in opposition to the civilization being created. However, developments in the revisionist Westerns and wider culture (such as the Keep America Beautiful poster campaign[13]) questioned this, as did the parallels drawn between the Vietnam War and the Westwards expansion. Was the transformation of America, dramatized in the Western, a just one? Was the cost of the civilized society worth the price paid?

This lack of a clearly defined set of oppositions, and of a clear other, leads to the lack of ideological reassurance in the Vigilante Thriller, in which the world is not transformed nor new consciousness gained. The protagonists shed their civilized aspects but, unlike the Western hero, fail to 'transform the world'. Civilization has been achieved, but distinctions of otherness, of right and wrong, have collapsed as the underpinning mythology has been pulled away.

* * *

The Vigilante Thriller is a product of its times, drawing from existing genres but not replicating them. Partly this is an act of generic transformation, partly it is a response to the ideological upheavals and the time and the changes in the American film industry. Part One has explored the context of these films, how they were received and how they grew out of, and in response to, the times in which they were made. As texts they are drawing from a range of influences and interacting with a range of social and political issues. Part Two considers how spectator theory further illuminates this cinematic cycle.

---

[13] As a side note this campaign, referenced in the posters in *Joe*, demonstrated the general confusion over how to represent Native Americans at this time. The image seemed to present a Native American weeping over the state of the environment; however, the actor presented, Iron Eyes Cody, 'was actually born Espera De Corti, an Italian American who literally played Indian in both his life and onscreen' (Dunaway 2015: 79).

PART TWO

Spectatorship

FIGURE 2 *Travis Bickle spectates in* Taxi Driver *(Columbia Pictures, 1976)*.

The cinema is attended out of desire, not reluctance, in the hope that the film will please, not that it will displease.
(METZ 1975: 19)

Having examined where the Vigilante Thriller came from, we now turn to close analysis of the films using the contextual understandings to inform questions of identification. Here the ways in which a culture structures its oppositions and the concept of the other are essential in conceptualizing the ambivalent relationship the spectator has to the figure of the vigilante. At once attractive and repulsive, the vigilante reveals the complexity of the ideological crisis and the shifting dynamics occurring in American cinema that arose in response to the times. Therefore, Part Two comprises textual analysis of the films, guided by the critical and contextual research. The purpose is to illustrate potential readings of the films both in relation to and untethered from their contexts, to open new ways of considering the films apart from previous discourses. This analysis contests the claims by contemporary reviewers that the films were communicating a settled set of ideological positions (particularly their supposed fascism) and attempt to open new ways of considering the films apart from their context.

Central to this is the concept of film violence. Consideration of film violence is essential to understanding the Vigilante Thriller as they are films that are, to a great extent, structured around violence and sold on the appeal of violence. Two of the films have been implicated in influencing real-life acts of violence: *Taxi Driver* in John Hinckley Jr's shooting of Ronald Reagan in 1981, and *Death Wish* for the subway shootings perpetrated by Bernard Goetz in 1984. That these links between film violence and real-life violence were made, both in the press and the courts, suggests the importance of the issue of film violence (and violence in the media more widely) and how violence sits within wider cultural debates (as do the writings of the contemporary critics). This wider debate had developed throughout the 1950s and 1960s, which saw an increased academic interest in the representation of violence in film and TV and an increase in popular concern. Writing in 2004, J. David Slocum reviewed various surveys and analyses from the previous sixty years which are dedicated to the supposed link between media representations of violence and the real thing (and many of which still underpin current discussions). He suggests,

> Today, the invocation of 'film violence' continues to tend strongly towards a critical and public discourse premised on the issues of the behavioural 'effects' of viewing (putatively) violent movies. In so orienting discourse, the trope of 'film violence' effectively delimits the scope and focus of attention to cinematic brutality and bloodletting. It also enables the ready attachment of moral judgements – of Hollywood film being 'good' or 'bad' for its violence – to these supposedly more objective or scientific evaluations. (2004: 33)

It is important, therefore, to detach analysis of film violence from the wider moral debates to allow us to challenge these assumptions – instead, considering the role of film violence in relation to representation, character and narrative and then its relationship to the spectator. The intersection, between changes in American society and the representation of violence in film, cannot be ignored as it directly influences the spectator's understanding (and the critics'). In this context film violence could have become symbolic of wider cultural and moral changes. So, while acknowledging this relationship, we must also be able to detach from it in the analysis of film violence, allowing us to see the violence in textual terms, to begin with, before returning to the cultural influences.

One key element in the consideration of film violence is the problem of how film violence is discussed, described and delineated. This presents a problem of discourse, which we can see in some of the contemporary reviews discussed in Part One – violence is an elastic concept which embraces different representations in different contexts and presents a challenge to how we accurately discuss such ideas. After all, *Tom & Jerry* cartoons are violent but not in the same way as *Straw Dogs*. Stephen Prince suggests the term 'ultraviolence', derived from Anthony Burgess's *A Clockwork Orange* (and used in Kubrick's 1971 film), for describing the cinematic presentation of violence that emerged in Sam Peckinpah's films (including *Straw Dogs*) which aptly defines how film violence had shifted by the early 1970s. Prince's decision to use this term acknowledges a shift in the representation of violence, with the prefix 'ultra' (a synonym for extreme) indicating a significant aesthetic development. This change emerged out of the shifts in censorship and classification that occurred in the late 1960s and was met, in some areas, with alarm for both its cinematic and cultural implications (as seen in Part One). Prince gives a model for discussing film violence, dividing it into two areas: the referential component (the act represented) and the stylistic encoding (how the act is filmed and presented on-screen) (2003: 34–5). This relates closely with the concept of modality as presented by Hodge and Tripp (1986). They assert that the level of reality that a text suggests to its audience (its modality) helps to align the audience's reactions to, and understanding of, the violence depicted. These frameworks allow us to discuss the differences in the representation of violence across the films and to connect these to concepts of spectatorship, allowing for a more complex understanding of the reception of film violence to emerge.

Considering the representation of violence in the Vigilante Thrillers leads to a wider analysis of how the spectator's gaze functions in each film. An essential part of this is to understand the role of the respective protagonists. Protagonists are not simply the main focal point of identification: they are the fulcrum around which the narrative is structured. Narratological theory suggests that the protagonist carries the ideological weight of the film, with the narrative arc serving to represent the values of wider society. After Todorov we can think of the traditional protagonist as an agent of equilibrium that works to restore that state from the disruptions that incite conflict. Within the Vigilante Thriller it is evident that this archetypal role is continually challenged with neither protagonists nor the narratives themselves, achieving the closure required to institute a new level of equilibrium. For this analysis, theories of identification and spectatorship are used, including those of Metz, Mulvey, Branston, Casetti and Brannigan, to explore ways in which a film can be understood.

The exploration of concepts of madness is a reaction to the descriptions made by several contemporary critics of audiences displaying alarming, hysterical responses during the films (such as Kael's description of Times Square audiences during *The French Connection*). Fuery's work in *Madness and Cinema* (2004) explores the relationship between cinema and madness in the sense that both create alternate meaning systems outside everyday reality, allowing us to explore these ideas further. Fuery's examination of the representation of madness includes the enacting of transgressive and obsessive acts, and certainly, the protagonists' behaviour in the Vigilante Thrillers could be defined as transgressive and obsessive and with terms such as 'manic', 'obsession' and 'schizophrenic' used in both the marketing and reviews for the films. As madness is a relevant concept in investigating these texts, Fuery gives us a way to discuss the representation of character but also offers a way to frame spectatorship by dividing spectating positions into three types based on three types of madness: the psychotic, the neurotic and the hysteric spectator. The final of these, the hysteric spectator, allows discussion of audience behaviour during the films and a way to explore how spectators relate to and enjoy transgressive behaviours represented on-screen.

Traditionally, analysis of film presents a dichotomy between the spectator (the individual) and the audience (the mass), and the analysis of identification in cinema is bound to several theories emerging from Freudian and Lacanian psychoanalysis. Key to this is a conception of the spectator and their direct relationship to the screen, a relationship theorized as a fixed, private and individual gaze. Elements of Freud's Oedipus complex (and in particular the concept of the primal scene) and Lacan's theory of the mirror stage (in which the subject attains self-identification) have been insightfully applied to spectatorship, especially in exploring concepts of voyeurism and identification. There are, however, issues with these ideas, especially as they conceive the spectator as solipsistic when films are experienced in the group environment of the cinema. Anyone who has had their engagement with a film interrupted by the audience will know that the power of others to influence and disrupt spectatorship can be very strong (although since the advent of VHS in the 1980s and subsequent developments in digital media, the context for viewing is extremely variable). The predominant psychoanalytic theories are complimented, therefore, with reference to Fuery's ideas concerning neurosis, hysteria and psychopathy as these allow for an engagement with the audience/group context but also for an investigation and analysis into the protagonists of the films and their actions (within the context of transgression). Equally important is the influence of the semiotic school which sees the audience's understanding as informed by their own experiences apart from the film-text (that the film-text does not exist in isolation).

As many critics of these films discussed the audiences' potential reactions, further exploration of this issue is pertinent, and it links clearly to the idea that the audience might be inspired to act or have their political views influenced. A useful overview of the arguments contemporary to the films is given by Eves (1970) giving us a sense of the discourse of the time, whereas Blackman and Walkerdine (2001) give a history of the debates surrounding audience behaviour that makes compelling arguments detailing the flaws in applying various audience theories. The latter also discuss the formation of the 'normal' subject in twentieth-century psychology, which in turn leads to the formation of the other (and ties to madness, for what is madness but an abnegation of the normal?). The formal analysis of opposition (extrapolated from work done in Part One regarding the Western) is essential to understanding these films and the construction of their characters. This in turn leads us to relate the Vigilante Thriller to the work of Žižek (2008), Richardson (2010), Mercer (1994) and Izod (2001). Žižek explores different forms of violence, ranging between that of the state and the individual, and the othering process that occurs in society to make the former morally allowable. Richardson gives an overview of how Hollywood has traditionally represented groups typed as other. Mercer's work is referenced in his explorations of the simultaneous attraction and repulsion of the other which helps us to explore how films that contain acts that run against cultural norms can be simultaneously enjoyed and kept distant. Izod helps us place these oppositions into a specifically American framework, using Jungian structures to help explain and explore oppositions.

Part One established the narrative image of these films, ideas that will be returned to in Part Two, and the dialogue that exists between the narrative image and the films will be explored in relation to violence and spectatorship, further questioning the predominant analyses of the films. Constructing an understanding of the spectator, contemporary to the films, is a key element of this. Data does not exist for identifying the spectator(s) of these films in demographic terms; however, they can be theorized through interpellation, the Althusserian concept of how a text 'hails' its audience. This shows how the films approached their audience and how the texts invited interpretation and understanding. Research by Krämer, using an audience survey from 1973, suggests that male audiences preferred 'Westerns, drama and suspense', whereas women liked 'love stories, drama and musicals' with women objecting 'most strongly to sex and violence' (1999: 95). Broadly speaking, we can assume a largely, but not exclusively, male audience for the films examined here. Previous chapters established the points of social anxiety that existed in American society when these films were released and their cinematic and generic context. Like the times in which they were made, these films are fraught with contradictions and neuroses (represented in part through their protagonists); the films attempt to reconcile the pre-existing conception of the American masculine ideal in a new and conflicted context.

Finally, this work will return to the question suggested by many of the critics, one that draws together the issues that have been at play throughout this work: Are the films fascist? The resultant complexities require us to understand something lacking from the writing of the original critics: how fascism functions as both a political and rhetorical construct. We have seen how this term is one that can be understood in many ways (a problem acknowledged as far back as the 1930s by Orwell), and works by Weber (1964), Passmore (2002) and Costa Pinto (2011) will give us both a historical and modern understanding of the term and its uses, with Churchwell (2019) adding a specifically American context to the term's use. This ties to a further analysis in which the wider invocation of political terminology is revealed in its complex, and contradictory, employment in rhetoric and brings the study back to the question of how these films were consumed within their contemporary context.

Part Two then is concerned with the text/spectator interaction, with specific emphasis on textual elements that arose from the critiques covered in Part One. These elements, pertaining to representations of violence and the spectator's identifications, have been selected to interrogate the initial critical response to the films and to extrapolate alternate readings in the light of contextual sociopolitical changes. This will then turn to an exploration of the protagonists of the films and how they subvert notions of the hero.

4

Violence

I intend it to have a cathartic effect. Some may feel a sick exultation at the violence, but he should ask himself, what is going on in my heart? I want to achieve catharsis through pity and fear.

(SAM PECKINPAH, QUOTED IN BOUZEREAU 1996: 127)

Defining film violence is problematic as it operates in more than one way. When a film is described as violent, or more violent, a referential judgement is made without specifically defined criteria. Is a film more violent because it has more incidents of violence, the violence is shown more explicitly, or because the violence accurately replicates real life? This is complicated further when personal experience of violence is considered. Indeed, this experience may be entirely mediated; it could be that any given member of the audience has no real-world referent to the violent acts shown on-screen.

Prince splits film violence into two elements: 'the stylistic encoding of a referential act, thus one can speak about the act, the behaviour, the referent, and one can speak about the stylistic encoding' (2003: 34–5). Film violence is, therefore, broken down into two areas: the referential component (the act depicted) and the stylistic amplitude (the aesthetic style employed in depicting it). Two separate films may depict the same referential component, for example a shooting, but the stylistic amplitude could differ greatly. Compare, for instance, the finales of *High Noon* and *Dirty Harry*. In both the antagonist is killed by the protagonist in a scene in which a hostage is used as a human shield. However, in the former a single camera shot is used in which Will Kane fires his gun twice and Frank Miller falls dead. There is no visual sign of impact on Miller's body. In the latter, the film is edited into several shots that emphasize Callahan's gun (using a close-up as it fires), then cutting to a medium shot of Scorpio being thrown violently backwards into a lake with blood spurting from a wound. The stylistic amplitude has increased considerably, although Callahan fires one shot less than Kane. As Prince explains, 'Amplitude is a function of two elements – graphicness and duration. The more graphic a violent act, the more detailed its depiction and the greater its stylistic amplitude becomes. The degree of graphicness is directly related to film technique' (2003: 35). Returning to the final shooting in *Dirty Harry*, we can see how the violent act is not only presented differently but that it also takes up more time: 'The more camera set-ups that a filmmaker uses to convey a violent act and incorporates into the editing, the more extended the screen time of that violence' (2003: 35). It is therefore possible to distinguish between what is shown and how it is shown. This allows a more accurate discussion of what is being represented, but it does not link clearly to spectatorship. The concept of modality, which returns somewhat to narrative image, offers a way to integrate the spectator into this discussion.

It is suggested here that the historical spectator's reaction to film violence is, in part, conditional on their expectations of each film. Therefore, the violence as represented in *Death Wish* is approached differently from that in *Taxi Driver*. Although this is partly driven by narrative structure, it is also set before the spectator takes their seat. Previously it has been shown how each film addresses its spectators in different ways through narrative image. Modality (Hodge and Tripp 1986), a way of judging the 'reality' of a text, becomes important here as, in many ways, it is set before the film begins (through the narrative image). Clues from the text contribute to this; some films use visual and auditory codes to create a high modality, such as the imitation of documentary techniques in *The French Connection*, whereas others suggest a lower modality through more obviously cinematic and fantastic techniques, such as Bill Compton's murder of Frank in *Joe*.

The relationship, in terms of identification and emotional response, of the spectator to film violence is complicated by the actions depicted, and the way in which they are filmed, but also by the modality of the text itself and the audience's anticipation of violence. In discussing *Dirty Harry*, Lovell observes that the film 'is organised formally on the basis of creating tension out of an anticipation of violence' (1975: 39) and that 'the general narrative interest of the film depends on both maintaining and delaying this anticipation' (1975: 39). All these films are viewed by audiences that want to see violence on the screen (an offer made clear in their narrative images), and their narratives are built around the movement towards violence, although they differ in how that desire is met and in how violence is presented, both in style and in referent. To aid this discussion violence, as defined here, are acts between one character and another, or to themselves, which cause physical harm (and the depiction of the act), including the results of such acts and the attempts. This is to make the following discussion more specific and avoid debates about violent language and attitudes. This also reflects the concerns of the critics, who pinpointed the representation of physical acts. One way to consider this is the body count in each film (the number of deaths). This reveals that in *Joe* nine characters are seen to die or can be assumed to be dead. In *Straw Dogs* the figure is seven, eight in *The French Connection*, seven in *Dirty Harry*, nine in *Death Wish* and four in *Taxi Driver*. From this we could infer that *Taxi Driver* was the least violent, but in truth this tells us very little. Although none of the films reach double figures for deaths, their depiction differs greatly as does the nature of the victims. The fan-site All Outta Bubble Gum (ASHPD24, 2010) suggests that *Star Wars* (George Lucas, 1977) has an onscreen body count of 151, but this film was not associated with any critical opprobrium for violence. This is due to the genre of the film, science-fiction/fantasy, its modality (low) and the fact that many of the victims are either masked or alien. The referents are removed from real life and the aesthetics place these acts in a context far removed from the spectator's life. Therefore body counts, although useful, fail to tell the whole story. Table 3 catalogues the violent acts in the films, with a timecode of when they occur, to aid this analysis.

These lists deliberately de-contextualize the violent acts and remove the stylistic and narratological elements. Their purpose is to allow understanding of the difference between representation and referent, but also to think about structure and character. They also highlight the inaccuracy of contemporary reviewers such as John Coleman, who, in *The New Statesman*, described *Straw Dogs* as 'two hours of gratuitous violence' (quoted in Barr 1972: 19). From these lists *Taxi Driver* appears the least violent in terms of screen time. However, the length of the final shoot-out (about five minutes) with the detail of the violent actions affects this. In comparison, the shootings in *Death Wish* are typically filmed in medium shot, with no anatomical detail of wounds. It is arguable that the frequency of violence creates a differing reaction in the spectator than sudden unexpected moments that have not been presaged. Both *Straw Dogs* and *Taxi Driver* hold back violence, building the narrative towards extended scenes with multiple acts. In the other films early scenes of violence are causal acts that drive the films forwards. The position of the spectator is then shifted depending on expectation, experience and narrative.

Violence in *Joe*

The occurrence of violence in *Joe* is sporadic, but, as often in these films, the suggestion of violence is often present. Nowhere is this more obvious than in Joe Curran's basement where he keeps a 'well-balanced' collection of weapons (some from the Second World War), including a gun he got 'From a dead Jap in Okinawa'. This imagery is attached to the image of Joe Curran himself, reinforced in his first appearance by the image of the flag raising on

TABLE 3 *Violence Lists*

Joe

Frank injects heroin into his arm.	0:06:26
Melissa has a 'freak-out' in a store, pushing items off shelves. She is restrained, in a kindly way, by the store assistant.	0:14:35
Bill attacks Frank then kills him by repeatedly bashing his head against a wall then hitting him in the face.	0:22:27
Joe and Bill violently interrogate two hippie girls by slapping, throttling and restraining them. Joe threatens to 'Beat the shit' out of one.	1:32:57
Final Shoot-out: Joe and Bill attempt to regain their money from the hippy commune. Joe kills three hippies (all shot in the back). Bill watches as Joe kills two more (all unarmed). Bill shoots one in the back as he flees. Three more hippies enter. Bill shoots two in the doorway, then follows and shoots Melissa in the back.	1:35:19

Straw Dogs

Tom Heddon slaps the pub landlord.	0:06:44
A dead cat is found by Amy in the farmhouse wardrobe.	0:42:00
Amy is raped by Charlie Venner.	0:55:11
Amy is raped by Scutt.	1:01:37
Flashback to the rape scene.	1:08:00
Henry Niles strangles Janice Heddon.	1:16:40
David's car hits Niles.	1:17:45
Charlie Venner hits Niles with a cloth.	1:20:30
David beats away hands from a window.	1:28:29
Tom Heddon shoots Major Scott.	1:30:01
David slaps Amy.	1:35:34
David ties Scutt's hands to a window frame, leaving his neck against broken glass.	1:37:09
David slaps Niles.	1:38:36
David throws hot oil onto invaders' faces.	1:39:39

TABLE 3 (Continued)

Tom Heddon shoots his own foot.	1:41:57
David beats Chris Cawsey to death (with a golf club).	1:42:53
Scutt attempts to rape Amy.	1:43:58
Charlie Venner shoots Scutt.	1:44:54
David and Charlie fight on the stairs, David kills Charlie by trapping his head in the mantrap.	1:44:54
Amy shoots the final invader who is attacking David.	1:48:14
The French Connection	
Nicoli shoots a Policeman in the face.	0:03:07
Sonny rousts a Black suspect in a bar.	0:04:21
The suspect cuts Sonny's arm with a knife.	0:04:41
The suspect is caught and beaten by Sonny and Doyle.	0:05:23
Doyle rousts a bar, threatening the Black patrons.	0:25:26
Two dead car-accident victims shown.	1:02:59
A mother pushing a pram is shot dead by Nicoli.	1:04:10
On an elevated train a Policeman is shot by Nicoli.	1:08:39
A train conductor is shot by Nicoli.	1:12:24
Doyle shoots Nicoli in the back.	1:14:16
A shoot-out at a drugs warehouse (multiple people are shot).	1:34:03
Doyle shoots Mulderig by mistake.	1:36:52
Dirty Harry	
Scorpio shoots a woman on a rooftop.	0:01:38
During a bank-robbery Callahan shoots the getaway driver, his passenger (both are left dying) and the final bank robber (left alive). All the robbers are black.	0:11:33
Callahan fires his empty gun at the final bank robber.	0:12:56
Scorpio looks for targets in a park.	0:20:20
Callahan is beaten by four men in an alley, after he spies on Big Mary.	0:26:20

TABLE 3 (Continued)

Callahan punches a potential suicide jumper.	0:28:15
Scorpio's next victim is found (a young Black boy).	0:32:19
Roof-top shoot-out between Callahan and Scorpio.	0:38:00
A Policeman is found dead in an alley (killed off-screen by Scorpio).	0:40:00
Callahan uses a bag to fight off muggers.	0:51:17
Scorpio beats up Callahan.	0:56:15
Gonzalez (Reni Santoni) and Scorpio exchange fire – Gonzalez is hit. Scorpio is stabbed in the leg by Callahan.	0:57:25
Kezar Stadium: Callahan shoots Scorpio in the leg. Callahan then stands on Scorpio's wound.	1:06:12
A dead girl's naked body is removed from a drain.	1:07:41
Scorpio is beaten up (by a Black man he pays to do this).	1:16:17
Scorpio assaults a shopkeeper by breaking a bottle over his head.	1:22:24
Scorpio threatens a female school bus driver with a gun.	1:22:49
Scorpio hits two of the children on the bus.	1:29:44
Scorpio fires at Callahan (through the school bus roof).	1:31:36
Callahan chases Scorpio: they exchange fire.	1:32:40
Scorpio holds a boy hostage.	1:34:32
Callahan shoots, and kills, Scorpio.	1:35:08

Death Wish

Kersey's wife (Hope Lange) and daughter (Kathleen Tolan) are attacked by three white men. The wife is beaten to death, and the daughter is daubed with paint and orally raped.	0:09:17
Kersey defends himself against a Black mugger (using coins in a sock as an improvised weapon).	0:21:11
Kersey shoots a white mugger in the park.	0:43:45
Kersey interrupts a mugging and shoots three men (two Black, one white).	0:47:26
Kersey is attacked on a subway train by two knife wielding assailants, both white. He shoots both of them.	0:55:09

TABLE 3 (Continued)

Kersey shoots two Black muggers in a subway station, chasing one.	1:04:01
TV report where a Black woman defends herself against muggers – she uses a hatpin.	1:06:05
Kersey shoots three muggers (one Black, two white); one survives. Kersey is shot in the exchange and chases the remaining mugger.	1:24:18
Kersey watches as a gang of young men rough-up a young woman in Chicago.	1:32:30
Taxi Driver	
Sport pulls Iris out of the back of Bickle's taxi.	0:29:53
A group of young men throw eggs at Bickle's taxi.	0:31:01
Bickle grabs Betsy's arm as she tries to leave their date at the porno-theatre.	0:34:58
Bickle threatens Palantine office staff.	0:37:55
Taxi passenger discusses what 'A magnum .44 can do to a woman's pussy', although it is unclear as to whether he will do this.	0:38:35
Bickle shoots a Black man who is robbing a store. Store owner then beats the man with an iron bar.	1:05:30
Two, unknown, men fight on the sidewalk.	1:11:54
Bickle shoots Sport, then the final shoot-out occurs. One man has his fingers shot off. Bickle is shot in the neck. Sport is shot dead by Bickle. A second man follows Bickle upstairs shouting, 'I'll kill you, I'll kill you.' Bickle is shot in the arm by a third man, who he then shoots in the face and body several times. The second man grabs Bickle, they tussle on the floor, then Bickle uses a knife to stab the second man in the hand. Bickle kills the second man by placing a gun against his cheek and firing.	1:34:15

Iwo Jima that is placed behind him on a rear wall as he sits in the American Bar and Grill. An association is created between Joe and violence, in which his desire to commit acts of violence is clear, although this is problematized when we consider the goals/aims of the violence. His acts in Japan exist within a wider context that gives the actions legitimacy, even if Joe's own enjoyment of killing is alluded to – in the final scene he states, 'At this point it can get to be fun.' Killing the hippies in the final scene does not share the wider moral context of the Second World War. Although this is not how all acts of violence are depicted throughout the film, it signals a correlation between character and theme.

The acts of violence are most often seen through the eyes of Bill Compton, and the spectator is invited to share his experiences and reactions. The initial act of violence that instigates the main plot, in which Bill kills Melissa's boyfriend Frank, is filmed using an over-shoulder shot from behind Bill (intercut with one reaction shot of Bill's angered face). The main action is blurred, as in Figure 3, with several frames superimposed over each other, giving the action an obviously cinematic quality.

The diegetic sound of Frank's pained reactions echoes, with high-pitched horns on the non-diegetic score. This construction repeats to some extent in the final sequence, in which the film takes Bill's point of view as he watches Joe shoot several of the hippies. The voice that appears in Bill's head (an alignment with his inner monologue) as he fires on the hippies, and the highlighting of his reactions and discomfort ('No more!') rather than Joe's (who is absent in the final moments), leads the spectator to relate most closely to Bill. The voice (Joe's, saying, 'It's your ass now Compton' and repeating other lines of dialogue from earlier in the sequence) dramatizes the conflict that Bill undergoes; Joe's desire for violence and hatred of the hippies are being well established. Finally, Bill shoots Melissa in the back, only realizing who she is after he fires. Here the camera moves to Melissa, rather than Bill, and the final lines of dialogue (again repeats we can infer are in Bill's head) place her in the centre of the narrative: Melissa asks, 'Are you going to kill me too?' Bill shouts, 'Melissa!' Melissa's death is one

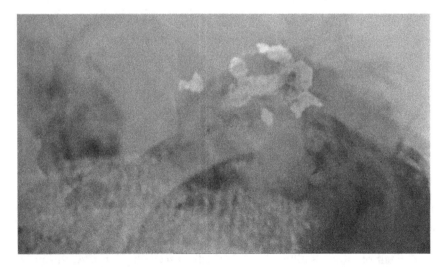

FIGURE 3 *Bill Compton kills Frank: overt technique used in the murder of Frank in* Joe *(Cannon Group, 1970).*

of only two in the film where any blood is shown; as she turns, her back is covered with it. Earlier we see Frank's blood on the wall after Bill has attacked him. These examples emphasize the violence, but generally the modality remains low. The killing of the hippies in the commune house is largely shot in medium shot, with little detail. Each is killed instantly with a single shot, and no physical damage is shown. Allied to the diegetic sounds an impressionistic sense of violence is created, rather than a realistic one. The stylistic amplification is low throughout.

Joe Curran himself stands as a nexus for the violence in the film. Bill's killing of Frank is shown as accidental, an act full of rage in which he follows up the initial bashing of Frank's head against the wall by kicking and punching him while he is prone on a mattress (the same one that Frank sleeps on with Melissa – a suggestive link between sex and violence). Bill's reaction is one of panic, his confession to Joe accidental. It is Joe who expresses excitement and pride in the act, one that he both admires and is jealous of. His weapons collection, of which he is very proud, suggests a fetishization of guns, a reaction perhaps to his own social/familial emasculation. The guns become part of a hyper-masculine code, alongside his physical job. A confusion also exists about the meaning of violence, or at least about who commits it and for what reason. The song Hey Joe by Dean Michaels[1] discusses how the changes in the world might 'make you want to go to war, once more', and how we should 'back our boys in Vietnam, show this world we'll fight for freedom'. The codes of violence are complicated here. For Joe, his actions in the commune correlate to his acts in Japan, with his own pleasure blurred with the ideological meaning of the acts.

Violence in *Straw Dogs*

When considering *Straw Dogs*, it is worth noting what Peckinpah had to say about his intent. He was a vocal defender of his films, and although we should not accept his comments without questions, they do offer some interesting points for analysis. Speaking to William Murray, in a *Playboy* interview originally published in 1972, Peckinpah discussed *Straw Dogs* and his approach to filming violence. He advocated the argument that film violence is cathartic, and to produce this cathartic response required a development in the representation of violence on-screen:

> You can't make violence real to audiences today without rubbing their noses in it. We watch our wars and see men die, really die, every day

---

[1]Not related to the song made famous by Jimi Hendrix.

on television, but it doesn't seem real. We don't believe those are real people dying on that screen. We've been anesthetized by the media. What I do is show people what it's really like – not by showing it so much as heightening it, stylizing it. Most people don't even know what a bullet hole in a human body looks like. The only way I can do that is by not letting them gloss over the looks of it, as if it were the seven o'clock news from the DMZ. (2008: 103)

Several issues can be drawn from Peckinpah's discussion. One is the issue of reality which, in Peckinpah's terms, becomes a contradictory proposition. On one side the spectator is more aware of the reality of violence through the increased representation of it through news media; however, this depiction has denuded the spectator's sense of the significance of violence. As well as this, there is a lack of detail in the depiction, the lack of the 'bullet hole'. Peckinpah's goal was to reinvest meaning into film violence, something achieved through greater stylization which, ironically, makes the violence appear less real. This is as at the heart of much of this discussion, the question of representation and effect. The stylization pursued by Peckinpah, and evident in *Straw Dogs*, is defined by Stephen Prince as 'a montage-based aesthetic, characterized by multicamera filming at varying speeds and rapid cutting, to break with realism in order to substitute a stylized rendition of violence' (1998: 48). This accurately characterizes Peckinpah's desire to sacrifice realism for emotive effect, to create the emotional impact of real (first-person witnessed) events. Barr adds to this in discussing the differing reactions to *Straw Dogs* from critics than to *A Clockwork Orange*. Despite both films having similar acts depicted in them, the former was reviewed negatively, the latter positively (as per Part One). For Barr, the positioning of the camera explains this:

The 'eavesdropping' effect of the telephoto lens, used as it is here [in *Straw Dogs*], is now part of the basic language of the camera. We are distant-yet-close, as when watching an outside broadcast on television: the distance repeats the scene's autonomy, the closeness involves us in it, and this involvement is enhanced by the nervous way the camera has to respond, at this distance/focal length, to the camera's movement. In contrast, with an extreme wide-angle lens we are close-yet-distant, perspectives exaggerated, creating an effect (again, as in many scenes in *A Clockwork Orange*) of peering in through the glass of a goldfish bowl: we may only be an inch away, but the world is remote from us, alien. (1972: 22)

The critics responded more positively when distanced from the violence in the film, when not placed into it by the direction. Peckinpah's desire to place the spectator 'close' to the action and to move through differing points of view is key to understanding the violence in *Straw Dogs*.

Much of the alarmed reaction to *Straw Dogs* was in response to the rape scene that occurs fifty-five minutes into the film. Attention is drawn to the scene here to highlight inconsistencies in how this sequence has been perceived. It must also be acknowledged that the topic of rape has a strong political charge which, as illustrated in Part One, was changing in the 1960s–70s. This makes an objective discussion of the topic difficult. This is especially pertinent when inconsistencies of the reviews are taken into consideration (acknowledging that the contemporary critics did not have the opportunity to rewatch the scene in the ways that modern technology allow). Several critics, including Kael, expressed that the second part of the rape, by Scutt, was more horrifying as it was anal intercourse. This reaction is based solely on the fact that Amy is turned onto her stomach during this part of the scene. This reaction highlights the polysemic nature of textual criticism, but also its emotive element – almost as if the rape itself must be made more horrific by accruing more actions than the sequence displays. Alongside this is the assumption that the representation of an act is also an approval of the act. Indeed, is rape an act that can be portrayed without the risk of being branded approving or exploitative? In giving an overview of the rape scene, Weddle suggests, 'It starts out as a rape scene, turns into a sad and tender love scene, then veers hideously back into rape when a second villager, Norman Scutt, shows up with a shotgun in hand' (1996: 36). This suggested elision of consensual sex and rape is further discussed by Linda Ruth Williams:

> All the time she [Amy] screams 'No, no, no', as her actions are saying 'Yes, yes, yes' – fear is turned into arousal. It's an image of the complicit rape victim that's as old as misogyny, here all the more astonishing for the audacity and clarity with which it is represented. . . . In the *Straw Dogs* discourse, rape is not *necessarily* negative – it depends on who's doing it to you. (1995: 26)

The criticism here is as much of the history of the depiction of rape itself which pivots around the question of consent (as evidenced in Brownmiller's research). However, it is evident that both Weddle and Ruth Williams' readings oversimplify the sequence and isolate it from the context in which the film presents it.

Throughout the film the relationship between spectator and characters is continually problematized and this is seen with the rape. The traumatized reaction of Amy during the church fête later in the film attests to the mental damage done to her during the sequence and contradicts ideas that Amy enjoys it. There is also a lack of consideration of the role of cross-cutting within the sequence, to an isolated David in a field (tricked into being there so Amy would be isolated at the farmhouse) and flashbacks to David and Amy in bed together. Stephen Prince offers a detailed, shot by shot, analysis of this sequence as a subjective montage. His analysis highlights important aspects of the sequence, particularly the emphasis on Amy's point of view, and how cross-cutting creates parallels between David and Charlie Venner: 'A close inspection of the shot series within the rape sequence where this associative intercutting occurs reveals several interesting features of design. A rapid series of shots conveys Amy's welling terror and her rushing thoughts as she makes the connections between David and Charlie' (1998: 75). The reactions of Amy are therefore more complex than enjoyment or terror. She elides David and Charlie – her response is based on the realization of this. This is further complicated by the view of Amy's body presented, in which the spectator is simultaneously asked to identify with Amy (through flashback and reaction shots) and desire her (through an objectifying gaze). At the same time David's isolation and humiliation (neatly summed up by the flaccid neck of the duck he has shot) suggest sympathy with him. As Bliss points out, 'Like the shower scene in *Psycho*, the voyeuristic element of the *Straw Dogs* rape scene directly implicates the audience in its concerns' (1993: 152). Following from Barr's discussion of Peckinpah's technique, the full complexity of the scene is revealed – the spectator is a voyeur aligned with the lust of Venner and Scutt, Amy herself and her distress and confusion, but also David in his isolation and humiliation (though this is through implication). The later scene at the church fête replays the rape as more clearly traumatic, revising its meaning and clarifying Amy's response removed from the confusion evident in the scene itself. The repeated close-ups on Amy's face remove doubt as to her feelings. Prince reads similarities between the rape and the fête:

> The images demonstrate that Amy's anxieties are being aroused not just from the memory of the rape but by present surroundings. The children's noise-makers – rolled paper tubes they blow into and which become elongated and erect when making noise – assume an increasingly phallic quality. Amy makes this association, as the intercutting of the boy with the noise-maker and her rape images indicate. (1998: 82)

The clarification and revision offered by the later sequence demonstrate the danger of discussing film violence in isolation, removed from the narrative. The associative imagery in the fête replicates motifs of violence and invasion that run throughout the film. The mantrap from the opening scene sits within the farmhouse, over the hearth, a constant reminder of violence (and of emasculation in its evocation of vagina dentata). The boundaries of the farmhouse are consistently invaded, figuratively by the workmen's gazes, and literally when Cawsey steals Amy's underwear and the dead cat is found, prefiguring the rape and the final siege. The sense that Amy exists as part of the house returns to the oppositions of the Western; however, this is subverted by the focus on her reaction, leading to a collapse of oppositions. In this space the inherent threat of rape from the Westerns is made real. Peckinpah suggests that Amy and the house stand for one another (through the invasion imagery), but this is subverted through the complexity of Amy's reaction and her own violent acts during the siege. Amy is not the house, but she is violated physically and emotionally.

Violence is figuratively present in *Straw Dogs* when it is not being overtly depicted. The tension between the villagers, the threat of Henry Niles and the threats to him, and the ever-present workmen reiterate this, as do the arguments between the Major and Tom Heddon. The final scene of the film, the siege, is the culmination of this. The action, as outlined earlier, is filmed in the subjective montage that Prince defines. However, understanding the violence is further complicated by the differing motivation and identifications on offer. Although the spectator is essentially encouraged to be within the farmhouse, and by association in alignment with David and Amy, the breakdown of the relationship between these two (and the cutting between them) makes retaining a point of identification insecure. David's decision to harbour Henry Niles further complicates matters (although the spectator knows Niles killed Janice, David does not). David remains unaware of the rape suffered by Amy, and he is ignorant of the invaders' acts of violence, whereas Amy is not. This confusion culminates as Amy, shotgun in hand, chooses between shooting Charlie Venner and David, her confusion held in close-up, and she moves the gun-barrel between the two. Pierre Greenfield describes the problem of identification thus, 'Like David, we cannot help but feel a kind of exhilaration amidst all this death. If we are honest with ourselves at least, we recognize it, and the recognition is disturbing in the extreme' (1976: 34). This returns to the spectator's proximity to the violence and the sharing of multiple points of identification. The suggestion that the film invites pleasure in the violence as well as revulsion (through close-ups of wounds) helps to explain the varying and confused reactions. Peckinpah is willing to acknowledge that violence is not only horrific but also exciting, denying the spectator a secure approach to the text. Despite this, and Prince's argument that the subjective montage highlights Amy's reaction during the rape, why then did so many critics react to the film as if the rape and the final siege were part of some machismo ritual? The narrative image of the film suggests an answer. Taglines such as 'The knock on the door meant the birth of a man and the death of seven others' anchor the film, offering a preferred reading of the text that simplifies the complexity of the narrative and the relationships. The images of Hoffman presented on posters and the film's rating/certification further prime the spectator for the occurrence of violence and centre their attention on David, rather than Amy. This creates a simultaneous desire and repulsion – the spectator has taken their seat in response to the narrative image, expecting the film violence. However, the narrative image can never securely demonstrate the intensity of the experience that will follow. Special Notices were displayed in theatres before the film was shown that stated, 'Straw Dogs unleashes such dramatic intensity that this theatre is scheduling a 5-minute interval between all performances.' This message, reminiscent of Hitchcock's marketing campaign for *Psycho* (1960), further entices and repels, and affects the spectator's view of the narrative. They are waiting for the violence that has been promised – it is one of the main aspects of the narrative image. Therefore, to object to the violence seems perverse, unless it is to link to a wider cultural malaise. Indeed, the clear desire spectators showed, by watching the film, suggests that the critical reaction was not necessarily about the film but about that desire to watch.

The film violence in *Straw Dogs* is a delayed gratification and as such has a higher intensity. The modality of the text complicates this. Much of Peckinpah's aesthetic technique, whether subjective montage, slow motion or the use of squibs to simulate impact, were still new. This novelty is difficult to interpret in terms of modality, but the techniques used could suggest a lack of understanding in the reviewers, that the newness was itself problematic.[2]

Violence in *The French Connection*

The status of violence in *The French Connection* differs markedly from *Straw Dogs*, not just within the film-text but also in the narrative image and modality. As seen in Part One, the marketing for the film stressed its relationship to real events, something confirmed by the directorial style used by Friedkin which imitates documentary/news-footage. The lack of an established star (Hackman was yet to achieve that status) further heightened the modality, allowing the actors to be subsumed into their roles. *Straw Dogs*, in casting Dustin Hoffman (already a star), created an instantaneous dialogue with its audience over the nature of the main character, especially as Hoffman was not known for violent roles (although knowledge of Peckinpah's films would have pulled against this). With *The French Connection*, neither the star nor the director carried much expectation. Therefore, the modality of the film rises, something enhanced by Friedkin's technical choices. These techniques are distant from the subjective montage of *Straw Dogs*, suggesting an objective spectatorship position. As Mask

---

[2] It is worth noting, however, that as early as 1972 Peckinpah's approach to film violence was being satirized. The sketch 'Sam Peckinpah's Salad Days' that appeared in Series Three of *Monty Python's Flying Circus* shows a garden party turned into a massacre. This includes a cut to a woman's horrified reaction and slow-motion inserts of blood flowing from wounds.

records, 'In an effort to give the film a documentary-like aesthetic, Friedkin instructed cinematographer Owen Roizman to eschew the tradition of lighting and blocking and to film the event before them as if they were news reporters arriving at the scene of the crime' (2007: 66). The link to news reporting is especially pertinent as it immediately conveys a higher modality to the film, linking to the spectator's existing experience in other media. Friedkin had previously worked as a documentary maker and researched for *The French Connection* by spending 'a year riding around with Egan[3] in the 81st Precinct' (Shedlin 1972: 6). The moments of procedural detail that follow Doyle and Russo on stake-out (such as the detail given to their recordings of Boca's diner) further enhance this – these sequences do not move the plot forward so much as establish the working codes of the Police. The image used on posters for the film, in which Doyle shoots Nicoli in the back, both conflicts and reinforces this level of modality. Action and violence are clearly signalled as is the ambiguity of Doyle (enhanced by the tagline 'Doyle is bad news, but a good cop'). The in medias res aspect of the image, with Nicoli's body reacting to the shot, gives the sense of a stolen moment, frozen from reality rather than posed for the cameras. The visible grain in some of the poster images reinforces this and suggests newsprint. Violence is central to the narrative image of *The French Connection*, but so is the suggestion of a high modality.

The first violence in *The French Connection* occurs three minutes and five seconds into the film. The moment is important for several reasons, not least because it has no direct relationship to the plot. (It is neither causal nor reactive.) The antagonists are glimpsed in this sequence, but the location of Marseilles is far removed from most of the film. Primarily the purpose of this sequence is to foreground violence and to suggest its immediacy, brutality and casualness, something that primes the spectator for the rest of the film. Rather than building towards violence, *The French Connection* opens with it. The opening shooting occurs after a sequence of mostly long and medium shots in which the camera is mainly handheld. The undercover Policeman, although shown in close-up, remains nameless and motiveless. His death is sudden and unconnected to the rest of the film. (It is referred to obliquely in the following scene.) It does, however, illustrate the levels to which Charnier's operation will go, and it conditions the spectator to expect sudden contextless violence. The shooting includes several reaction shots, but identification is difficult due to the lack of character information. The quick cuts, between the Policeman's face, Nicoli's appearance, a close-up on the gun, then back to the Policeman's reaction with blood spurting from his neck and onto his face,

---

[3] This refers to Eddie Egan, who featured in Robin Moore's non-fiction book which inspired the film and the character of 'Popeye' Doyle. He appears in *The French Connection* as Walt Simonson, Doyle's superior.

are sharp and sudden. Immediately after the Policeman slumps into the right of the frame a moment occurs that both diffuses the violence and signals a callousness: Nicoli tears off and eats some of the baguette the Policeman had been carrying and eats. This juxtaposition of violence with the banal is something that continues throughout. Later when Doyle, Russo, Simonson and Mulderig share expositional dialogue, the film repeatedly cuts to the aftermath of a car crash in which two people have died (bloodily). There is no reason for this scene to take place at the car crash, and the images of the bodies are unrelated to the narrative. What they do, however, is suggest that violence is ever present and often senseless. During the car chase, which develops from a pursuit on foot to one in which Doyle drives a car while Nicoli rides an elevated train, a variety of unnamed characters are killed by Nicoli, including a mother pushing a pram, shot by mistake as Nicoli aims at Doyle. In the film's final sequence Doyle shoots Mulderig, another accident, and an irony as Mulderig has continually questioned Doyle's competence and safety. For none of these deaths is an aftermath considered; they simply happen then the film and the characters move on. In the case of Mulderig's death, Doyle ignores the body and continues his ineffective pursuit of Charnier. The ending, in which the spectator is informed by text of the fate of the characters, offers no resolution in the traditional sense but does conform to the higher modality of the film – real life lacks the neat closure of classical narrative. In *The French Connection*, violence is rendered every day. Later, in this work, the character of Doyle will be considered further, especially his treatment of different social groups and his motivations, but for now it's enough to draw distinctions with *Straw Dogs* and *Joe*; *The French Connection* presents the spectator with high modality film violence that is often unrelated to plot advancement.

Violence in *Dirty Harry*

The opening of *The French Connection* distances the spectator from the action using long shots and objective positioning. *Dirty Harry* does the opposite, placing the spectator into a subjective position after the initial prologue of the memorial board for San Francisco Police Officers killed in the line of duty. This subjective position is that of the antagonist. Indeed, throughout the film the spectator is offered the position of the antagonist and protagonist, Scorpio and Callahan. This querying of the spectator's subject position, and its eventual resolution (with the death of Scorpio), creates a problematic alignment of spectator and character. The memorial board opens the film, signalling risk and death, which then fades to the image of a rifle barrel. Here the spectator becomes the target, seen in Figure 4, powerless in front of the long barrel that juts towards them.

FIGURE 4 *Scorpio aims at an unknown woman and the spectator in* Dirty Harry *(Warner Bros, 1971)*.

FIGURE 5 *Scorpio's gaze in* Dirty Harry *(Warner Bros, 1971)*.

The next shot Figure 5, however, moves to a point of view down the telescopic lens of the rifle – now the spectator takes the powerful position (that of Scorpio) and shares the gaze towards the powerless female victim (rendered powerless by her unawareness of the gaze, but also her partially naked, slim, body).

The victim is unidentified, but the non-diegetic music suggests romance; violence and desire are elided. The next shot, an over-shoulder of Scorpio, retains a superior position and a subjective alignment as Scorpio, and the spectator stares onto the rooftop where the victim swims. We return to the front of the barrel, then to the point of view. As the bullet is fired, we have a close-up of the trigger being pulled, then we cut to see the victim who struggles, then dies, for a few seconds (from a similar angle to the point of view). The woman herself, young, blonde and in a swimsuit, immediately suggests a masculine scopophilic gaze explicitly tied to violence. The fact that Scorpio's face remains obscure further allows alignment with his subjective view. (Indeed, he lacks much more than racial identity in this sequence, due to his long hair.) The girl has no identity, and she functions simply as an object for our shared gaze, and to be the victim – an inevitable status conferred by the rifle itself. This emphasis on looking, and on sharing the gaze, continues throughout the film and complicates the violence while suggesting links to masculinity. In the next scene, Callahan arrives at the crime scene, his eyes obscured by sunglasses – the effect of which is to draw attention to them.

Throughout the film Callahan is portrayed as having superior observational powers to those around him. When he argues with the mayor about the shooting of a rapist, it is Callahan's observation of 'intent' that leads him to 'shoot the bastard'. Later, when he interrupts the bank robbery, it is his observation of the car's running engine which leads him to call in the crime. After Scorpio has escaped from a rooftop, Callahan comments that the officers supposed to stop him 'were probably talking instead of looking like they were supposed to'. Callahan finally warms to his partner, Gonzalez, after the latter visually identifies a suspect briefcase. The parallels between Scorpio and Callahan, suggested by their similar gazes, were signalled in the marketing campaign ('Dirty Harry and the homicidal maniac. Harry's the one with the badge') and in their shared 'distaste for authority' (Street 2016: 77). However, the film also delineates a divergence between the two, and this separation suggests two forms of violence: legitimate (Callahan's) and illegitimate (Scorpio's). Partly this comes from Callahan's status in the Police (despite his tense relationship with his superiors), which lends a social justification to his acts if not necessarily a moral or legal one (especially considering the contextual debates), at least until he violates regulations by torturing Scorpio. Several scenes highlight the correlations and divergences between the two. When Scorpio attacks Callahan in Golden Gate Park, he derives a clear sexual pleasure (including innuendo-filled dialogue – 'My, that's a big one' in response to Callahan's gun). Later he pays a Black man to beat him up and his face registers pleasure as he spits out racist insults. These scenes are shown clearly to the spectator in medium and close shots. Callahan, however, registers less pleasure especially in the scene in which he tortures Scorpio. Here the camera withdraws from Kezar Stadium denying a view. (Ironically, this occurs in a public space designed for spectating.) Callahan does take pleasure in the threat of violence (during the famous bank-robbery sequence where he asks a robber if he 'feels lucky') but not the enactment of it. The pleasure that Scorpio displays effectively sanctions Callahan's actions: 'the film cynically but effectively sets up . . . a villain so base and repugnant that no measure of brutality could seem excessive' (Horsley 1999: 90).

The narrative image of the film emphasizes violence, especially highlighting Callahan himself (who is, in all the posters, depicted holding his gun, often aiming it outwards). Taglines such as 'Detective Harry Callahan. He doesn't break murder cases, he smashes them' and 'Detective Harry Callahan. You don't assign him to murder cases. You just turn him loose' use language that signals violence. The casting of Eastwood will have brought a clear level of intertextuality, especially through his association with Westerns and War films (such as *Where Eagles Dare* (Brian G. Hutton, 1968) and *Kelly's Heroes* (Brian G. Hutton, 1970)), both genres in which the action and violence are central. Jake Horsley notes that

> a Clint Eastwood movie always features Clint Eastwood *as* Clint Eastwood – that's what people come to see. It isn't necessary for Eastwood to *act* in order to fill out his role. In *Dirty Harry*, for example, we never feel we are seeing a real San Francisco cop but only a Hollywood idealization of such a cop, all out fantasies (and fears) embodied in a single icon. (1999: 89)

Although Horsley's analysis neglects two films that demonstrate Eastwood's willingness and ability to play with his persona, in the self-directed *Play Misty for Me* and *The Beguiled* (Don Siegel) both released, like *Dirty Harry* in 1971, he pinpoints one of the main attractions of Eastwood's film – his star persona. What then of modality? The relationship between a star (with whom the spectator has a pre-existing relationship) and the level of reality of a text varies depending on the star. De Niro was known to be subsumed into character. Eastwood conversely creates a distancing effect simply by his appearance – he stands for ideas and values perhaps, but not necessarily performance and character. When viewing Eastwood, in whatever role, the spectator is consistently aware of the actor, simultaneous with watching the character and becoming involved in the diegesis. This tension lowers the modality of the film and pushes the pleasure of the text more towards ritual, similar to the pleasure of genre. Even films such as *Play Misty for Me* that cast Eastwood in roles against type become commentaries on his usual persona.

The violence in *Dirty Harry* and the question of legitimacy[4] are further complicated by a hierarchy established in the victims of Scorpio. The first victim is nameless, a single white woman. The second is a young Black boy whose death is seen through the impact it has on his mother. The final victim, the young girl, is white and middle class. She is raped and left in a drain. Her body is glimpsed in long shot with music that uses a sorrowful

---

[4]Tasker suggests that Callahan's violence is legitimized by the urban environment. The finale, outside of the city, makes it 'asocial' (2015: 114).

motif. It is this final murder that comes to justify Callahan in his pursuit of Scorpio. Scorpio's threat to a young white boy justifies his murder. The differing emotional values and screen time given to each death remind of the reporting of Kitty Genovese's murder, the nature of the victim impacts on the level of outrage and response to the crime. In *Dirty Harry*, there is a suggestion that the life of white victims has a higher value, and that the greatest violation of this body is sexual. The famed sequence where Callahan confronts bank robbers confirms this somewhat, in the way that Callahan toys with one of the robbers (played by Albert Popwell). The famous speech, where Callahan asks if the robber 'feels lucky', invokes the spectre, perhaps, of the public lynchings discussed in Part One – this is a very public moment of violence, violence as a public spectacle. That all the robbers are Black certainly invites this comparison, although other moments in the film offer a counterpoint to this, not least Scorpio's targeting of Black people and his own clearly racist views. The scene which follows the robbery shows Callahan's friendly relationship with a Black doctor (they grew up in the same neighbourhood) offers a further counterpoint to this reading.

Violence in *Death Wish*

Of the films in this study, *Death Wish* was most routinely condemned by critics for its depiction of violence. In a similar way to *Straw Dogs*, much of the criticism concerned the rape scene, but there were also concerns about the nature of the acts committed by Kersey and his choice of victims. (Victims is used advisedly – Kersey's moral status is something returned to later in the chapter.) However, these criticisms ignore mediating factors of ritual and star persona. As seen previously, *Death Wish* imitates and references the Western in many ways. (Cawelti goes as far as to call it a 'modern urban western' (2004: 160).) However, as *Death Wish* does have several key differences from the Western, we cannot assume that violence operates in the same way. Kendrick suggests that 'In the traditional or classic western (primarily those produced before the 1960s), violence is the chief means by which good and evil are distinguished. While the old adage suggests that the white hat denotes "good" and the black hat denotes "evil", the principal factor in distinguishing between the two is arguably *restraint*, particularly in the use of violence' (2009: 72). For Kendrick, the villain is 'a figure of excess in the western, deploying violence to satisfy his own desires' (2009: 72–3) and 'if the hero is to use violence, then it must be seen as legitimate and "pure", which necessitates the violence to be circumscribed' (2009: 73). This formula of film violence is replayed in *Dirty Harry* in the comparison between Callahan's precision and Scorpio's imprecision, and to some extent this model also works for *Death Wish* if we see the society that Kersey lives in as inherently violent, rather than focused on one individual villain or gang. Kersey's opposition is to the extremities of violence present in New York. In this context, where violence is everywhere and is capable of transgressing boundaries of home, Kersey's reactions appear restrained. He is never the instigator; his acts are reactive (although he does travel to areas of New York where attacks are likely). The violence, although imitating the Western, is elevated in its stylistic component but conforms mostly to similar situations of gunfights and threats with knives. The motivations of Kersey, however, problematize the film violence. Nominally motivated by revenge, Kersey never endeavours to trace the men who attacked his wife and daughter; rather, he seeks any criminal who is willing to attack him or others, leading to a more complicated view of morality than allowed by the contemporary critics. Cobley suggests:

> What is morally right for Paul [Kersey] stems from the fact that the body politic is not concerned with individual cases of crime. The contradiction of the narrative appears when the vigilante becomes a celebrity, demonstrating clearly that society at large *is* concerned, however, with the doing of justice. If *Death Wish* is anti-liberal in any sense it is *knowingly* anti-liberal, exploring like *Dirty Harry*, the inner contradictions of the contemporary liberal consensus (2000: 173).

Death Wish points to the failure of the liberal consensus to cope with the rise of crime during the 1970s, while simultaneously exploiting the moral panic the rise has caused.

The celebrity status that Kersey attains throughout the film further complicates the depiction of violence by providing a critique of the news media's response and exploitation of events – simultaneously debating the legitimacy of the acts while using them to increase sales/ratings. This situation of Kersey's actions in a 'real' debate runs at odds, however, with the narrative image of the film. In ways similar to Eastwood, Bronson had an established screen persona that subsumes any character he played. This was acknowledged in the film's marketing with the tagline 'Charles Bronson is the vigilante, city style!' Previous films, such as *The Mechanic* (Michael Winner, 1972) and *The Stone Killer* (Michael Winner, 1973), had established Bronson as a strong, quiet and violent character (at odds with Kersey's middle-class, conscientious objector views), and he had gained fame as a cornerstone of several successful ensemble action films through the 1960s (such as *The Magnificent Seven* and *The Great Escape* (John Sturges, 1963)). The attraction of a Bronson film was Bronson himself, and it guarantees Kersey's transformation. This knowledge, alongside some melodramatic directorial choices such as the creation of the Hawaii prologue, helps to lower the modality through the overt display of convention.

The ritualization and distancing from violence have further implications when linked to the rape scene that initiates the plot. One of the most significant differences between Brian Garfield's original novel and the film is the decision to include a depiction of the rape. In the novel Kersey (known as Paul Benjamin) learns of the rape after the fact, and the rape is not described. By choosing to depict the rape, the spectator's relationship to Kersey's actions is transformed. As Harding suggests, the scene is essential to justifying Kersey's subsequent actions: 'The attack on the women is the film's central sequence, and by its nature presents problems of direction; how violent should the rape scene be? Too violent and it will become merely disgusting; not violent enough and the basis for Kersey's later behaviour will be weakened' (1978: 104). Therefore, up to a point, the greater the traumatic event, the greater the cathartic release and the greater the justification for the violence that follows. The rape scene allows the audience to identify with Kersey and to enjoy his acts, even though they are not directed at the rapists themselves (the lack of characterization of the muggers/attackers in the films allows an elision – like Native American braves in the Western, they are all the same). His actions are therefore presented as just and right as in the American Frontier tradition (which he discovers for himself during his time in Tucson). The amalgamation of the attackers reinforces the sense that violence is everywhere – therefore any criminal will do.

Examining the rape scene directly, we can see how Winner directs the action in the film and how he tends to eschew subjective camera techniques in favour of an objective approach. Only in one moment is a subjective view used, giving us Kersey's wife's point of view, as she watches the daughter's attack. This then cuts to the wife's reaction shot. We are not, however, given the daughter's point of view or reaction. Indeed, the daughter is not given a subjective angle in the scene. Later, when in a mental institution, she is unable to speak. Her character exists without agency, unable even to comment on what she wants. The build-up to the attack crosscuts between the assailants and the wife and daughter in equal measure, prioritizing neither and certainly not offering the subjective montage of *Straw Dogs*. The rest of the film largely follows Kersey, but the direction lacks consistent subjective techniques. The rape scene also asks questions of the spectator and their desire to look, as the film violence depicted serves to justify the spectator's enjoyment of Kersey's response. Assuming the spectator knows about Bronson's star persona (which seems likely), the desire to enjoy Kersey's acts drives a demand for the rape and for it to be particularly unpleasant. This renders the female members of Kersey's family as nothing more than plot devices, causes for effect.

The criticism of the film violence of *Death Wish* also ignored the changing mental state of Kersey. He moves from non-violent to anxious and alarmed by his own violent acts (vomiting at one point), to later cruising for violence around New York, then finally entering into a play-acting of fantasy Western violence in the closing scenes. This degeneration comes to mirror the degeneration of the Western ideal and the Frontier Myth. Slotkin explains how the displacement of Western codes into an urban environment shifted meanings:

> The displacement of the Western from its place on the genre map did not entail the disappearance of those underlying structures of myth and ideology that had given the genre its cultural force. Rather, these structures were abstracted from the elaborately historicized context of the Western and parcelled out among other genres that used their relationship to the Western to define both disillusioning losses and the extravagant potential of the new era. Violence remains central to these new genre-scenarios as it had been in the Western, but the necessity for violence was no longer rationalized by an appeal to the progressive historical myth of the westward expansion. (1992: 633)

Kersey's actions are removed from the Western myth, transforming the text/spectator relationship. This is referred to self-reflexively in *Death Wish* when the Wild West show, in Tucson, affirms the traditional genre codes but also highlights the artificiality and ridiculousness of them. Although at first Tucson appears as an idealized frontier, it is far from it. Kersey is there to plan a housing project, arriving by plane. Jainchill is a parody of a cowboy, wearing a cowboy hat and gun but driving a car (albeit one with bullhorns on the front), as are the actors in the show. The Western is consistently revealed to be fantasy. Finally, Kersey comes to imitate the Western hero calling for young urban men far removed from the myth to 'draw' their guns. Slotkin elaborates:

> What makes the urban vigilante genre different from the Western is its 'post-frontier' setting. Its world is urbanized, and its possibilities for progress and redemption are constricted by vastly ramified corporate conspiracies and by monstrous accumulations of wealth, power and corruption. Its heroes draw energy from the same rage that drives the paranoids, psychopaths, mass murderers, and terrorists of the mean streets, and their victories are never socially redemptive in the Western mode. In these respects, the world of the urban gunslinger film is cognate to that of the horror and 'slasher' film, typified by *The Omen* and *The Texas Chainsaw Massacre*. (1992: 634)

The imitation of the mythic code of the Western is evident in *Death Wish*; however, the film continually exposes and undermines that mythic code. As such, Kersey's acts become a simulacrum of the Western hero, but one that is undermined by the lack of 'social redemption'.

Violence in *Taxi Driver*

Structurally *Taxi Driver* offers different aspects to examine in the representation of violence. In terms of incidence, it resembles *Straw Dogs* in that acts of violence are slowly introduced, but the threat of violence is ever present. The film also has structural links to the Western (especially *The Searchers*), as identified previously, which links it to the ritualized violence of *Dirty Harry* and *Death Wish*. The narrative image was conflicted. Trailers suggested a trajectory towards violence for the protagonist, but the dominant image in posters isolated Bickle against a backdrop of New York. De Niro had had some success in *Mean Streets* (Martin Scorsese, 1973) and particularly in *The Godfather Part II* (Francis Ford Coppola, 1974), but had not attained the level of stardom of Hoffman, Eastwood or Bronson.[5] The previous films, however, would have created an intertextual link to other films where violence plays a central part (both are gangster films). The lack of clear generic elements in the film's marketing, the lack of clear antagonist/protagonist opposition and the uncertainty surrounding the protagonist's motivation all complicate the spectator's understanding of the film violence.

To understand film violence in *Taxi Driver*, we must return to Slotkin and the concept of violence as redemption. Although *Taxi Driver* does not uncritically replicate this idea, the concept underpins the narrative and Bickle's actions. This places violence as an inevitable resolution for the protagonist but, as in *Death Wish*, the relationship of the protagonist to reality is questioned. Kolker explains that '*Taxi Driver* rigorously structures a path to violence that is separate from community, separate from the exigencies of any "normal" life, separate from any rational comprehension and need, but only the explosion of an individual attempting to escape from a self-made prison – an individual who, in his madness, attempts to act the role of a hero' (1980: 182). Only one scene occurs in *Taxi Driver* in which Bickle is not present (where Sport and Iris dance), and his voice-over is a consistent presence, offering commentary and interpretation of the narrative. The structure of the film, in which progression of time is unclear, disassociates events, replicating Bickle's own mind. Within this the violent events that do occur can seem unprovoked or unheralded. In a similar way to *The French Connection*, violence occurs without provocation and at the margins of the narrative: events in the background such as two old men fighting in the street and young men throwing eggs at the taxi's windshield. In this New York, violence is all-pervasive. One of the more striking moments in which the threat of violence is represented is when Bickle carries a passenger who wants to kill his own wife: 'This is the longest sequence devoted to any of Travis' fayres. As the film's turning point (prior to Travis' late recognition of the transition: "Then suddenly, there is a change"), the scene is remarkable for its representation of

---

[5] As identified in Part One, De Niro first appeared in Quigley's listings in 1977, the year after *Taxi Driver*'s release.

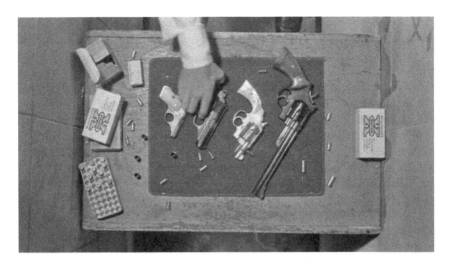

FIGURE 6 *Bickle's selection of guns at the shooting range. From left to right: Sterling Arms pistol, Walther PPK, Colt Detective Special, .44 Magnum.* Taxi Driver *(Columbia Pictures, 1976).*

violence' (Fuchs 1991: 42). In this sequence the passenger is played by Scorsese himself, his speech explicitly linking sex, jealousy and violence. Although there is no visual representation of violence (indeed we cannot know if the passenger makes good on his threats), violence is described. The line 'Have you ever seen what a .44 Magnum can do to a woman's pussy?' presages a change in Bickle's mindset. It connects the sex he watches on-screen in porno-theatres to his violent desires driven by his rejection by Betsy. The passenger's line '*That* you should see' is a come-on to Bickle but to the spectator as well – an invocation to look at the horrific. The gun fetishism displayed in this scene and later when Bickle buys his own guns references back to *Dirty Harry* (Bickle chooses Callahan's .44 Magnum as one of his weapons), but also to Westerns through the Derringer-like Sterling Arms pistol, Police procedurals with the Colt Detective Special and the James Bond films through the presence of a Walther PPK, shown in Figure 6.

This intertextual dialogue with previous violent films helps establish Bickle's desire to be a hero, or at least to see himself as one. The association of violence with sex is furthered in the final scene which occurs on the street and in the building where Iris and Sport work (imitating his earlier journey as a potential customer), interrupting Iris with a customer. The desaturation of the final scene (to avoid classification issues (Taubin 2000: 21)) gives it a visual separation from what precedes – a culmination of the narrative, but somehow apart.

There are elements of critique when *Taxi Driver* is watched after *Death Wish* and *Joe*, in the way it inverts the representations of violence. In *Taxi Driver* the incidence is less, but the stylistic component is more detailed, using close-ups and special effects to show the physical effect on characters (including when, in medium shot, a characters' fingers are obliterated by a gunshot and blood sprays from the wound site). The differences between Bickle, Kersey and Joe Curran are instructive; Curran fought in the Second World War, Kersey had been involved in the Korean War (albeit in the Medical Corps), conflicts seen as legitimate and successful. Bickle claims to have been involved in Vietnam, which his jacket and insignia patches attest to. The image of the Vietnam War as unsuccessful and illegitimate places Bickle's relationship to violence in a different vein from the others' – suggesting that violence is unsuccessful in resolving problems and invoking the issues and discourses covered in Part One. Peter Boyle appears in *Taxi Driver* as Wizard, an older figure who counsels Bickle and expresses liberal values, a character seemingly drawn in opposition to Joe Curran. There is also no direct catalysing moment in *Taxi Driver*, such as the attack in *Death Wish*. Bickle's violent urges grow throughout the course of the film, rather than as a response to violent events. Bickle's final redemption, in which we see newspaper cuttings acclaiming his actions as heroic, shows a disassociation between his actions as seen by others and his motives. The media representation simplifies his actions to that of a Western-style hero from a captivity narrative (re-enforced by the voice-over from Iris's father), missing his sexual motivations and frustrations. Here the complexity of film violence is revealed and critiqued – the actions are reinterpreted by the media's own desire for a simplistic narrative.

In terms of realism, *Taxi Driver* presents more complexity. The aesthetic component bears relation to *Straw Dogs* and *The French Connection*, and the specific descriptions of firearms and the use of New York locations shot in detail (often from Bickle's point of view in the taxi) suggest a high modality. However, the films' structure, in which time is represented elliptically, complicates this as does Bickle's voice-over. The final image of the shoot-out, in which the camera floats above and then out of the room in which Bickle sits covered in blood, breaks with the rest of the film which has largely been from Bickle's subjectivity. The line in the film's trailer, voiced by an anonymous announcer, that claims Bickle is 'preparing himself for the only moment in his life that will ever mean anything', highlights the importance of the build towards the final shoot-out but also the centrality of violence to Bickle's character. In the fractured, decaying world that Bickle lives in, violence comes to have more meaning, an almost nihilist view.

The narrative's trajectory towards violence also complicates meaning in its links to desire. As with all the Vigilante Thrillers, the audience's desire to see violence is problematic for many critics. Scorsese's own reaction to how spectators received the film elucidates this:

I was shocked by the way audiences took the violence. Previously I'd been surprised by audience reaction to *The Wild Bunch*, which I first saw in a Warner Brothers screening room with a friend and loved. But a week later I took some friends to see it in a theatre and it was as if the violence became an extension of the audience and vice-versa. I don't think it was approval, some of it must have been revulsion. I saw *Taxi Driver* once in a theatre, on the opening night I think, and everyone was yelling and screaming at the shoot-out. When I made it, I didn't intend to have the audience react with that feeling, 'Yes let's do it! Let's go out and kill.' The idea was to create a violent catharsis, so that they didn't find themselves saying 'Yes kill'; and then afterwards realize, 'My God, no' – like some strange Californian therapy session. That was the instinct I went with, but it's scary to hear what happened with the audience. (Thompson and Christie 1989: 63)

We return then to the question of catharsis, raised by Peckinpah at the beginning of this chapter. Scorsese's reaction to the audience's response also raises questions of how a group behaves compared to an individual, and how the cinema audience as a mass reacts.

* * *

The purpose of this overview of violence has been to problematize the original critical reactions and many of the later analyses. Film violence operates in different ways within different films, affected by multiple factors both within and without the text. When describing Don Siegel's directorial characteristics, Alan Lovell suggests that the function of violence in Siegel's films is to 'define the nature of his heroes' as it is an 'expression of their temperament' (1975: 25). It is a contention that works for each of these films, and the violent acts they commit help to define their characters and draw attention to differences between them. It is through the protagonists that the spectator understands the film. As we move to consider ideas of identification and gaze the relationship between spectator and text will develop.

5

Establishing the gaze and identification

Analysis of the gaze(s) employed in these films begins with the openings of each film. Consideration will be given to the gaze as it is constructed through cinematography, sound, mise en scène and editing. This in turn will lead to discussion of identification, based on how the spectator is positioned. This is not to suggest that each film necessarily retains the same subject position for the whole film. However, it helps to fix the spectator's position for the remainder. This, an aspect of interpellation, sets the text/spectator relationship for the rest of the film.

A textual/paratextual relationship exists during the openings, between the establishment of the film's diegesis and the extra-diegetic formalities that acknowledge a film's artifice and creation (such as titles). Titles and credits allow the spectator to be introduced to the text, but their existence simultaneously acknowledges its constructed status. Francesco Casetti investigates this:

> Moments of looks into the camera, titles addressing the viewer, voice-over narrations, or again, credits at the film's beginning and end are exemplary; they are moments that lay the cards on the table and offer a game to those who want to play it. The credit sequences are particularly instructive: placed at each extremity of the film, and reproduced on posters and advertisements at the entry to the movie house, they function, in a most obvious manner, as an elastic border between two universes, between an interior seeking to escape its limits and an exterior wanting to penetrate into the discourse of the film. (1998: 48)

The function of titles and opening sequences is partly one of ritual, an extension of the film experience, but also to condition the spectator – who becomes aware of the transition into the diegesis. Here interpellation takes place, the text/spectator relationship is outlined, and a subject position suggested. Each of the Vigilante Thrillers suggests complex subject positions; indeed, the very idea of positioning/alignment is problematized, and the suggestion of a clear ideological reading is compromised. The following examination of each film's opening sequences establishes this.

Joe begins with an indistinct shot of a waterfall over which the titles are superimposed. After the producers' names, Peter Boyle is listed first, establishing him as the star, consistent with the narrative image. As the waterfall comes into focus, the title appears in a type that is both indicative of the hippy generation and, through its colour scheme and star in the centre of the O, of traditional patriotism. The opening lines of the non-diegetic song ask, 'Where are you going? Tell me what you want to be.' In Figure 7 we see how Melissa enters the frame, into the O, and a freeze-frame highlights her appearance.

Here she becomes an object of the gaze, but also a target, with the O standing as a sight (linking back to imagery in the theatrical release poster). Melissa's appearance demonstrates a confusion of codes important for the film but also links to the Vigilante Thriller more widely. Her eyes are heavily lined with make-up, creating a child-like appearance, reinforced by her long hair. As Melissa exercises her own gaze (which the spectator briefly shares), her eyes rest on childhood images (a shop display of teddy bears) while the non-diegetic song implores her to 'grow-up'. Throughout this sequence she

FIGURE 7 *Melissa's status as target and source of conflict/confusion is signalled in the title sequence in which she appears in the centre of the O/target in* Joe *(Cannon Group, 1970).*

FIGURE 8 *Melissa and dolly in* Joe *(Cannon Group, 1970).*

remains isolated, but the song (a ballad) suggests hope and love. Another freeze-frame fixes her. When the title sequence is over, the film cuts to her shared room with Frank and an abrupt juxtaposition is created in which she is sexualized as she undresses and gets into the bath (with Frank). Frank's antagonistic reactions to her disrupt the peace of the title sequence, re-enforced by references and images of the 'Cookie-Jar' (their drugs). Melissa then becomes both a child and an image of sex, shown again in Figure 8, in which she cuddles her doll while lying on a mattress with Frank, and later referenced where she applies make-up (badly) in the drugstore while high.

This confusion continues throughout. Idealized images (of Melissa, of traditional home life, of upper-middle-class business) are repeatedly exposed as shams. The spectator is given one position, only to have it undermined later. The romanticized image of innocence in the opening gives way to drug-dealing and an abusive relationship between Frank and Melissa (in which he dominates) in which her love is unrequited. (Frank even fails to consummate it while high.)

Fifteen minutes in, the narrative switches to focus on Bill Compton, after which Melissa becomes largely excluded from the narrative. All of this is against the background of a strong hermeneutic code; who/where is Joe? Having established the character in the title and the narrative image as central, his absence until the twenty-sixth minute serves to emphasize this mystery but removes him from being a secure point of identification. That falls more clearly to Bill (emphasized in the scene in which he kills Frank). Joe's character is anticipated by the spectator but also alienated from them. It is also clear that Melissa's status is to represent a problem – causing conflict and worry but not a developed character in herself. Although we look at her, we rarely look with her, and she takes up little of the remaining screen time. Her emphasis in the opening creates her as a nexus for the narrative, a causal factor. It is because of her that the narrative occurs, and it is her death that will close it. She is representative of a conflict, in which innocence is corrupted and the opening allows for that corruption to be seen, as she moves from a point of innocence to degradation with Frank. The hippy counterculture is specifically undermined here, but later developments in the film follow this pattern of exposing all cultures, rather than simply demonizing one.

The opening of *Straw Dogs* creates conflicting subject positions in several ways. It offers a variety of points of identification through several points of view. Edits confuse eyelines, suggesting and denying relationships and links. The titles seem conventional, as a prelude to the narrative, but by being superimposed over blurred images of trees and children playing in a graveyard, several important themes are presented: nature, death and childhood games (with a heretical element in the juxtaposition). The titles set Dustin Hoffman/David Sumner as the protagonist (given the prominence of his name after the production company and before Peckinpah's), but the following shots pull against this. The blurring of the first shot, then the dissolve to the second, which also focusses-in and draws attention to the cinematic apparatus, suggests the mechanism itself as an independent point of view rather than one of subjectivity. This tacit acknowledgement of the film's construction then makes way to shots that highlight various gazes, using subjective angles to query where the spectator should locate themselves in the action, creating links between characters through mismatched eyelines and reaction shots. Bliss explores the movement from out of focus further:

> We see children playfully circling around a gravestone, certainly a prescient image in light of the various horrible deaths the film metes out. The director begins the shot by having it photographed out of focus, gradually sharpening it throughout the title sequence until by the sequence's end, when Peckinpah's name appears, the background image is sharp and clear. (In a comparable fashion the film's undercurrent of sexually created and sustained violence becomes clearer the closer we come to the revelatory end). (1993: 142–3)

The next shot, the title sequence having ended, is a slow zoom from a high angle onto the children playing. The opening shot of the titles is replayed, but in focus this time, before a cut to an establishing shot of the village from an unlikely, if not impossible, angle from the church tower. A close-up of two children looking around a doorway suggests an eyeline to David Sumner, crossing the village in medium shot while carrying a box of groceries. One child's surprised reaction indicates David's separateness from the village, as does his costume. (His urbane dress of brown knitted jumper and pale trousers contrasts with the other men who dress predominantly in dark clothes of rough materials.) Shots of other children watching suggest more inquisitive gazes towards David, until the film cuts to Amy (introduced via close-up onto her bra-less chest), creating confusion as to who is the subject of these various gazes. The shot of Amy, which tilts up from her chest to her face, clearly highlights her body as a scopic object. As she smiles, the film cuts to Charlie Venner exiting a phone box with a look of surprise on his face. A link between them is suggested (that Venner is in Amy's point of view, although this contradicts the possible eyelines). However, the next shots, of Amy walking and carrying the mantrap with Janice, are intercut with a close-up on a lone elderly male. The angle on Amy changes (now from high in churchyard), which further confuses spatial relations between characters and disrupts focalization. As David, Amy and Venner converge, spatial confusion continues; David and Amy look left to right, while Venner looks right to left. The eyelines and relations are only resolved in a following long shot.

The mise en scène also confuses but serves to foreshadow later events. Amy, while looking at David, moves towards Venner. The camera holds David on the opposite side of the car. As Amy and Venner talk, a cut to David reverses the angle of the previous shot giving David the appearance of being on their right, rather than on their left as before. The following shots settle into more conventional continuity, but frame Amy and David separately. Hoffman's stardom surely allows the spectator to identify him as the protagonist, but the use of various angles, gazes and confused continuity destabilizes this. The opening view of Amy, concentrating on her breasts, sets up a scopophilic gaze (returned to subsequently in the film) that the spectator is invited to share, but not in a way that anchors it to a particular character. A closeness between Amy and Venner is suggested through angles and shots, David's consequent exclusion, and difference from the villagers, is taken further in the next scene when he goes into the pub and buys cigarettes (pointedly asking for 'American' ones). The small alien details (such as cows in the high-street), the old age of some of the villagers and the poverty of their dress, not only alienate David but potentially the spectator, suggesting an alignment with him. This, however, is undermined by one element; David is not wearing his glasses. Throughout this sequence he squints, suggesting an unfocused, unknowing and un-detailed gaze.[1] Therefore, his point of view is complicated, and the spectator is denied a secure position. The mantrap that Amy carries (a gift to David) simultaneously indicates the violence to follow and undermines the scopic gaze to which she is subjected – the threat of emasculation is present.

---

[1] This references to the film's US theatrical release posters in which David stares out of the image through broken glasses.

The opening of *The French Connection* has been discussed in detail already (in relation to violence) in which the Marseilles prologue establishes the style and tone of the narrative. The opening of the narrative proper introduces the character of Doyle and his partner Russo in New York. The sequence is instructive as it simultaneously keeps the observational style of most of the film but includes some subjective point of view to align the spectator with Doyle and Russo, rather than their suspect. After a medium shot of Russo masquerading as a hot-dog stand attendant, Doyle is placed in the rear of the frame (in a Santa-Claus disguise surrounded by children). Close-ups establish the children gazing up at him and his point of view towards them, but his gaze is distracted as he looks through the window of the bar that he is staking out. Here his gaze is clearly highlighted. Similarly, when Russo enters the bar, the camera offers a handheld shot from his point of view, and a series of shots that track directly behind him. Never in this sequence are the views of the suspects in the bar given, nor are there reaction shots prompted by Russo's behaviour – he always remains in the frame. The subsequent chase highlights the intention of aligning the spectator with these two characters, offering a shot that follows Doyle and Russo onto an area of waste ground, placing the spectator with them. This camera movement remains on the edge of the waste ground, returning to an objective angle. During the subsequent interrogation, down a back alley, the sense of a forbidden gaze is evoked by the placement of the camera behind objects, such as a low angle from the bottom of a stairwell. The subsequent shots crowd the frame, with Russo occasionally out of focus, suggesting an unplanned aesthetic. All through this sequence 'impossible' shots (such as high angles from buildings) have been avoided, with a concentration on eye-level framing. *Straw Dogs* deliberately confuses the spectator's alignment; *The French Connection* is more secure but refrains from an explicit positioning of a subjective gaze. Alignment is, however, created through generic expectation and narrative structure but also through a secure sense of who is being followed and who is following.

With *Dirty Harry*, again the opening has been extensively analysed previously, noting the importance of Scorpio's subjective gaze and the suggestion of Callahan's (through his sunglasses and his discovery of Scorpio's firing position). This develops further in the next scene where Callahan investigates the crime – here the split between Scorpio's illegitimate gaze and Callahan's legitimate one is delineated. As Callahan investigates, the titles play, emphasizing Eastwood as the star but also his character as the focal point for identification through the title of the film and the placing of him centre frame. The camera follows Callahan as he works. The titles, suggesting the film is beginning properly, allow for a distance to be made between the spectator and Scorpio – having been invited to share, and indulge in, this illegitimate gaze, the spectator is returned to a 'normal' subject position in which Callahan is quickly established as the protagonist. Largely, the film will continue this by following Callahan and sharing his gaze. However, there are sequences that return to Scorpio's gaze, reminding the spectator of his illegitimacy but also of the correlations with Callahan. Despite the division/opposition between the two gazes, there are shared elements, especially in the scopic drive (returned to later). Suffice to say, here the main focalization is on Callahan, despite initial sharing of Scorpio's gaze (which may indeed be distancing due to the character's non-normative elements).

Death Wish opens with shots that identify the gaze of Paul Kersey as important and places his wife Joanne as the object of his gaze (which is then imitated by the voyeuristic way in which the attackers follow her and her daughter). As Joanne emerges from the sea, the opening shot objectifies her implying his gaze, and the following reverse angle shows Kersey's reaction (and his pleasure as he looks). Intensifying this he takes pictures of her, after instructing her to 'Hold it right there' several times.[2] Joanna's body is highlighted in the dialogue that follows, with Kersey's approval of it clear (his right to do this is unchallenged). This sequence very much accords with concepts of the male gaze, in which the female figure is held for the pleasure of the male character/male spectator. This prologue, followed by a montage of the couple on holiday, is not in Garfield's novel. The addition creates a clear idyll to be contrasted with the later introduction to New York (heavily tinted and with an atonal sound that disrupts the previous non-diegetic soundtrack) but also establishes a conventional relationship between Kersey and his wife – married, heterosexual and with him in control (the only caveat being that Joanne insists they have sex in the hotel, not on the beach as they would have when they were younger). The establishing shots of New York that follow the Hawaii prologue also contain the film's titles and call attention to a traditional cinematic structure. The protagonist is clearly identified (the film's star, the main male character, whose gaze we share briefly), but the camera generally remains objective. The shot of the Kersey's cramped taxi ride (as opposed to the expansive Hawaii beach) highlights their situation and reaction, but the lack of over-shoulder or point-of-view shots avoids a total subjective alignment. The spectator, through clear focalization and cinematic technique, is hailed to see the film as a film within existing familiar traditions. Ironically, this approach is as distancing as it is inclusive; it simultaneously puts the spectator at ease (they will be able to follow the text) while reminding them of its obviously constructed nature. This is most evident in the scene in which Kersey watches a news report on his television. The report cuts from the interviewee narrating her own resistance to mugging, to a flashback of the events – something impossible for the TV news to do – a conventional narrative device that signals the constructed nature of the text.

---

[2]This dialogue foreshadows Kersey's use of clichéd Western phrases later in the film.

Taxi Driver opens, after several credits, with a low shot of a taxi emerging out of steam from manhole covers. This, however, is not a familiar image of the Yellow Cab, as Kolker observes: 'The smoke is yellowish, and the taxi that emerges from it is not so much moving as looming, viewed from a low angle and travelling at a speed too slow and regular for it to be an "actual" cab on the street' (1980: 187). This image, instantly familiar in iconography but unfamiliar in construction, suggests a tension between the known and unknown. As the titles continue, the film cuts abruptly to Bickle's eyes, held in close-up and saturated by red light. These eyes are restless, as the red vanishes and other neon colours flash. Although the cut leads the spectator (as does the film's title) to presuppose that these are the eyes of the taxi's driver, the image reflects and imitates the position of the spectator themselves, in which the colours of the screen project on their eyes. A triple gaze is suggested: an otherworldly view of the taxi, Bickle's restless gaze, the spectator's own. This relationship between reality and cinema is repeated throughout as 'Scorsese frames the world as if all of it is a movie. Inside his cab Travis is as much the spectator as he is in his seat in the nearly empty porn theatre. The windows and mirrors of the cab turn the real world into a reflection that he observes without being observed' (Taubin 2000: 24). The shot of Bickle's eyes is followed by one looking out of the windscreen of the taxi (the cut suggesting this is Bickle's point of view) now driving through the rain, disassociated from the previous image by the change in non-diegetic soundtrack and lighting. A cut brings a similar view, but here the image has been blurred, a gaze that has been distorted and distressed. Another shot again suggests point of view, watching people across a street. The steam imagery returns as does the red light. After another cut, we return to Bickle's eyes, again restless, again in a red light. The sequence ends with a dissolve through steam to the taxi office. Assessing the gaze in this sequence is problematic. There is no direct cause and effect between the images, rather a set of associations created through the montage aesthetic. The cuts between Bickle's eyes and the point-of-view shots suggest a direct relationship (of viewer and gaze), but the lack of specific context between subject and object undermines this. The light sources are unclear, as is the focus of Bickle's gaze. The moving eyes suggest an inability to settle. The very first shot, from a low angle, establishes the taxi as a central motif in the film's narrative (as does the title), but the lack of a clear view into the taxi disassociates it from the other images. Taubin explains this sequence: 'It suggests that what we're about to see is some kind of hybrid of an urban horror film, an urban road movie and a psychodrama with neo-noir overtones. It also suggests that the film will be dominated by a subjective point-of-view filtered by and reflected in the windows and mirrors of a taxi from hell' (2000: 34). The music similarly contorts meaning, switching from the film's brooding main theme to its love motif and back without clear association to the imagery, other than switching initially over Bickle's eyes. This suggests disassociation, as does the use of shifting film speeds. Here the spectator is not allowed to settle into a clear subject position (although in a different way to the multiple points of identification in *Straw Dogs*); instead, *Taxi Driver* questions the reality/authenticity of the subjective gaze. Further to this, the violation of established narrative form that the sequence represents invokes a dream-logic, an idea confirmed by Scorsese: 'Much of *Taxi Driver* arose from my feeling that movies are really a kind of dream state' (Thompson and Christie 1989: 54). Modality becomes a question here. Given the dreamlike opening, a suggestion of a lower modality is made. However, simultaneous to this is the understanding that an intensely subjective gaze is being constructed, in which reality is filtered through the protagonist's mental state.

These opening sequences serve to introduce the spectator to the films' narrative schemas but suggest differing points of identification and focalization. Each, however, directly forms a dialogue with the nature of the gaze, how characters look and are looked at. *Joe* highlights the centrality of Melissa as a figure of objectification, but one that is restless and lost with her own questioning, peering gaze while the film's suggested protagonist's gaze is rarely shared. *Straw Dogs* denies us a clear position but suggests themes of voyeurism. *The French Connection* uses a series of objective techniques, occasionally using subjective techniques to indicate identification. *Dirty Harry* provides an illegitimate gaze which is superseded by a similar, legitimate one. *Death Wish* stresses Kersey's heteronormative gaze towards his wife, the film clearly placing him as an active protagonist. *Taxi Driver* disregards a traditional shot construction by confusing the gaze of the spectator and the protagonist (in themselves and with each other). This range of gazes/points of identification invites the spectator to take several different positions in consideration of the films, points which develop as the narratives progress.

6

Functions of the gaze and identification

Having established how each film creates subject positions, we shall now go deeper in discussing how these positions are built upon and explored throughout the films, with questions of identification being explored more fully, and how the gaze shifts within the films, suggesting and complicating the relationship between the spectator and key characters. This includes, but is not limited to, the protagonists who are the main points of identification, and by questioning the spectator's relationship to them, we will further question the suggestion of settled ideological viewpoints.

The delayed introduction of Joe Curran acts partly as a hermeneutic code. Despite his centrality to the narrative image, his appearance is delayed until after twenty-six minutes in which the main causal elements of the plot (Melissa's relationship to Frank, Bill's murder of Frank) have already occurred. Previously Melissa has been the centre of the narrative (although as we have seen, she functions partly as an object), offering one insecure point of identification. The introduction of Bill, and his wife Joan, occurs at fifteen minutes. Their initial appearance demonstrates concern for their daughter, the scene taking place in a hospital. That the nurse is Black and clearly caring and competent helps to inflect the later introduction of Joe, creating a distance between the text and the character. The Currans' concern, however, is undermined in later scenes in which their desire for self-preservation overrides worries for their daughter. This unpicking of the sympathy for characters remains a predominant technique in *Joe*, in which early sympathy is undermined by later events. For Melissa this is done by proxy through her hippy friends and Frank; the former who are willing to steal and entertain Bill and Joe in return for drugs, the latter in his drug-dealing (which Melissa goes along with). Three ways of identifying with the film are created: one that follows Melissa (and by proxy the other hippies, suggesting sympathy for their murder, if not their actions), for Bill and Joan (whose concerns are primarily ones of class and status preservation) and finally Joe (and to some extent his wife Mary Lou (K. Callan)). I would suggest that the primary focus for identification is Bill (it is through his eyes that most of the narrative unfolds, especially his dealings with Joe), but the film allows for other identifications to be built, particularly with Joe as he is a more active protagonist than Bill (and we know from the film's narrative image that he has been cast as such, with the film's reception confirming that audiences identified him in this way).

The first words we hear Joe speak (addressed partly to the barman but also to the spectator through a close-up on his face) are

> The Niggers. The Niggers are getting all the money. Why work? You tell me. Why the fuck work when you can screw, have babies and get paid for it? Welfare, they get all that welfare money. They even get free rubbers. You think they use them? Hell no, the only way they make money is making babies. They sell the rubbers. And then they use the money to buy booze. Nobody has a right to booze unless they earn the money. It ought to be a law: you don't work, you don't drink. Yeah, the Social Workers, the ones in welfare, how come they're all Nigger lovers? You ever noticed that? All those Social Workers are Nigger-lovers. You find me a Social Worker that ain't a Nigger lover and I'll massage your asshole. And I ain't queer!

The rhetorical passage ends as Bill (who Joe also addresses as part of his general audience) enters the bar. The dynamics of the other people in this

FIGURE 9 *Joe passively stares at the screen (watching a Western) in* Joe *(Cannon Group, 1970).*

scene are important as they illustrate several things. No one responds to Joe. Indeed, the barman who makes up his putative audience walks away to take Bill's order. Joe continues to speak, with the camera taking an angle indicative of Bill's point of view. The content of the speech is provocative, including several fault lines in American culture (race relations, welfare, sex and homosexuality: '42% of all Liberals are queer. That's a fact. The Wallace[1] people did a poll.'), but it becomes background as soon as Bill enters the bar. The camera follows him to the phone, all the while Joe continues. When Bill leaves the bar, having accidentally confessed to killing Frank, the camera follows him returning to his car, then cuts to his home and Joan. The next cut brings us to Joe in his home watching TV (the show sounds like a Western). Figure 9 shows Joe's passive figure, his gaze fixed on the screen.

His blank face is open to interpretation – could his mind be on Bill's earlier confession? Or is it simply watching gormlessly? Joe's status here, and throughout, becomes problematic. Signalled by the narrative image as the protagonist, his introduction places him as a secondary point of identification to Bill. He espouses controversial rhetoric angrily (including his view on hippies), and it's clear that the other people in the bar are not interested (the barman going so far to give Joe a quarter to play the jukebox, so he quietens down). His mispronunciation of 'orgy', giving it a hard 'g', is comedic, suggesting he's a fool. How then can Joe represent a point of identification when much of his introduction seems clearly alienating and/ or ridiculous? From this point, the film becomes about Joe and his home life. We see him working in a foundry, then his relationship with Mary Lou (which is kindly). Their conversation begins about dinner, then she gives a detailed account of the soap operas she has watched. Things change when Mary Lou discusses their children (tellingly absent from the film) and the 'Coloured' people who have moved into the street. Joe retreats into his basement where he cleans his rifle. This sequence helps to articulate Joe's frustration and impotence, with his retreat to the basement a reaction to the changes in society around him (the shifting ethnicity of his neighbourhood, his son going out with a girl who wears an 'Indian headdress'). His anger dominates, with Mary Lou given the role of an appeaser. Here Joe's anger and frustration provide an avenue for identification, despite his alienating introduction. He also verbalizes opinions little heard in films. The spectator may not agree with all he says, but some will agree with some of it or at least recognize the problems that exist. However, this exists within the film's deliberate undermining of him in later scenes in which he is seen to be socially inept (much of the film shows class comedy between the Currans and the Comptons, with the Comptons' reactions being given primacy), violent and sexually disappointing (told by a young hippy girl that he 'just broke

---

[1] A reference to Governor George Wallace.

the world speed record' during sex). He is a figure of continual inadequacy, and his gun fetishism suggests a phallic anxiety. His initial speech couches his racial hatred in terms of sex, so too his hatred of hippies and their orgies. His class aspirations and worship of Bill suggest a hatred of his own situation and his low pay. Bill in turn becomes a spectator of Joe during their burgeoning friendship; Bill mitigates some of Joe's views and actions and Joe allows Bill to indulge his pleasure and satisfaction at killing Frank. *Joe* is complex in how it offers several points of alignment (in particular Joe and Bill) and offers several points of keying (Melissa, Joan, Mary Lou), but never gives a concrete sense of allegiance partly through the shared screen time of the main characters but also through the way the text undermines each of them.

As already explored, the opening scene of *Straw Dogs* suggests a variety of subject positions, despite the narrative image's placement of David Sumner as the protagonist. The overt manipulation of the spectator into multiple and contradictory perspectives continues, particularly in several scenes examined here. In these scenes, the act of looking is highlighted, particularly in the way that the gaze of certain characters penetrates and invades the farmhouse (foreshadowing the final siege). These invading gazes provide alternative viewpoints but also highlight issues with the representation of Amy and her body. Often this gaze is voyeuristic and scopophilic. Mulvey explains there are

> two contradictory aspects of the pleasure structures of looking in the conventional cinematic situation. The first, scopophilic, arises from the pleasure in using another person as an object of sexual stimulation through sight. The second, developed through narcissism and the constitution of the ego, comes from identification with the image seen. Thus, in film terms, one implies a separation of the erotic identity of the subject from the object on screen (active scopophilia), the other demands identification of the ego with the subject on the screen through the spectator's recognition of his like. (1975: 487)

It makes sense, therefore, to take a twofold approach in this discussion: identifying elements of scopophilic separation and those of ego identification. Amy stands as the primary object of the scopophilic gaze (as per the opening sequence), and at various points in the film is subject to David and the villagers' gazes, as well as that of the spectator. The simplicity of this is questioned, however, by the ways in which the spectator is encouraged to identify with Amy (such as the subjective montage technique used in the rape scene and the church fête), and the fact that the gaze that regards her is not always voyeuristic (she is often aware of it). This awareness of the gaze has implications for where power is located in the relationship of subject and object. Added to this is the ambivalence and ambiguity of

David. His behaviours are consistently distancing for the spectator through his motivations, actions and his gaze. Despite his status as the nominal protagonist, his role as the point for ego identification is constantly problematized.[2]

Amy's body is a site of desire and conflict throughout the film. In some senses the violation of her body, both literally and voyeuristically, mirrors the situation of the farmhouse. That the workmen (Venner, Scutt, etc.) desire her is signalled in several ways: reaction shots that show the desire on their faces, the rape scene, Scutt's attempt at another rape during the siege, and the theft of her underwear by Chris Cawsey. This is not to say that the film invites the spectator to be complicit in these gazes. The first shot of Amy, as explored earlier, suggests the scopic gaze as it places her body before her face. Later this is queried via Amy's role in relation to the workmen's gaze. During the scene when Amy returns to the farmhouse (on twenty-seven minutes) she exits her car, adjusting her tights as she does so. The workmen (shown in a reaction shot) plainly stare at her. Amy enters the house upset and complains to David that 'They were practically licking my body'. David's indifferent response provokes her to go upstairs and take a bath. As she proceeds to the bathroom, she removes her jumper, revealing her naked chest. At this point she pauses by a window in full view of the workmen (violating David's earlier demand that she closes the curtains). The workmen look at her; she looks back and then continues to the bathroom. The spectator is offered two views here, that of the workmen and that of Amy. A third could be included when considering that the sequence eschews any particular point of view, a voyeuristic gaze is suggested but not one that aligns with the characters, as illustrated in Figure 10.

A low angle has shown that the workmen are on a rooftop, whereas in this shot the camera is placed low alongside the car. This view is one that only the spectator experiences and is also more revealing than previous shots from the workmen's point of view, here showing Amy's underwear. The alignment with the workmen is broken, as the spectator is given a more invasive angle. This perhaps makes the spectator complicit with the workmen's voyeurism, and it certainly signals the manipulation of the spectator's gaze. This is perhaps symbolic of the workmen's desire/fantasy, but it is broken by her reaction and discussion with David. The subsequent sequence where she undresses upstairs offers an overt view of her body to the spectator first, then as she moves to the window (Figure 11), the workmen's view is invoked, then confirmed in a reaction shot.

---

[2] I should make it clear that I make no assumptions in this analysis of the audience's sex. As Carol Clover points out, identification is much more complicated than women identifying with women and men with men, although this does not contradict the idea of a male subject position (1992: 20).

FIGURE 10 *A privileged view of Amy. Although the workmen's gaze is suggested, this angle is impossible from their position.* Straw Dogs *(Cinerama Releasing Corporation, 1971).*

FIGURE 11 *An act of provocation or defiance or both? Ignoring David's instruction to close the curtains, Amy pauses in front of the workmen, actively engaging the gaze she complained about before.* Straw Dogs *(Cinerama Releasing Corporation, 1971).*

Rather than being the voyeuristic gaze suggested when Amy was in the car, here she is presented as in control of the gaze, both that of the spectator and the workmen. This creates a tension between scopophilic desire and ego identification. This act by Amy is one of defiance towards David (ignoring his instruction), reinforced by her throwing her jumper onto him, but the image of Amy in the window does not suggest exhibitionism per se because of her posture and facial expression. The provocation comes from her semi-nudity and the implied gaze of the workmen, but her actions simultaneously question her erotic role.

Amy's status as the object of the gaze is, of course, only one side of the equation. How she is looked at is also an essential consideration. In *Way of Seeing*, John Berger set out an established formula for the presentation of women and men in art in which

> Men act and women appear. Men look at women. Women watch themselves being looked at. This determines not only the relations between men and women but also the relation of women to themselves. The surveyor of woman in herself is male: the surveyed female. Thus, she turns herself into an object – and most particularly an object of vision: a sight. (1972: 47)

A key idea here is the representation of Amy as a woman who watches herself 'being looked at'. Amy's face bears witness to others' gazes; she is acutely aware of her status as an object of the gaze. Returning to the sequence when she exits the car and subsequently shows herself by the window, we see a clear structure of a privileged gaze of the audience (the low angle on her legs/her removing her jumper), then the worker's reaction, then her reaction to their gazing. She is aware of the gaze, constructing herself as 'a sight'. This status as an object to be looked at is later transgressed when she is raped by Venner and Scutt. Events are then initiated that cause the siege. Similarly, Niles kills Janice when she allows his gaze for her to become tactile. (Ironically, he does not look at her when he strangles her – his attention is elsewhere as he fears discovery, of being seen with her.) Looking is one thing, moving beyond looking leads to destructive events. A question then remains: Is Amy responsible for this, or is this structure an inevitability in this masculine-dominated society? It is notable that there are few women with speaking roles in the film, and that the Heddon family is motherless. Stephen Prince discusses the importance of the anthropologist Robert Ardrey on Peckinpah: 'Like Peckinpah, Ardrey argued the folly of denying the inevitability of violence in all human groups' (1998: 105). Is Amy a provocateur who deserves her fate as many of the critics would suggest? Or, in highlighting the invasive gazes that she is subjected to, does the film reveal the inherent violent threat contained within the gaze without seeking to endorse it? The subjective montage during the rape, and the later flashbacks, attests to the latter. Amy's emotional response (albeit confused) is at the heart of these sequences. The spectator is invited to share the workmen's gaze, a sharing that implicats the spectator in the same desire and the violence that follows. This is not a comfortable concept. As Barr (1972) explained, the spectator is not allowed to remain at a safe distance; they are close to these actions and therefore implicated by them.

Trencher's Farm is the film's main location and is where the most significant events take place. It is consistently a site of conflict, both large and small; between David and Amy, between David and the Reverend Hood, when Amy is raped, and the final siege. It is also a site that helps us integrate how the gaze functions in *Straw Dogs* as it is continually invaded by various gazes (through doors and windows), consistently drawing attention to its penetrated nature. The difference between the interior and exterior is also key, with the effect this has on the gaze made clear. Figure 12 illustrates David's point of view out of one of the farmhouse windows.

This image relates back to David's squinting in the opening sequence and helps represent his general ignorance (confirmed by his absence during the rape scene). Figure 13 shows an example of David's poor gaze, as he strains to see out of the farmhouse.

This functions as a metaphor for his lack of knowledge and awareness. This screenshot also places the urbanite figure of David inside a rural home space. (The gingham curtains could be a reference to the Western farmhouse.) We return here to the concept of the farmhouse as a feminine space, part of the civilization-versus-wilderness opposition from the Western. David's

FIGURE 12 *David's gaze from inside the farmhouse, in* Straw Dogs *(Cinerama Releasing Corporation, 1971).*

FIGURE 13 *David squints as he looks through the farmhouse window, signalling his poor gaze, in* Straw Dogs *(Cinerama Releasing Corporation, 1971).*

placement within the space is clearly uncomfortable (as Amy reminds him, 'Every chair is my daddy's chair', not his), and the house can be seen as representative of emasculation, especially in the mantrap/vagina dentate that sits above the hearth (given as a present from Amy to David). What then of identification? If we are to align ourselves with the nominal protagonist David, it is to align with a character who is blind to the situation in which he lives.

The gazes that penetrate the household, and that hold Amy in scopophilic interest, offer other possible routes for identification. Despite the subjective montage technique used during the rape sequence, placing Amy's emotional reaction to the fore, other scenes do suggest some alignment with the workmen, the Heddon family and their associated group. Twenty minutes into the film, a scene occurs that raises the question of identification with these men but creates a sense of alienation from them by suggesting that their gaze is unnatural. In this sequence, brother and sister Bobby and Janice Heddon spy on Amy and David, who are preparing for bed. From this hidden point of view they watch David undress, and we are given a clearly voyeuristic angle, as seen in Figure 14.

The mirror allows fuller access to the bedroom, with the reflected view used several times in the scene. Cuts between David and Amy, and Janice and Bobby, allow for two points into which the spectator can project themselves. The two areas, however, remain distinct. David and Amy are here private, unknowingly displaying their anxieties and the tension in their marriage (seen in his exercises and their chess game). Amy's glasses suggest her attempt

FIGURE 14 *David undresses, seen from Janice and Bobby's point of view*, in Straw Dogs *(Cinerama Releasing Corporation, 1971)*.

to project an intellectual image to match David (who teases her about the chess). The subsequent love scene begins in humour after David has rejected Amy's approaches. He gains control first by rebuffing and belittling her, then mock searching for a missing chess piece, then physically asserting himself over her (literally lying above her) and taking sexual control (this is done to his, not her, agenda). The view outside, from Janice and Bobby, provides a complex imitation of this. At first, Janice is alone. Bobby surprises her, mock throttling her from behind (an act of control, and a foreshadowing of Janice's death). Janice's response is humoured, suggesting a normality to this violent approach (which perhaps foreshadows Amy's own conflict in the rape scene, and her throttling by Niles). Their talk has a coy but sexual nature; 'Do you fancy him?' Bobby asks. 'He's sweet, I think' answers Janice. Here David becomes the object of Janice's gaze. (Amy is mostly in bed and covered during the scene.) As Amy and David begin to have sex, Janice becomes more excited and Bobby draws closer to her, suggesting a mutual arousal and an incestual link between them. Janice's gaze has become deeply problematic here: although her desire for David may be considered normal, her sexual closeness to her brother is not. This leaves the spectator with few choices. Inside the farm, we are experiencing David's power game and anxieties. Outside, we are exposed to aberrant desires. The incestual theme is echoed throughout the local Cornish community. Janice's desire for David (notice it isn't physical but rather because he is 'sweet', suggesting the local men aren't) is later problematized when he rejects her attentions at the fête, and she moves on to Niles, who murders her.

The Cornish community is deliberately drawn to be alienating. Clover outlines a type of family that appears in 1970s Horrors such as *Deliverance* (John Boorman, 1972), *The Texas Chainsaw Massacre* (Tobe Hooper, 1974) and *The Hills Have Eyes* (Wes Craven, 1977):

> In horror country dwellers are disproportionately represented by adult males with no ascertainable family attachments. . . . These men do no discernible work and are commonly shown lying about the home farm in the middle of a workday – usually singly, sometimes in groups. When we do see country families, something is always terribly wrong with them. One standard problem is a weak or missing father and correspondingly too-powerful mother. . . . More commonly, however, the problem is patriarchy run amok. (1992: 125)

There are conspicuously few mothers in *Straw Dogs* and few women at all. Tom Heddon, chief agitator at the siege, is Clover's unproductive male (with no job to speak of), and the workmen are slow and eventually dismissed. The village pub is an area in which they congregate, one into which women do not go often, standing in for the home farm. The village is presided over by Major Scott, a patriarchal (though physically debilitated) figure of law, who conflicts with Tom Heddon's opposing father figure. John Niles, Henry's father, is ineffectual, failing to rein in his son. Amy pointedly refers to her father but never her mother. As Clover describes, the result of this male-dominated culture in which 'patriarchy has run amok' is that 'One way or another, in short, country parents produce psychosexually deformed children. The ubiquity of degenerate specimens (the retarded Matthew of *I Spit on Your Grave*, the genetically deficient banjo player in *Deliverance*, Henry in *Straw Dogs*) is the material expression of family wrongness (inbreeding being one form of wrongness)' (1992: 125). Having established the village as such a place, it is unlikely that its inhabitants become a secure or wanted site of identification for the spectator. To do so would be to link themselves to a society of incestuous degenerates. This leaves us with the putative protagonist David. As we have seen, his gaze lacks clarity (both figuratively and literally).

As already established, *The French Connection* generally eschews a direct subjective camera and establishes an objective, documentary/news footage style. This is significant given that the film is overtly concerned with looking and the power of the gaze. Drawing from elements of the Police Procedural, a great deal of the film presents the 'real' activities of the Police, such as the stake-out scenes. This concentration on verisimilitude establishes high modality but detaches sequences from the narrative drive. This sense of detachment lacks a focus for the spectator, which correspondingly could create problems with identification. However, the spectator has been primed by the narrative image to identify Doyle as the protagonist, and as the film develops, he emerges clearly as such, but this identification proves problematic when we consider the nature of Doyle's characterization. Throughout *The French Connection* Doyle engages with practices that are problematic with regard to identification and pleasure. This includes overt racism (towards Black, Italian American and French people), his past being brought into question (with the suggestion he has killed a colleague), and how he chases and harasses single women. To further our understanding, an appreciation of identification, as linked to Lacan's mirror stage via Metz, is useful. Fuery outlines this:

> Metz is concerned with a truly Lacanian project, which includes the analysis of the positioning of the subject in relation to the cinematic signifier. This leads him to the theme of the mirror, and specifically to Lacan's theory of the mirror stage. Metz's theorising (at times via Jean-Louis Baudry) on how identification operates, and for what reasons, commences with a comparative positioning of the spectator of a film and the formation of the subject through the mirror stage. The self-reflexivity of the mirror stage becomes the self-consciousness of the spectator as he/she negotiates the position of the self in terms of the film and meaning. This allows Metz to make the conceptual leap that identification for the film spectator is actually a self-identification. (2000: 25)

Does Doyle provide this mirror for the spectator? It is questionable when we consider how the film simultaneously aligns and alienates (and, of course, the subject does not have to like what they see in the mirror). This suggests an interaction of objectivity and subjectivity, or 'intersubjectivity' (Brannigan 1992: 101). Whereas *Straw Dogs* suggested a range of subjective views, *The French Connection* directs the spectator through the process of external focalization, inferring identification with the protagonist rather than directing it. Combined with the film's narrative image in which the spectator has already been primed to both identify and be alienated by Doyle ('Doyle is bad news – but a good cop'), *The French Connection* avoids direct identification. Instead, the film offers a complex system of identification that balances an overall objectivity with subjective elements and suggests the spectator understands the film through allegiance, rather than alignment. This structure allows identification with Doyle but also allows for a significant distance in which the spectator does not have to identify continuously. Returning to the scene in which Doyle is introduced, we find a clear example of this element of identification. Throughout the early parts of the scene, it is Russo, not Doyle, who is most active. Like us, Doyle is a witness to events. As the scene develops, Doyle becomes more aggressive and active. His Santa-Claus suit and positioning in the frame give him more space on-screen, and he is taller than Russo and their suspect. Even though Doyle is in the background, he dominates the frame, with the positioning of the characters making a clear lead for the eye to him. This domination of the frame continues, making Doyle the more active of the two possible protagonists (Doyle and Russo) and narrative convention (along with the narrative image) confirms this.

The manipulation of the gaze throughout the film also helps to align the spectator with Doyle, and to a lesser extent Russo (who operates as an alternate point of identification, another subjectivity who, at times, objects to Doyle but most often acts as a supporter). Partly this is accomplished through an opposition formed with the antagonist in the film, Charnier. Charnier's qualities hold many of Doyle's in relief. Much of this links to voyeurism, a central concern in a film that uses objective techniques (that 'hide' the construction of the film) and one that follows an investigation in which looking for evidence is a central concern. Mulvey suggests that voyeurism 'has associations with sadism: pleasure lies in ascertaining guilt (immediately associated with castration), asserting control, and subjecting the guilty person through punishment or forgiveness' (1975: 14). The nature of Doyle's work is voyeuristic, suggesting an element of power and knowledge. This the spectator shares through allegiance, but the limitations of this gaze, and of Doyle's, are also exposed.

The main gaze in the film is established as Doyle's after the opening in a sequence where he and Russo attend a nightclub (based on Doyle's hunch; he ignores Russo's knife injury in his determination). Despite Doyle's methods being called into question throughout the film, especially by Mulderig, the demands of the narrative dictate his effectiveness. This legitimizes Doyle's gaze even when it contravenes laws. This is illustrated in a moment of external focalization in the nightclub. Although no optical point of view is offered, the alignment with Doyle can be inferred from the structure of the sequence, cutting from Doyle's face (Figure 15) to the object of his gaze.

Variation in sound levels in this sequence, implying distance from Doyle, emphasizes alignment. The close-up on Bocca emphasizes the power in Doyle's gaze: his attention to detail and his precision, but also his obsession. Due to narrative and genre convention, the spectator associates power with this view, knowing this will lead somewhere. This adds a legitimacy to Doyle's voyeurism that otherwise would be lacking (a similar association occurs in *Rear Window* (Alfred Hitchcock, 1954) where LB Jeffries's spying on his neighbours becomes morally legitimate when his fantasy of murder comes true. Just as the narrative of *Rear Window* requires a murder to allow our identification with Jeffries to be sustained and legitimized, so the narrative of *The French Connection* requires Doyle's suspicions to be proven right).

Mulvey (1975) discusses how the gaze operates from a position of power in which the subject who gazes controls the object which is looked at. Although Mulvey's analysis is directed towards a feminist critique of

FIGURE 15 *Doyle gazes in* The French Connection *(20th Century Fox, 1971)*.

Classical Hollywood cinema, in which the male/female division is seen as one of active/passive and bearer of the look/spectacle, the correlation between looking and power is clearly active in *The French Connection* in the opposition of Doyle and Charnier. Voyeuristic power depends on secrecy, on the gaze being unknown. However, and despite early success, Doyle's gaze is repeatedly manipulated by Charnier, reversing the power structure. This then corresponds to the spectator's gaze. Having aligned with Doyle, they are then simultaneously distanced from it. This is most evident in the sequence where Charnier dines in a restaurant and Doyle watches from across the street. This sequence also intensifies their opposition, recalling the opposition between civilization (the urbane Charnier) and wilderness (the wild and misbehaving Doyle). We can see in Figure 16 Charnier and Nicoli enjoying a fine dining experience.

In the centre of the frame, Doyle huddles in a doorway. This conforms to the nature of the sequence, a stake-out, and the contrast suggests the unrelenting nature of Doyle's work (and obsession). Cross-cutting in this sequence, in which Charnier enjoys luxuries such as wine, isolates Doyle outside in the cold (a contrast intensified when he bites, then throws away, a piece of flaccid pizza). Doyle knows where Charnier is, but no shot suggests the reverse. Doyle then follows Charnier into the subway where Charnier's gaze is increasingly emphasized. Figure 17 illustrates this as he looks into the mirrored surface.

A reversal then follows in which the supposed power conferred on Doyle by his gaze is shown to be a sham, as Charnier fools Doyle into embarking then disembarking a subway train. The final reveal of Charnier (gazing

FIGURE 16 *While Charnier and Nicoli dine, Doyle stands in the background of* The French Connection *(20th Century Fox, 1971).*

FIGURE 17 *Charnier uses the mirror – he controls the gaze, in* The French Connection *(20th Century Fox, 1971).*

through the train window seen in Figure 18) illustrates his power: Doyle and the spectator have been manipulated all along.

This sequence provides some key meanings for the function of the gaze in *The French Connection*. Previously the film has constructed a gaze of which Charnier is unaware, placing power with Doyle. This sequence

FIGURE 18 *Charnier waves at Doyle, and us, expressing his power and manipulation of the gaze in* The French Connection *(20th Century Fox, 1971).*

reverses that sense of power: Doyle is not following, but rather being led. Despite Doyle's attempts to evade identification (removing his hat and coat), Charnier easily loses him on the subway. Doyle has become the object of Charnier's gaze, instantly unmanning him. This, by proxy, likewise turns the spectator into the object. The distance we have kept from Doyle, through allegiance rather than alignment, is intensified here. Moments of subjectivity are used throughout to focus our allegiance on Doyle, and this sequence intensifies our sympathies. However, the use of objective techniques, so that full alignment does not take place, allows Doyle's problematic behaviours to remain distanced.

The resistance/manipulation of Doyle's gaze remains throughout the film as Charnier escapes. Despite a reclaiming of power by Doyle (signalled by his discovery of the drugs in the car and in his imitative wave to Charnier before the final raid), Charnier is not caught. Indeed, Doyle's gaze fails once again when he shoots Mulderig, mistaking him for Charnier. Doyle's refusal to stop at this moment, continuing his pursuit, suggests desperation and a complete castration of his power (reinforced by the credits delineating his fate). Throughout the film, Charnier has retained power over Doyle, despite Doyle's gaze. In the sequence where Doyle chases Nicoli (in car and train respectively), shots repeatedly emphasize Doyle's persistent gaze as he follows his suspect. The sequence ends as Doyle shoots Nicoli. Charnier exists beyond this gaze; therefore, he cannot be controlled. As an ending, this is deeply problematic for the spectator. Their sympathies have been with Doyle. However, the distance retained in the film, through the objective techniques and an emphasis on allegiance, not alignment, allows the spectator a mental get-out. The film fades as Doyle continues pursuing Charnier, his fate told through text rather than action.[3]

In *Dirty Harry* we have already seen how the film creates parallel gazes between Callahan and Scorpio, with the former being typed as legitimate and the latter illegitimate (in respect of what they gaze on, and the pleasure, or not, they gain from this). In exploring this further, we can see how the film continues in the same vein as the opening sequence in developing this. It is clear, throughout the film, that both Callahan and Scorpio are voyeurs, and both gain power from their gazes. However, before investigating this in detail, it is worth discussing how the dedication that opens the film addresses the spectator. The camera pans and tilts slowly over a memorial to San Francisco Police Officers. The dedication reads, 'In tribute to the police officers of San Francisco who gave their lives in the line of duty.' This tribute suggests a direct link between the film and reality; this is a real memorial with real names. The earliest date, in 1878, ties the film directly to history. This connection with reality is further conveyed by Siegel's shooting style, using recognizable public locations (such as Golden Gate Park and Kezar Stadium), with natural lighting aiding this. But the dedication both reinforces and alienates us from ideas of high modality by invoking the fictions of the Western genre through the date of 1878, reinforced by the casting of Eastwood. It suggests that the film takes place within a real world, but that the narrative is drawing on existing generic structures and fictions. The seven-pointed star on the board is as much a convention of the Western as is the saloon. A tension is created as reality and fiction are collapsed. The star fades to Scorpio's rifle, an intrusion into this nostalgia. The opening sequence sees Scorpio use a telescopic lens to target a lone female swimmer. This 'normal' act of looking is contrasted with Scorpio's abnormal desire to kill the object of the gaze. Later in the film Callahan re-enacts this twice, one while being a 'Peeping Tom', another while using binoculars to search an area of San Francisco for Scorpio. Callahan's gaze, unknown and from a position above, imitates Scorpio. However, his goals and engagement suggest difference.

In the first instance of Callahan's voyeuristic gaze, the object is 'Hot' Mary, who Callahan spies after following a suspect down an alleyway. Watching through a window, as in Figure 19, he finds that the suspect is not the killer but a man returning home.

With Callahan's face hidden and his eye staring through the gap between the curtain and the window frame, voyeurism is clearly shown. This view is

---

[3]It is worth noting that *The French Connection II* (John Frankenheimer, 1975) was advertised on some posters with the tagline 'This is the climax!' acknowledging the problems that some spectators experienced with the lack of traditional closure.

FIGURE 19 *Callahan spies on 'Hot' Mary in* Dirty Harry *(Warner Bros, 1971).*

replicated in a reverse angle from Callahan's point of view, the net curtain in the foreground. Despite it being clear that this lead is not helpful, Callahan lingers, straining to stay balanced on a trash can and preserve his view. His gaze is finally broken when members of the public attack him, denouncing him as a 'lousy Peeping Tom', a phrase that echoes Callahan's own words to the mayor when he discusses investigating 'prowlers and peepers'. This moment exposes Callahan's voyeurism, somewhat undermining his gaze, but also legitimizes it by confirming his heterosexuality (as opposed to the problematized sexuality of Scorpio). The object of his gaze is well known to the men who attack him, and her epithet 'Hot' Mary confirms her as a known object of desire. As Callahan scuffles with the men, she leans out the window showing herself naked from the waist up. This act of brazen display suggests a want or desire to be seen. The attack on Callahan, which stops when Gonzalez appears, suggests to us that the power of the gaze is not total – Callahan's desire to watch is what makes him vulnerable.

A later scene involves Callahan and Gonzalez on stake-out hoping to bait Scorpio out into the open, and imitates the opening of the film in several ways: Callahan's point of view is a clear subjective angle focalizing on his reactions. (We never see his partner's view on events in this sequence.) The binoculars frame recalls the telescopic lens from earlier, but Callahan's gaze is not fixed, it roams. After following several people, Callahan's gaze comes upon a window in which he spies a young woman seen in Figure 20.

He watches as she disappears from view, then reappears naked and lets two visitors enter the apartment. His reaction to this is unclear. At first, he appears disgusted. However, he then smiles and says, 'You owe it to yourself to live a little, Harry.' He renews his gaze, only to have it interrupted by the noise of a door opening. His reaction is significant. He is willing to be distracted from his job and this clearly links, in his dialogue, the act of looking to pleasure. In a similar way to the earlier scene with 'Hot' Mary, he

FUNCTIONS OF THE GAZE AND IDENTIFICATION

FIGURE 20 *Callahan's point of view takes the scopic gaze during* Dirty Harry *(Warner Bros, 1971).*

is diverted, and his gaze is interrupted (as is the spectator's). Are we being saved from our own desire to look at her? Both moments are extraneous to the plot but do suggest a heterosexual desire on behalf of Callahan, one that stands at odds with Scorpio, whose gaze targets different sexes and sexualities, and in this scene, he looks through binoculars, not a telescopic lens on a rifle. Callahan's gaze is not destructive, whereas Scorpio's targets women, gay men, priests and children all the same and in ways that suggest sexual gratification conflated with violence.

Although we are initially aligned with Scorpio in the opening sequence by point of view, a simultaneous distancing occurred as we were also the object of his gaze (albeit briefly at the beginning). During the opening his identity is largely hidden. During his second, but failed, attack we are given a clearer view and the subjective gaze has moved to an objective one. Given an androgynous appearance (round face and long hair), Scorpio collects several signifiers that work against each other to defy obvious interpretation. He is introduced in this sequence with a close-up on his highly polished military boots, and his handling of his rifle suggests professionalism[4] although later in the film he sports a peace sign as a belt buckle and his

---

[4]Director Don Siegel suggests this about Scorpio: 'No verbal exposition is ever given, but to those who might have questioned his strange attire, it is possible that in his tilted fashion he could have returned from Vietnam bearing a crazed grudge' (Siegel 1993: 370). Generally, however, Scorpio is read simply as representing the countercultural left, despite his targets, opposing him against the 'right' Callahan. Street, however, suggests that Scorpio's living conditions may make him one of San Francisco's 'indigent poor' made homeless by urban renewal (2016: 77–8).

long hair places him within the counterculture fashion. In this sequence the target of his scopic gaze is now a Black male homosexual. Is this desire, or a technique to alienate the spectator from Scorpio's gaze? Initially while his gaze was heterosexual, we were allowed to share it. Here we are distanced from him as both his appearance and his choice of target violate norms of the masculine gaze. As the potential victim flirts with another man, we are given Scorpio's point of view, again through the telescopic lens, but repeated cuts to his face and his emotions of frustration when his target walks out of view and pleasure when he re-emerges are distancing. The implication of non-heteronormative desire takes the initial alignment that was offered and renders it impossible. Considering this, Callahan's heteronormative/ heterosexual desires increase their attraction. Later Scorpio's sexual pleasure becomes apparent when he taunts Callahan over the size of his gun. He is further made non-normative through his high-pitched scream when stabbed in the leg by Callahan, and the pleasure he displays in being beaten by a Black man he has paid to do this (and who he racially taunts to increase the level of violence).

Later in the film, both Callahan's and Scorpio's gazes are drawn together when Callahan follows Scorpio around San Francisco. The places they visit, including a children's playground and a strip-bar, show the unnatural elements in Scorpio's gaze. Here Callahan's gaze becomes overtly controlling as Scorpio tries to evade it – only when Callahan's gaze is removed at the bequest of his superiors can Scorpio commit crimes again. This relationship, however, with Scorpio as bearer of the look, reasserts his unnaturalness, placing him into the feminine position implied by his soft features and long hair. At this point Callahan is drawn as normative, due to the extremity of Scorpio – therefore his gaze feels normative too, despite the excesses.

Of all the films in this study, *Death Wish* received the most condemnation from critics and the most simplistic criticism. These reactions are flawed, however, as they rely on surface reading of the narrative and ignore issues of how the spectator is interpellated. The film reads initially as a revenge narrative, reinforced by the rape scene as a causal event for Paul Kersey's actions. This, however, fails to notice that Kersey does not pursue the people responsible for the death of his wife and maiming of his daughter. It also avoids the complex debate on the media's relationship with crime that takes place. Essential to this is the spectator's relationship with Paul Kersey, and how they are, or are not, asked to align with him. The structure of the film offers what at first seems a simple level of focalization. We see, in the Hawaii opening, the opening shot, an implied point of view through Kersey's eyes of his wife. The remainder of the film generally avoids this. Typically, the film uses long or medium shot through a wide-angle lens. The spectator is also placed in a position of power over Kersey. The spectator watches the attack on his family, Kersey does not. Indeed, he is the last to know (informed by his son-in-law who is drawn in the film as generally inadequate and impotent).

FIGURE 21 *A powerless Paul Kersey observes the hospital in* Death Wish *(Paramount Pictures, 1974).*

Kersey, on his return to New York from Hawaii, is addressed as someone ignorant of the true nature of the city, described by his colleague Sam as a 'bleeding-heart liberal' for expressing sympathy for the 'underprivileged'. Kersey's boss reinforces this in his description of the city as 'the war-zone'. There is something impotent about Kersey himself in his lack of knowledge, ordered by his son-in-law (who calls him Dad) to meet him at the hospital. During this sequence Kersey is consistently passive, baffled by the events around him. Figure 21 shows his isolation and exclusion as he sits in a hospital waiting room.

But this is also the moment that Kersey's view of the world begins to change. He spies an injured man, stating: 'There's a man over there, he's bleeding. Nobody comes.' A close-up on his face is now used as he is given the news of his wife's death. At this point the spectator's relationship with Kersey is problematic. The filming techniques are largely objective, only moving to the close-ups on Kersey's face at the end of the sequence. We remain superior to him in our knowledge, both of the attack as it happened and our understanding that something like that would happen from the narrative image. However, this is undercut by the casting of Bronson, who remains, intertextually, a strong and dominant figure.

From the funeral onwards, the relationship between Kersey and New York and Kersey and the spectator shifts. He visits a Police precinct, and the camera uses more over-shoulder and reaction shots. He/we are exposed to the victims and suspects of crime. Then, twenty minutes into the film, a change occurs in Kersey's gaze, one that the spectator is invited to share. At

FIGURE 22 *Kersey watches TV resting in a passive pose in* Death Wish *(Paramount Pictures, 1974)*.

FIGURE 23 *Becoming active Kersey look out of his window in* Death Wish *(Paramount Pictures, 1974)*.

first Kersey watches TV slumped on his sofa as an advert plays for a bank. The voice-over for the advert asks, 'Are you getting the most out of life? Are you satisfied, fulfilled, happy?' The idea of artifice is interrogated here as Kersey moves from looking at the TV set and takes a place looking through a different screen, his window, as illustrated in Figures 22 and 23.

FIGURE 24 *Kersey admires the Wild West show in Tucson in* Death Wish *(Paramount Pictures, 1974)*.

It presents a separate window/screen into which Kersey looks. An opposition is created between his views of each screen, as if one is more real than the other, as if he is finally seeing reality. This is counterpointed, however, by the spectator's knowledge that all in the film is artificial. Kersey, now standing, sees a gang vandalize a car. Previously we have seen him in cars, in offices, behind glass in the hospital. As he leans through his window, past the liminal space of the frame, he emerges from his ignorance and becomes possessor of the active gaze. This sits closely with the active scopic gaze seen in the opening sequence of the film where the spectator shares Kersey's gaze. In between this scene and the opening, a distancing of the spectator from Kersey has occurred, one that imitates his own distancing from the reality that surrounds him. When he looks through his window, Kersey and the spectator are realigned. Another notable scene of spectatorship occurs in Tucson when Kersey chooses, at Jainchill's invitation, to watch a Wild West show. The location, a sometime film-set, signals an obvious artifice, as does the crowd of tourists (from which Kersey and Jainchill stand apart), and the echoing shows dialogue broadcast from the loudspeakers. Kersey's reactions and engagement with the show are evident through repeated close-ups in which he becomes more involved, even flinching when the false punches are thrown. Unlike the other spectators, including Jainchill, he does not clap at the show, he simply admires. The slight low angle elevates Kersey, connoting a new power as seen in Figure 24.

This power is confirmed when Jainchill takes Kersey to his shooting range. Using a vintage pistol (owned by a gunfighter) Kersey shows prowess with the gun, hitting the target dead centre first time. He then relates a

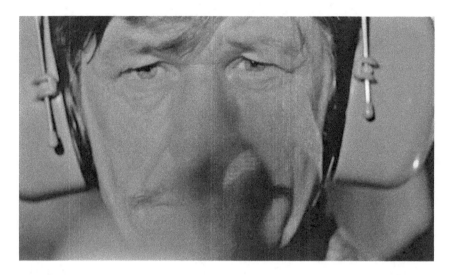

FIGURE 25 *Kersey's powerful gaze. The gun blurs to almost disappearing, highlighting his vision. He hits the target dead centre.* Death Wish *(Paramount Pictures, 1974).*

story about his relationship to guns, a negative one as his father was killed after being 'mistaken for a deer' by a hunter. The implication is clear. The gaze is powerful, but it must be looking in the right direction, as shown in Figure 25.

More than the other films, *Taxi Driver* develops a commentary on the nature of the gaze. Narrative and the subjective gaze are collapsed by an intense focalization through the protagonist Travis Bickle. This involves his presence in all but one scene, subjective camera techniques, and Bickle's voice-over that comments on the narrative, giving insight into his mind. Screens feature conspicuously: the windscreen of Bickle's taxi, the cinema screen in the porno-theatre, the TV and the mirror in Bickle's apartment. The relationship of the spectator to the screen is questioned throughout because Bickle *is* a spectator too. When he first enters a porno-theatre, the camera lingers on the projection equipment, reminding the spectator of their own position in relation to the cinematic apparatus. Never do we see the object of Bickle's gaze within these theatres; Bickle himself becomes the object of our gaze. Despite our subjective relationship with Bickle, the film, at times, reminds the spectator of their own distance from the screen. In two scenes director Scorsese appears. The second of these, in Bickle's taxi, we have previously discussed. The first occurs when he appears as an extra who stares at Betsy, alongside Bickle's gaze (and the gaze the spectator shares with him). This is the first moment the boundaries between screen and reality collapse. In Figure 26, we can see how multiple

FUNCTIONS OF THE GAZE AND IDENTIFICATION   187

FIGURE 26 *Scorsese, in the background as an extra, gazes at Betsy. This shot, from Bickle's point of view, is a clear subjective angle. However, Scorsese's appearance suggests both a parallel with Bickle and a distance. Like Bickle, his gaze follows her as she moves while Bickle's voice-over intones, 'They cannot touch her.'* Taxi Driver *(Columbia Pictures, 1976).*

gazes occupy the same space while simultaneously the mechanism of the gaze is invoked.

This moment occurs in slow motion with Bickle's voice-over explaining that 'They cannot touch her'. Who are *they* in this scenario? Literally the situation of the spectator is one in which touching is impossible, an invocation of Metz's imaginary signifier. The power of the gaze is suggested, but also its impotence. Later Bickle spies on Betsy while she is in Palantine's campaign office. He sits in his taxi drinking coffee using the same style of cup he drinks from in the porno-theatre. The implication is that both situations are the same. When Betsy appears at a distance, she seems perfect, the scopic object of the cinema screen. Later when she eats coffee and pie with Bickle, he stumbles, unable to communicate with her. Confronted with reality, rather than a screen image, he cannot cope. The fantasy he has created cannot be sustained by the real Betsy.

This division between gazing and the confrontation that results when the screen is removed repeatedly occurs in *Taxi Driver*. The spectator is continually reminded of the simultaneous control/impotence their gaze has. A notable shot occurs when the camera pans from Bickle on a phone to an empty corridor, removing him from the gaze and reinforcing the spectator's lack of control. The spectator objectifies and enjoys the fantasy of control but cannot influence the events that occur. Bickle's metaphorical failure to bridge the gap between screen and reality reinforces this. When he takes Betsy to the porno-theatre, it is unclear whether this results from his social unawareness (remembering that four years earlier *Deep Throat* had prompted round-the-block queues in New York helping to establish the phenomenon of 'porno-chic' (DeAngelis 2007: 75)), or a desire to confront her with his reality, perhaps to punish her for her failure to match his fantasy expectations of her. When greeting her the first time, he says, 'I think you're a lonely person . . . I think you need something.' This is evidently not true, shown by her relationship with Tom (Albert Brooks). It is Bickle's projection of himself onto her, a form of the same identification that occurs between the spectator and the screen.

7

Neurosis, hysteria and psychopathy

The recurring images of madness function as a discourse of power, attempting to control something that is, by definition, beyond such control.

(FUERY 2004: 24)

The issues of power and control are essential to the Vigilante Thriller; the attempt to control society is what motivates the protagonists. Their failure creates an ambiguity that problematizes the spectator's understanding of the narratives. The attempt to control the uncontrollable (whether it be social change, the drugs trade, inner-city crime or other people) can be related to ideas of madness. The gaze functions from a position of power, despite its simultaneous powerlessness (in that the spectator sits passively towards the screen), and this fracturing in which the spectator both believes and does not believe also resembles a form of madness; we gaze at a representation we know to be constructed, while often reacting in ways that suggest we are part of the diegesis. Audiences called out 'We're coming to get you Joe' and cheered Paul Kersey's subway shootings, then left cinemas to resume normal life. Lacan's mirror stage, in which the child acquires their identity through the mistaken belief they have mastery over the reflection (as other, not as themselves), has often been linked to cinema as a way of understanding identification through narcissistic projection (by Metz, Baudry, Mulvey and others). A mastery over the camera is assumed by the spectator giving them a god-like control. This, however, only functions when the spectator is unaware of the mechanics of the camera (as in classical Hollywood narrative). As we have seen, the Vigilante Thriller problematizes the gaze and identification by providing multiple points of identification and by disrupting the diegesis (breaking the primary identification with the camera and the control it suggests). The vocalization of the audience could be an attempt to regain this mastery over the screen, to assert power through consent and/or objection. The ego of the spectator is then inserted into the diegesis through their active participation, their threats to action a way of asserting their objection to the acknowledgement that they are indeed powerless, that they have no mastery over the image. Lack of clear resolutions in the films reinforces this – the cries of the audience acknowledging their impotence. At this point the spectator attempts to assert control over the film. This then links to the wider sense of impotence perceived by some of the audience in relation to the social changes discussed in Part One.

Fuery argues that spectating is an act of delusion in which meaning is constructed in ways that imitate aspects of neurosis, psychosis and hysteria. This framework is useful because it discusses representations of madness in film (and I will argue that the protagonist of each film displays symptoms of madness) and explores the interaction of the spectator and the film-text in ways that relate to the initial critical reaction, in which (some) spectators were assumed to be liable to imitate protagonists due to an inability to distinguish fantasy from reality. As Fuery describes, in relation to Lacan, this stands as a definition of psychosis, wherein 'the delusion is so powerful that there is a complete abandonment of reality' (2004: 96).

Before entering this discussion, it is worth considering the construction of meaning, something that is underpinned by the Symbolic Order:[1] 'when we are spectators we more than simply watch – we include our own psychic processes through the invention of the signifiers themselves' (2004: 56). Our understanding of signifiers is dependent on the culture in which we exist, the culture that forms the subject/spectator. However, with the films of this study the situation is problematized when we consider the ideological crisis occurring in American culture. In effect the Symbolic Order was changing, especially in the understanding of the law (as in the morals and ethics that underpin the culture). Feminism, Civil Rights marches and Black militancy posed a direct threat to the patriarchal structures of society in which the head figure was the white male. This shift in culture has an impact on the production of meaning and the structuring of representation.

Within the Vigilante Thrillers a series of transgressive acts are represented by both protagonists and antagonists. These representations suggest madness through the character's behaviour. Returning to *The Searchers*, we can see how elements of madness are interwoven into films that operate within established conventions and cultural norms:

---

[1] The Symbolic Order is 'Lacan's version of the cultural order' (Fuery 2004: 24), the rules that order and regulate society.

Many of the actions of Ethan Edwards in *The Searchers* (Ford, 1956) can be read as madness in part because of the nature of his deeds (obsession, violence, mania – there is even the sense of the schizothymic[2] within both character and narrative) and in part because it is a disturbance to the cultural icon of John Wayne. Yet, this is a film that is not readily categorized as one representing madness, even with its theme of the obsessive drive for revenge and the (psychical) recouping of John Wayne as Western (and American) hero (albeit confirmed as an outsider). In these terms how far removed is this from many of the slasher films of the 1980s and 1990s? These films may hint at the madness of the killers, but more often it is the themes of revenge, sexual transgression, and (occasionally) the supernatural that define the narrative and explicate the events. (Fuery 2004: 25)

Edwards's 'obsession, violence, mania' are clear but also resolved in the text when he decides to rescue Debbie rather than kill her. His final exclusion from society removes the threat that he represents, allowing the oncoming civilization to develop 'normally'. The Vigilante Thriller differs from this in how the resolutions of the films avoid Edwards's decision to be merciful and in the way he is excluded from society. The frontier is still available to Edwards, and there is a territory in which he can disappear and belong. However, in a modern urban society where is left for this escape? Even David Sumner fails in this endeavour; his retreat to Cornwall implies an attempt to escape the conflicts in the United States, but he only finds more conflict. The problems of these films can never be resolved as they are ones that exist in wider society, and they are the unending issues of drugs and crime. To believe they can be resolved is a form of delusion in itself. The endings of the films acknowledge the impossibility of resolutions (in the Todorovian sense) because they acknowledge that the problems are bigger than the interpersonal conflicts used metaphorically in the Western to stand in for wider social conflicts.

Neurosis

Neurosis has its origin in obsession:

For the obsessed, their desire exists, to a certain degree, beyond any moral imperative. It is an obsession first and foremost. It is only afterwards that

---

[2]Schizothymia is 'an introvert tendency or temperament that while remaining within the bounds of normality somewhat resembles schizophrenia (as in a tendency to autistic thinking)' (www.merriamwebster.com).

any sense of morality regarding the issues may follow. And yet part of the neurotic attribute of obsession is entwined in a moral universe, for the obsessions are usually linked to some sense of moral concern and/or fear, often stemming from a conflict with authority. (Fuery 2004: 51)

The morality of the Vigilante Thrillers, as discussed by critics, was of major concern. Beyond the question of messages taken from the films, a clear neurotic obsession with aspects of morality can be seen, aspects that link directly to the contemporary changes in American society. Each film displays anxiety towards aspects of law and order, but also gender, race and authority. Conflict with authority, whether that authority is present or absent, is a key element, a further link to power and the relationship of the protagonists to power. Within each film, alternatives to an endorsement of the actions of the protagonist are shown through their neuroses. The conflicts with authority figures suggest and make available a different viewpoint on the actions within the films, and on the protagonists themselves, 'a conflict based on the compulsion that is seemingly insatiable and originates from a conflict of pleasure and guilt, the inescapable compulsion and the forbidding authority' (Fuery 2004: 53). Can we see their acts as compulsive? Much depends on the rationality of the acts. For Callahan and Doyle (who both show compulsive voyeuristic behaviour, and in Doyle's case sexual fetishism for women in boots[3]) their discoveries of crimes/criminals legitimize their compulsions, but their quests run against the advice and instruction of authority figures. For the other protagonists, rationality is lacking. Joe Curran's shooting of the hippies displays a desire to satisfy a lust to kill (one that is projected onto the hippies whom he views both with hatred and envy). David Sumner's neuroses are evident in his baiting of traditional authority figures (particularly the Reverend Hood) and the compulsion to invade the local society (despite risks of harm). Kersey's compulsive desire to kill brings him into continual conflict with the Police (although there is approval from wider society and the media), but it brings with it risks of physical harm. Bickle's compulsions bring him into conflict with the authority figure of Palantine (who could be seen to stand in for all politicians) and the pimp Sport. He demonstrates compulsive behaviour in his consumption of pornography, and in the relentless taxi driving (avoiding sleep). This also ties to the voyeuristic behaviours of the protagonists, and their investigative/exploratory desires: 'Freud argues that true obsessional acts are auto-erotic, and that part of the repressed sexual development of this is tied to the scopophilic (the obsessed pleasure of

---

[3] In a deleted scene, available on the Special Edition DVD, released in 2003, Nicoli is shown as having a predilection for sado-masochistic sex adding a parallel with Doyle, who is left handcuffed to his bed by a woman he picks up.

looking) and epistemological (the obsessed pleasure for knowing)' (Fuery 2004: 52). Obsession is therefore linked to the gaze and knowledge. As we have seen, the protagonists are presented very much as looking characters but also knowing characters (even if this knowledge is erroneous). As Fuery observes, regarding *Taxi Driver*, this knowledge may be entirely solipsistic, 'Travis Bickle is convinced that only he has the true knowledge of the sordidness of the world. It is noteworthy that his diary entries and voice-overs contain no comments on the fact that no one else sees the world in this way' (Fuery 2004: 52).

Joe Curran is certain he knows about the changing world (bringing in evidence such as a poll by the 'Wallace people'); Callahan knows when a suspect is intending to commit rape; Doyle knows who is a suspect in the club where he spies Boca; Kersey knows who the muggers are and so finds them easily (possibly entrapping them); David Sumner professes knowledge and learning – in his academic work and his quoting of Montesquieu. Ironically (as we have seen), this knowledge is often erroneous. This is a form of obsessional neurosis, when an obsession moves from a normal state to when it 'comes to dominate all our action and thoughts, leading us to act in ways that are counter to everyday living' (Fuery 2004: 51).

'For Freud, *Angst* is either derived from a real situation, or it is derived from a neurosis' (Fuery 2004: 55). For the spectator, this angst is real, having origins in the changes of society; in the protagonists it is represented as an obsessional neurosis. Through spectating/identification a neurosis is created, double shared by the protagonists and the spectators. However, the spectatorship process suggests a level of mastery over the image, and that these films' popularity conveys a desire on behalf of the spectator to gain mastery over their angst (just as the protagonists pursue their obsessions to gain mastery over their changing worlds). The neurosis is worked out through the fantasy presented in the film through mastery of the image. However, this analysis is problematized by the elements of the films that draw attention to their construction. The realization for the spectator of their manipulation undermines their control; they cease to be masters of the image in that they are reminded of their manipulation. This tension between the Lacanian theory of spectatorship and the innovations in American filmmaking during the late 1960s and early 1970s calls into question the immersive qualities of film and rejects the fundamental cathartic notion that these films simply release the angst of the spectator. Rather, the films simultaneously represent and play on this angst while enforcing that it will not go away, that it cannot be controlled. Perhaps it is this element that most disturbed critics. Without finality and closure the suggestion that the spectator may carry the film with them outside the cinema has its origins. However, this fundamentally underestimates the spectator's ability to differentiate between the film and reality. This leads us to psychosis.

Psychosis

Psychosis is when delusion becomes dominant over reality, as in the latter two films where both Paul Kersey and Travis Bickle come to believe the world is different from how others see it. Kersey retreats to a Western code of ethics (evidenced through his use of clichéd dialogue), which occurs after the attack on his family. For Bickle it is from the first moments of the film, when the camera cuts to and from his reflected gaze and the exterior of the taxi. There are, however, elements of psychosis in the other protagonists, especially when we consider their externality from society: 'Lacan argues the psychotic finds him/herself as a foreigner in the world, and as such finds meaningfulness in everyday acts and objects, every moment and event' (Fuery 2004: 83). Each of the protagonists creates meaning from the world around them, in some cases to the point of delusion. This understanding, erroneous or not, separates them from others and confers upon them a special status.

David Sumner is the literal foreigner, but the others go through situations in which they are foreign in some sense. The class divide in *Joe* exposes both Joe Curran and Bill Compton as alien to each other's surroundings. Both are placed into this situation when they venture into the East Village (particularly in the sequence in a Japanese restaurant where they do not know how to behave). Earlier, we saw how Joe stares passively in front of the TV. Later he discusses soap-opera characters with his wife as if they are real. Joe himself is alienated from a society that is changing and in which his own children are beyond his control. He finds great meaning when 'Coloured' people move into the street, with Bill's acts being given great meaning for his own life. In a world of bureaucracy, both Doyle and Callahan are alienated and isolated. As Police Officers, their job is to find meaning in the everyday acts and objects such as Callahan's observational powers and Doyle's obsessive pursuit of Charnier (even beyond the confines of the frame and the film narrative) and the tearing apart of the suspect's car. Such is their confidence they know beyond question. It is their rejection of others' knowledge that allows them to pursue their goals (although, as we have seen, the completion of these goals is questionable). In discussing the ending of *The French Connection* Friedkin stated, in reference to Doyle, 'He's just killed a federal agent, he's a borderline psycho, who perhaps has become a total psycho; he's like Ahab after the whale. He no longer is concerned about human life, so he's shooting at anything he sees' (Shedlin 1972: 9). Kersey is alien to the urban world of the Subway and Central Park. Arguably Bickle is alien to everything he sees, his voice-over giving a constant insight into what he interprets from the world around him. When he approaches Betsy, he tells her:

> I think you're a lonely person, I drive by this place a lot and I see you here. I see a lot of people around you, and I see all these phones and all

this stuff on your desk, and it means nothing. Then when I came inside, and I met you I saw in your eyes, and I saw the way you carry yourself that you're not a happy person. And I think you need something.

The conversation demonstrates Bickle's certainty, his insistence on his view of reality. When the second date with Betsy goes badly, he sends her flowers and calls her on the phone, becoming angry when the version of reality he encounters is dissonant to the one he imagines. Partly this is to do with the fetishization of Betsy ('They cannot touch her'), in which a version of her is created for Bickle that cannot be related to the person he meets.

In discussing psychosis, Fuery refers to writings of Judge Daniel Schreber (writings then analysed by Freud) in which 'Schreber's interpretation of the world, and all the things done to him, are contextualized within a sexual dynamic' (2004: 80). A sexual dynamic is evident in all the Vigilante Thrillers, either in angst about rape (*Joe*, *Straw Dogs*, *Death Wish*, *Dirty Harry*), voyeurism (*Straw Dogs*, *Dirty Harry*) and the protagonists' own sexual behaviour and desires (Doyle's fetishism in *The French Connection*). Writing in *Jump Cut*, Marty Gliserman suggests a homosexual subtext in Kersey's relationships with Jainchill and Ochoa, one that finds expression in his attacks:

> The friendly male relationships Bronson has are, of course, with men of the same class. It is with those of the 'lower' social classes that the enactment of the homosexual fantasy through violence occurs. Class bias and hatred are implicit in this fantasy. Bronson walks in secluded places. As in any seduction attempt, he waits alluringly to be approached. His first victim appears to be an addict in need of money. After the shooting, Bronson returns home and retches. That's a more human and real response than he had to his own wife's death. This scene – minus the retching – is played out many times, variations on an urban-cowboy pornography theme. (1975: 8)

The manifestation of sexual anxiety links directly with psychosis as defined and understood by Freud. This is evident when we consider the nature of women in the texts. Women, recalling their character function in the Western (such as Martha in *The Searchers*), represent the Ideal law and the suppression of libido. Defence of them allows the preservation of Ideal law. In these films, preservation has failed or, in the case of Bickle, exists only in his psyche and not in the outside world.

Hysteria

The hysteric asks, 'What is my place in the world?' (Fuery 2004: 130). Fundamental to an understanding of hysteria is the question of what is good. According to Fuery, this is often expressed as the dichotomy between ideas of a Moral Good and the Good of the Self. Within the Western film these two ideas of good were able to coalesce; although the Good of the Self (the desire of the Western Hero is to be in the wilderness) was not the same as the Moral Good (the morality of civilization), the oppositions in the Western and the sense of narrative closure offered allowed them to coexist. The removal of this sense of closure in the Vigilante Thriller disavows any possibility that these two can coexist. In the modern landscape the morality of the Western, the underpinning myth structure of white America (and in particular white men), becomes a site of hysteria. This can be taken further when we consider that the definition of a wider social morality is itself in flux. Rather than asserting that society returns to the previous morality, or that it distances itself from it, the Vigilante Thrillers demonstrate the continual tension between meaning systems in conflict. It is important to remember that the protagonists are in general isolated from others (even those who are married are distanced from their own family life) and in some cases display psychotic behaviours that distance them from reality (both the reality represented in the films and the external reality of the spectator).

For Fuery this conflict becomes played out over hysterical bodies. Referring to *High Noon*, he explains that Will Kane's body

> becomes the site where all the issues of morality and ethics are played out, including the social (the inability and inaction of the townspeople), the sexual (his past sexual relationships as well as his current and future ones), and the personal. These are no more clearly demonstrated than in the countdown to noon scene, prefaced by his writing of a will, and closed by the sound of the train's arrival. In this sequence (and the surrounding ones), there are a number of shots which emphasise the body as vulnerable flesh (the shave, the cuts on his face from the fight, the flexing of the sore hand), even the shot of the empty chair (an absent reminder of Frank Miller) serves to position the body as the key signifier in the playing out of a cultural order of ethics. The lacuna of Miller's flesh drives the narrative as well as all the emotions. (2004: 125)

As we have seen, flesh is also an ever-present commodity in the Vigilante Thrillers. In *Joe*, Melissa's flesh is seen as something to be fought over. Bill's confrontation with Frank takes place over the bed where Melissa and Frank sleep together, Frank's goading of Bill taking on an Oedipal element. The flesh of the hippy girls is a site of desire for both Bill and Joe, but ultimately one of rejection and anger. Joe's own body becomes humorous in the love scene (the desire to keep his socks on) and unmanned by his poor performance and rejection. Young flesh is desired by the men but is also a point of conflict and violence in the form of Melissa. Amy Sumner's flesh is subjected to various gazes, a site over which David's and the workmen's desire and rivalry manifest. The siege of the farm takes various male body parts and exposes their fragilities. An early scene has David and Amy flirting with each other, with Amy playing younger and David stating, 'I freak out for eight-year-olds.' Popeye Doyle is shown to have a sexual fetish for young women in boots (pursuing one in the street), which results in Russo finding him handcuffed to his own bed. The film lingers on car-crash victims suggesting the vulnerability of the human body. Several innocent victims are killed, without the film following up on their deaths. In *Dirty Harry*, the bodies of the victims are a point of hysterical flesh, especially the teenage girl who has been kidnapped, raped and buried alive. The bodies of Callahan and Scorpio are both subjected to violence, particularly the latter (which in the way it is penetrated by Callahan's knife, and the high-pitch scream that follows, is feminized). The rape in *Death Wish* shows the female body under threat, and Kersey's assaults continually damage and penetrate other bodies. Kersey's daughter Carol is rendered voiceless by the assault – making her a body only (and eliminating any say she may have in Kersey's actions). Travis Bickle fixates over his own body through food, exercise and medicines. The bodies of Betsy and Iris become erotic fixations for him. Scorsese's second cameo in *Taxi Driver* demonstrates another example of hysteria in which a white businessman rants about his wife being with Black man, a scene which exposes a sexual hysteria at the heart of racism.

Impact on the spectator

As we have seen, the positioning of the spectator is a complex process that begins before the film and draws on a range of cultural and cinematic experiences and issues, including the angst of the spectator. It is a process that plays on neuroses and replicates elements of psychopathy (in its creation of an alternative meaning system within the film's diegesis) and hysteria through the externalization of emotion. As Fuery explains, 'cinema acts as a type of cultural sublimation, which can also be traced to the sublimations of the spectator' (2004: 62). In the group environment of the cinema, a cultural space, these sublimations are drawn from shared experience, shared angst. However, to suggest that the spectator would be moved to act, or act-out, following the viewing of these films is to deny the complexity of the power-play between text and spectator. It also assumes the development of a real psychopathy, as if the characters' madness projects onto the spectator irrespective of the textual systems, in denial of disavowal. Spectatorship requires disavowal which stems from foreclosure ('the rejection and fending off, of a part of reality' (2004: 90)). The spectator must disavow reality to engage with the film, 'When we watch a film, reality (that is, both the everyday as well as the Symbolic) is not repressed, rather it is fended off in order that a different reality (that of the film) can dominate. In this sense the spectator performs foreclosure in much the same way as the psychotic does' (2004: 91). Pleasure then stems from the disavowals that take place, investing in the fictional world presented to us. But this can go further:

> there are the disavowals that take place through the spectator's own histories of foreclosure. This is the spectator 'using' the film to disavow aspects of his/her own reality. This can be anything as simple as the disavowal of the Great Depression through elaborate musicals in the 1930s, through to a complex relationship of the spectator's 'acting out', psychically speaking, of the phantasies of the film's created world order. (2004: 90–1)

What then do the Vigilante Thrillers disavow? Partly it is the spectator's impotence, confusion and worry in the face of the social changes of the period. However, the films' presentation of the protagonists' inability to affect society at large, despite their personal effectiveness, undermines any sense of foreclosure. Fuery's analysis continues and somewhat answers this: 'Cinema's function is not foreclosure, but rather to perform a duality that may at times seem contradictory. Cinema must, at the same time, create the hole as well as the textual patch on the hole in the phantasy' (2004: 91). This duality is inherent in spectatorship. At once the spectator surrenders to the fantasy of the film-text while simultaneously remaining aware that it is not real (and particularly so with films such as these where questions of technique and focalization are foregrounded). To believe that spectators would imitate these films would be to believe that they could not perceive this difference. In discussing Lacan's theories on psychosis, Fuery states, 'There is no willing suspension of disbelief when we watch a film (or, to follow the historical origins of the phrase, read a novel for that matter), for like the psychotic what is at hand is the issue of certainty and the question of reality' (2004: 93). What these films do is ask the spectator to question certainty (in terms of moral certainty) and explore the relationship between fantasy and reality, culminating in *Taxi Driver* in which the protagonist cannot make that differentiation for himself.

The definition of madness relies on an understanding of the ordinary, of the usual. With the Symbolic Order in flux (as per the ideological shifts of the time) during the period in which these films were released, terms such as 'normal' become problematic. To fully understand this, we need to turn to the fundamental structures of society and the concept of the other.

8

Violence, identification and the other

The Christian motto 'All men are brothers' however, also means that those who do not accept brotherhood are not men. In the early years of the Iranian revolution, Khomeini played on the same paradox when he claimed, in an interview for the Western press, that the Iranian revolution was the most humane in all of history: not a single person was killed by the revolutionaries. When the surprised journalist asked about the death penalties publicised in the media, Khomeini calmly replied: 'Those that were killed were not men, but criminal dogs!'

(ŽIŽEK 2008: 47)

Otherness is nothing but the projection of our own otherness onto the canvass of another person.

(RICHARDSON 2010: 14)

The process of othering helps us to understand the concerns raised about violence and identification in the Vigilante Thrillers. The proceeding quote from Žižek explains this relationship – that violence towards the other is not violence towards a person, at least not in the sense that we regard the self, and as Richardson suggests, the other is built from the self. As we have seen, the Western of Classical Hollywood displays this in the often caricatured or characterless Native Americans. Discussing the Western in terms of Jungian archetypes, John Izod notes that 'The archetypal power of the Western myth that has always attracted readers and audiences to the genre may not have been true to the facts of the past, but it has been influential in forming the construction of contemporary American history', (2001: 37). The Western narrative is one of a journey to an Edenic space, extending 'the symbolism of the garden as the blessed place, a Paradise on earth, to include the farm, the smallholding, the wilderness, nature and even the desert' which symbolizes an 'idealised collective self' (2001: 37). This, a variation of agrarian/pastoral myths, worked as a mental set, if not as a reality, and underpinned the expansion Westwards. In this conception, the Native American male comes to represent the shadow projection of white European settlers, a symbol that carries the 'burden of white sexual guilt' (2001: 41) forming the Native American male as sexually rapacious and preferring white women (as per the Protestant Captivity narrative referred to in Part One). The Western narrative becomes one in which the hero fights for control of his unconscious desires for the supposedly sexually available Native American woman. The Native American is the locus for the projection of unwanted desires and values, of disorder and wilderness. Izod also notes that 'The white baddies in the classic Western are usually villainous because they embody some excessive appetites inimical to the puritan vision of the Western idyll – often their sin is the urban vice, greed. They look the obverse of the hero who, in the classical Western, keeps himself clean shaven and smart' (2001: 42).

How does this resonate in the Vigilante Thrillers? There are moments in each of the films where the victims of the Vigilante's violence imitate this classical othering. The costumes of Frank in *Joe* (and those that hang in the shop windows in the Village), Sport in *Taxi Driver* and the rapists in *Death Wish* reflect this. In *Death Wish* the behaviour of the rapists suggests a wildness (particularly when they whoop, holler and leap around the supermarket). Scorpio, in *Dirty Harry*, represents a confused gender/sexuality, and he is 'indeterminate' (Ryan and Kellner 1988: 44). The Workmen in *Straw Dogs* also display elements of this othering during the siege, with a suggestion of a regression to childhood (especially in Chris Cawsey as he rides a child's tricycle). Victims of Paul Kersey and Travis Bickle, and the suspects of Popeye Doyle, are generally faceless, lacking an identity that allows for identification. However, and in contrast to the Western, their otherness reflects and comments upon the otherness of the protagonists, who all display behaviours common to the other. *Taxi Driver* demonstrates how confused formations of the other had become, through Bickle's own otherness (depicted in his alienation, actions and voice-over), and how he others society and in particular Betsy through her, supposed, perfection (Fuchs 1991: 39). The negative elements of both Bill and Joe others them, such as Joe's racist and homophobic views and his sexual desire and general excessiveness (linking to the 'urban vice, greed'). In *Joe*, the lack of a secure point of allegiance in the film serves to allow each of the main characters to take the place of the other alongside the more obvious othering of the hippies. David Sumner is othered in relation to the culture of Cornwall and to the house (which is Amy's) – he is an urban character displaced to the wilderness, not of it in the way the Western hero might be. (He is useless at duck hunting and easily fooled by the local men during the hunt.) The antagonists are clearly marked by their sexual desire and objectification of Amy, a manifestation of excessive appetites. David's bullying of Amy and alienation of local figures, such as the Reverend Hood, furthers his own otherness from the Cornish location. The clear parallels between Callahan and Scorpio suggest Callahan's own otherness, as does his nickname, something that others him from his partner and the rest of the force. The death of his wife has left Callahan apart from society – his similarity to Scorpio emphasized by the parallel scopic gazes they enjoy. Doyle's obsession and sexual fetishism others him as a character, alongside his excessive violence and language. Paul Kersey adopts behaviours like those of the muggers he looks for by cruising the parks and subways of New York. His use of Western language alienates when placed into the urban setting, where it becomes incongruous, if not ridiculous. An alternative reading of *Death Wish* would see how Kersey becomes the antagonist, a serial killer being hunted by the Police (in particular, Lt. Ochoa, who would become the protagonist). Travis Bickle is alienated from society and reality; he exists on the margins and moves towards classically othered iconography in the adoption of Native American signifiers (such as the Mohawk haircut). He associates with groups but cannot see himself as part of them. All show the traditional figure of authority in American culture, the white male, displaying elements of the other once displaced onto Native Americans and other Western villains.

Lev discusses the links between dirt and otherness, suggesting that 'In *Joe*, and American culture generally, dirt seems to be connected with sex (as in "filthy pictures") and criminality' (2000: 26). However, Lev also acknowledges that 'dirty' is a term that can connote otherness in different ways:

> He is called 'Dirty Harry' because of his general misanthropy, because he takes all of the police department's dirty jobs, and because he does not stay within the limits of law and custom. A relevant usage of 'dirty' circa 1970 would be 'illegal, unethical, and violent', as in 'dirty' espionage or a 'dirty' war. Note that this is quite a different metaphoric use of 'dirty' from the 'dirty hippies' in *Joe*. . . . 'Dirty' is a rich, multivalent term in modern Western societies. (2000: 31)

The concept of dirt harks back to the opposition of wilderness and civilization of the Western and shows the continuing othering process of the protagonists and the worlds they inhabit – these are streets that cannot be 'cleaned', even by those who try to, in part because they are also 'dirty' (actually and/or figuratively). Although much of the concept of dirt can be tied to the urban environment, both *Joe* (in its closing scene) and *Straw Dogs* suggest that this dirt is not something that can be escaped or limited in its geography. Travis Bickle states that he wishes that 'Someday a real rain will come and wash all this scum off the street' without realizing his own place in the dirt.

As these figures are displaying elements of the other, the question of spectator's identification needs to be returned to. However, we must remember that othering does not eliminate desire and attraction; rather, these coexist. In discussing racial representation and fetishism, Kobena Mercer outlines the complexity of the image (referring to the works of Robert Mapplethorpe). Mercer's own position (as a Black gay man) is used to interrogate 'the problem of ambiguity and undecidability' (1994: 189) in textual readings. He also realizes the importance of the other in defining the self (in reference to Gayatri Spivak), 'Women, children, savages, slaves and criminals were all alike insofar as their otherness affirmed "his" identity as the Subject centred and stabilized in power by logocentrism, and indeed all the other centrisms, ethnocentrism and phallocentrism, in which "he" constructed his representations of reality' (1994: 215). The other helps define the self; the problematics of the other in the Vigilante Thriller reflect the problem of the self that existed during this time. That the spectator is capable of being both attracted and repelled by the image is a sophistication denied them by the contemporary critics and much of the continuing discourse surrounding film, and specifically film violence. It also returns to neurosis and the 'curious mix of disgust and pleasure within the compulsions' (Fuery 2004: 53) of the neurotic obsessional.

Part of the question of attraction/repulsion can be answered by a version of self-destruction that occurs in each of the films, a process that allows the otherness of the protagonists to be symbolically allowed and denied. In writing about *Taxi Driver*, Žižek suggests that Bickle wants to destroy himself as much as anyone else:

> Crucial here is the implicit suicidal dimension of this *passage a l'acte*: when Travis prepares for his attack, he practises drawing a gun in front of the mirror: in what is the best known scene of the film, he addresses his own image in the mirror with the aggressive-condescending 'You talkin' to me?' In a textbook illustration of Lacan's notion of the 'mirror stage,' aggression is here clearly aimed at oneself, at one's own mirror image. Travis, heavily wounded and leaning against the wall, mimics with the forefinger of his right hand a gun aimed at his bloodstained forehead and mockingly triggers it, as if saying, 'The true aim of my outburst was

myself.' The paradox of Travis is that he perceived himself as part of the degenerate dirt of the city life he wants to eradicate. (2008: 179)

Bickle's self-destruction is evident through the use of the mirror and his later symbolic suicide when he mimics shooting a gun at his temple. But this analysis is useful too when considering the other films of this study. In each of the films an element of self-destruction/self-loathing is evident. In *Joe*, Joe Curran seeks to change his life through his shadowing of Bill Compton, expressing the loathing of his own class and family life, and he is motivated as much by jealousy of the hippies as disgust. Bill Compton yearns for his youth, away from the confines of his upper-middle-class life, and finally shoots his daughter Melissa, bringing about the end of the life he has previously sought to protect, destroying his future. David Sumner destroys the life that he has accrued, abandoning the home he has defended and leaving his wife behind. Harry Callahan murders his parallel self, Scorpio, then throws away his badge, the symbol of society and of his legitimacy. Popeye Doyle, in his failure to capture Charnier, disappears in the final frame of the film, an unresolved figure whose career is over. Paul Kersey undergoes a rebirth, but one that leads into a psychotic fantasy of the Old West. None of the films resolves in a way that leaves the protagonists complete or in any way 'normal'. The characters are embedded in the worlds they wish to destroy – and thus destroy part of themselves.

This crisis of self points to a wider failure, that of grand narrative (also known as metanarrative or master narrative). Grand narratives, as defined by Jean-François Lyotard, are narratives whose function is to legitimate the history of a society, providing ideological structures to the audience. However, 'In contemporary society and culture – postindustrial society, postmodern culture – the question of legitimation of knowledge is formulated in different terms. The grand narrative has lost its credibility' (Lyotard 1984: 37). As we have seen, one of the core grand narratives of America, the Western, had by the 1970s lost its legitimacy, unable to bear the ideological shifts of the world around it. Within the Western the structural oppositions that form the narrative had become difficult, if not impossible. As it was true for the Western, so it was true for many of the myths and structures underpinning American ideologies.

This failure of grand narrative, and its implications for identity, has its most cogent expression in *Taxi Driver*. Barbera Mortimer discusses how *Taxi Driver* embodies a postmodern attitude to the self, explaining that 'Postmodern theory asserts that the subject as coherent, integrated, discoverable self is a fiction of modernity; subjectivity is understood to be organized through signification and therefore to be externally rather than internally "driven"' (1997: 28). Mortimer sees Bickle as a character attempting to create himself drawing from narrative forms, 'In the film, taxi driver Travis Bickle (De Niro) attempts to script himself as hero of a narrative – specifically, the story of his own life' (1997: 29). Bickle draws his identity from popular culture, 'Such "textual personae" as the western hero, the traumatized Vietnam veteran, the political assassin, the gangster' (1997: 30) but also as a romantic hero, with Bickle turning 'to violence after failing at his attempts to become the romantic lead in the story of his life' (1997: 29). Ironically, the celebration that emerges in the wake of the final shoot-out (assuming that the sequence is not a dying fantasy) finally creates Bickle's identity for him, 'the newspapers grant Travis a centrality and agency within their narratives that his own life could never offer him. Becoming the taxi driver who battles gangsters gives Travis a coherent identity constructed through popular discourse' (1997: 30). Similarly, in *Death Wish* the news reports of Kersey's violent activities construct him as a hero, using Western iconography, just as he has constructed himself as a hero based on the Wild West show he watches in Tucson.

If, finally, we see ideological incoherence in the Vigilante Thriller, then this is surely a reflection of the times in which they were made, times when the grand narratives of the past were no longer sufficient to support the emerging changes in American society. The harking back to the Western can only fail to resolve the issues the films bring forward; as a genre cycle, it is ideologically ill equipped for the society, and problems, emerging in the 1970s. These films offer little in the way of solution, and the narratives turn inwards at the end, exposing and problematizing all that went before. Unlike the Western hero, the Vigilante Thriller protagonists are not apart from society, but they are a part of society's problems.

Conclusion

> Triumph of the Will *illustrates a textual rendering of the good and power. The film does not in itself bring into question the morality of Nazism and fascism because it functions within the context of the good. This is not simply the process of ideology and glorification; it is the attempted absenting of the capacity to see this as anything but part of the good.*
> (FUERY 2004: 116)

> *Eleven years later [after* Death Wish *was released] Bernard Goetz shot people in the subway. He's a very slow learner if it took him eleven years to follow this film.*
> (MICHAEL WINNER QUOTED IN TALBOT 2006: 66)

> *In a few short months, Hinckley watched* Taxi Driver *(1976), a film in which Robert De Niro played a seriously disturbed Vietnam veteran named Travis Bickle, at least sixteen times. According to one of his attorneys, Hinkley 'became Travis Bickle; he* was *Travis'.*
> (GIBSON 1994: 233)

'Fascism' is an elusive term. Both George Orwell, writing in 1944, and Michel Foucault, in 1980, recognized that the term has, in its rhetorical use, become unanchored from meaning. First applied to political movements in Italy in the 1910s, the idea of fascism spread quickly across the world as a reaction to the liberalism and individualism embodied in laissez-faire capitalism (Weber 1964: 13), but each iteration is different to the last. Therefore, Italian fascism and German Nazism are not the same but share similarities. Passmore sees several elements as key to a workable definition of fascism: nationalism, hostility to socialism and feminism, a 'mobilized nation' which depends on the 'advent to power of a new elite acting in the name of the people, headed by a charismatic leader and embodied in a mass, militarized party', and a tendency towards conservatism (although this can be overridden when and where required) (Passmore 2002: 31).

America itself, although never having a fascist government, has a history with fascist ideology. Sarah Churchwell outlines the rise of fascist groups in America during the interwar period in *Behold America* (2019). Much of this springs from the concept of being 'One Hundred Per Cent American', a concept of racial purity focused on '"Nordicism" [which] held that people of Northern Europe were biologically superior' (2019: 58). Arising, in part, due to immigration to the United States, the term 'Nordic' 'was used to describe anyone who was blonde, white, or "Caucasian", or "Anglo-Saxon", or Northern European, as well as anyone who was actually from Norway' (2019: 59). Evidently excluding anyone non-white, this included other groups that failed to meet the level of 'One Hundred Per Cent', including the so-called hyphenates. The first hyphenate group was African Americans, but they were joined by Jewish Americans, German Americans, Italian Americans and Irish Americans (the latter two groups suspected of allegiance to the 'Pope over the president, while Jews had long been said to be a "nation within a nation", "mercenary minded – money mad", "unmergeable", "alien and unassimilable"' (2019: 47)).[1] The impact of these beliefs was most obvious in the revival and growth of the Ku Klux Klan (KKK), during the period after the release of *Birth of a Nation* (D. W. Griffith, 1915), and the emergence of American Fascisti or Black Shirts[2] (American fascist groups) and the German American Bund (effectively the Nazi Party in America) among other groups. Despite its growth, from 34 members in 1915 to almost 500,000 nationwide by 1921, and the acquisition of significant political power, the KKK was in decline by the 1930s as the other groups arose. (The clear ideological similarities between these groups were not lost on commentators at the time, however.) With fascist rallies commonplace throughout the 1930s, some as large as 20,000 participants (2019: 251), and demands for America First isolationist policies (promoted throughout the early twentieth century including during the 1930s by William Randolph Hearst and Charles Lindbergh), the Japanese attack on Pearl Harbour in December 1941 brought the popularity of such groups to an end. The KKK experienced some expansion during the 1960s[3]

---

[1] Rather tellingly Native Americans were not cited.
[2] 'They were not Italian-American followers of Mussolini; they were nativist supporters of a home-grown American fascism' (Churchwell 2019: 185).
[3] During the 1960s Klan membership 'reached an estimated 35,000 to 50,000' (Bullard 1997: 24). By the early 1970s this had declined to 6,500 although by the late 1970s this had risen to 10,000. 'Much of the Klan's gain was due to an improved public image fashioned by David Duke' although this failed to transfer to success in the political arena (Bullard 1997: 32).

in response to the Civil Rights movement and government legislation and its support for George Wallace's presidential bid (Passmore 2002: 105), but the significance of fascism as an organized political movement had waned. The term clearly had not lost its rhetorical significance, however, despite its unanchored use. The point of a 'One Hundred Per Cent' American has some significance with the Vigilante Thriller when we consider the ethnicities of their protagonists, stars and directors.

Joe Curran, Jimmy 'Popeye' Doyle and 'Dirty' Harry Callahan are all marked by an Irish Americanness through their names and, for the latter two, through their association with the Police (a traditional link). Both *The French Connection* and *Dirty Harry* have Jewish directors, as does *Death Wish*.[4] Hoffman's star image was, and is, linked to his Jewishness. Although born in the United States, Charles Bronson, originally named Charles Buchinsky, had Lithuanian heritage and had played a wide range of ethnicities during his career before *Death Wish*, including an Irish Mexican in *The Magnificent Seven* and a half Native American in *Chato's Land*. Finally, *Taxi Driver* was directed by an Italian American, and former Catholic seminarian and starred an Italian American. These elements inflect the accusation of fascism levelled at the films; within the terms of the 'Nordicist' nature of American fascism these films fall short.

The Vigilante Thrillers emerged during a time of ideological conflict and confusion in American culture, when the underpinning myths that had defined and driven a society had been thrown into doubt. This time was no doubt one of great anxiety, fuelled by military failure in Vietnam, economic failures and rises in crime, in which issues of race and gender came to the fore. By considering the issues that caused controversy with the Vigilante Thrillers, the roots of the objections voiced by critics can be found, but also the loose rhetorical position of the term 'fascist' can be determined. Fascism's objection to feminism can be read into the films, as can the use of violence (and its link to law and order) and racial faultlines; however, as an analysis, this reveals a lack of depth and precision. The authoritarian side of fascism is not present in the films – indeed, each film displays a consciously antiauthoritarian stance, with authority figures seen as a root cause of many problems. The limited success of the protagonists in achieving their aims fails to support an endorsement of violence. The film that most closely contains a figure that links is *Joe*, but Joe Curran himself is presented throughout the film as idiotic and mistaken. His family life (a mainstay of fascism) is dysfunctional at best. Indeed, families are largely absent from the films, only depicted as a source of motivation in *Death Wish* or as dysfunctional in *Straw Dogs* and *Joe*. It is fair to say that the concerns represented in the films

---

[4]One of the issues some American reviewers had with Winner's direction of *Death Wish* was his Englishness, suggesting this led to Winner misunderstanding New York culture.

are like those of fascism, including the concept of nationality (embedded in the anxiety concerning identity), but this does not suggest that the films endorse (or even represent) fascist ideals. Are fascist readings potentially open? Yes, but only if isolated aspects of fascist ideology are considered, and the problematizing features of the films are ignored. Ironically, the reviews display a key element of fascist ideology, as they are 'contemptuous of mass society' (Passmore 2002: 11). In this the critics are working in a familiar mode, one that sees the mass audience as deeply threatening and problematic.

Slane sees this loose definition of fascism as a key element in the definition of democracy in the United States throughout the twentieth century. In this process fascism becomes democracy's other, one that 'exposes some of democracy's own deeper historical contradictions by taking them to extremes' (2001: 5). In reference to Raymond Williams, Slane discusses how the fear of fascism/Nazism is tied to a fear of the masses, an inherent anxiety in democracy. These masses were imagined as 'consisting of devalued groups (especially women and members of the working class, who were often imaged as sexually debauched and morally bankrupt)' (2001: 6). The rhetoric employed in creating an opposition between democracy and fascism is selective, creating a sense of 'sexual decadence that served the American national/democratic image of purity and moral rectitude' (2001: 6), despite the Nazis' conservative values concerning the family. Going further, Slane discusses, in reference to the writing of Postcolonial theorist Homi Bhabha, the concept of homology (here the identification of self with the nation) which argues that 'the imaginary construct of the nation parallels the illusory unified image of the self-produced in Lacan's notion of the mirror stage: for Bhabha, the nation is a "differentiating sign of Self, distinct from the Other or the Outside," where members identify themselves with the perceived collective qualities of the nation through the establishment of an "Other"' (2001: 7–8). Ironically, this othering ignores similarities between democratic structures and those of a fascist state, 'The process of casting fascism as democracy's opposite often tries to deny these structural commonalities [between democracy and fascism] by either emphasising those democratic ideals that are indeed dramatically opposed to fascism (i.e., democratic pluralism) or fabricating an opposition through the selective imaging of fascism' (2001: 5). The concerns of the Vigilante Thrillers clearly tie to this image of self-definition when tied to national identity.

Several factors are thus evident in this discussion. That the shifts in American society create a crisis in the other (which reflects a crisis in national identity and the failure of pre-existing metanarratives), and that part of the rhetoric surrounding this process reflects a wider desire to invoke fascism and far-right politics in attempting to other a particular group. This has two aspects: othering the protagonists of the films and othering the audience of the films. The latter effort, to other the audience, was not new and sits within a long history of seeing the mass audience as a threat. The work of

Blackman and Walkerdine (2001) explores the history of how the mass has been seen as separate from the individual within the twentieth century, an understanding that relates to the othering process. By basing the concept of 'normal' on the individual subject, the group is othered and the mass is an irrational body, opposed to the rational individual:

> The government of reason placed reason and reasoning as naturalistic phenomena, with which upper-and-middle-class white men were most endowed. This natural rationality was needed for a rational-liberal government to work. It required men of reason to do the governing and the Others (women, children, and the dangerous classes and colonial peoples) at least to be made reasonable even if they could not be remade into quasi-bourgeois individuals. (2001: 33)

The mass, made of the other that is not the individual, is easily led, irrational, animal and instinctual. This attitude, originating in the works of Gustave Le Bon and Freud, prejudiced the development of theories in which the masses were vulnerable to media manipulation.

During the 1960 and 1970s the experiments of Albert Bandura explored supposed links between media violence and aggression:

> In the experiments the children are exposed to an actor acting aggressively towards a Bobo doll, a plastic doll that springs down and up again when it has been struck. The children are then led to another room full of the props that are at the actors' disposal. The children's aggressive behaviour is then measured. Bandura's objective was to see whether children would imitate or model the aggressive behaviour that they had experienced. The conclusion of these studies was that the 'experience helps to shape the form of [a] child's aggressive behaviour'. (Blackman and Walkerdine 2001: 40)

However, these studies, and similar ones of the period, have methodological problems, in particular the removal of context from the viewing situation, and they hypothesize that these conclusions can be expanded from their artificial laboratory environment to a wider social model. As discussed by Eves (1970), this form of effects theory was the dominant discourse in understanding media violence at the turn of the decade, led in the public domain by figures such as Dr Fredric Wertham (United States) and Mary Whitehouse (United Kingdom), who used little in the way of evidence.[5] Despite Eves's conclusion that there is no evidence of a causal link from violence in the media to that in society, she acknowledges that

---

[5]Eves (1970) also discusses Bandura's work (Bandura et al. 1963) identifying the limits in experiments that took children from 'a familiar world of established relationships' (Eves 1970: 36).

there was a 'widespread belief that there is a link' (1970: 42). This belief has existed since the beginning of mass media. In reviewing the history of this view in the UK, Julian Petley ties it to elitism, noting that these effects are only suggested to impact on the 'underclass' (1997: 87). Writing from an American perspective, Derek Nystrom suggests that film critics of this period, writing for national publications, were both from and writing for the middle class, making distinctions between their audience 'the knowing spectator and less sophisticated, tacitly lower-class viewers' (2009: 16). Film becomes part of a history of media effects, reaching back to Penny Dreadfuls and Music Hall, in which the poorer and excluded elements of society are supposed to be suggestible and unable to understand the difference between the medium and real life. Murdock explores this further, explaining that 'The dominant "effects" tradition has proved so resilient partly because it chimes with a deeply rooted formation of social fear which presents the vulnerable, suggestible and dangerous as living outside the stockade of maturity and reasonableness that the "rest of us" take for granted. "They" are the "others", the ones "we" must shield or protect ourselves against' (1997: 83). The presentation of the masses as irrational and uncaring recalls the Kitty Genovese case, in which a perception of the people who lived in a poorer ethnic area of New York created a narrative, rather than the facts of the event. A discourse emerges, in which the masses are irrational and problematic. Through this they are consciously othered, and the natural accusation of the othering process is fascism, according to the rhetorical structures in American politics (whereas UK critics avoided this accusation). A confluence of otherness occurs in which the typical other of American political discourse (fascism) meets the other of the mass film audience – they become naturally associated through the Vigilante Thrillers. In the films this othering process is discernible through the protagonists/antagonists themselves and the processes of identification and attraction/repulsion.

Smith highlights the problems associated with the interpretation of fascism in *Dirty Harry*:

> *Dirty Harry*'s effect, and the cultural controversy that the film caused, are to a large extent a function of the movie's belonging to a long history of generic and formulaic production in which the narrative structures bear the same or a similar ideological weight. *Dirty Harry*'s unusually spectacular resonance has to do with its intervention on that level: the politics of the film itself are unusually elaborated and exhibited, and the representations of violence that it includes are ones that exceed by far the conventions of cinematic verisimilitude at the time. Equally, the resonance is increased by the film's unusual propinquity to issues that were currently controversial and unsettled in the realm of public or civic discourse; in other words, the film's reception is also very closely dependent upon the particular historical moment to which it attaches itself. (1993: 94)

Smith places *Dirty Harry* within the larger tradition of narrative conventions of Hollywood cinema, the film as an extension 'of a populist line in Hollywood movies among whose main effects is to underscore an ideology of individual power and rectitude and to promote a distrust of institutions' (1993: 93). Therefore, the messages of the film are consistent in part with Hollywood tradition – it is the context of the film that provokes the reaction as much as the film-text itself. Ironically, in Smith's view, a tension exists in which the espousal of vigilantism becomes, if simplistically, itself a vindication of democracy and anti-fascist in the sense that moral conscience leads to vigilante actions, rather than Callahan toeing the line of a dominant state. If these elements are consistent with Hollywood's traditions, why was there no controversy before, particularly given the similarity with the Western? I would suggest it is partly the historical setting and mythologizing effect of the Western genre, which serves to remove the ideological issues from being taken as commentaries/effects on modern society. This distance allows the genre to be seen as detached from contemporary life (although as we have seen during the 1960s the Western itself was transforming and leaving behind many of the aspects that were beginning to cause discomfort with critics and audiences). Fuery's comments about *Triumph of the Will* that open this Conclusion demonstrate how the films of this study lack the 'capacity to see this [Nazism and fascism] as anything but part of the good'. The alternative spectating positions available, driven by the different techniques and gazes employed, prevent them from being fascist texts. They allow for alternative readings. Their very construction facilitates this.

The decline of the Western as a film genre is also a failure of metanarrative. The Western exists within the metanarrative of Manifest Destiny, the nineteenth-century belief that the westward expansion through America was ordained by God, legitimizing the forced removal, and murder, or Native Americans. Attempts by politicians to reposition this expansionist ideology to Vietnam, or to space as in John F. Kennedy's invocation of a 'New Frontier' (Slotkin 1992), had failed and, in the failure of the Vietnam War, exposed the violence and prejudice underpinning the myth (reiterated in the growing concern for Native American rights reflected in many revisionist Westerns). The Western film, as seen in Part One, was in drastic decline during the 1960s, the historical setting no longer providing a buffer to its inherent ideological issues. Attempts to reconceptualize the genre, as per Sergio Leone's *Dollars Trilogy* or the revisionist Westerns, had some short-lived success but are effectively critiques of the underpinning mythology and are therefore unable to replace it. The Vigilante Thriller attempts to transpose many of the concerns of the genre to contemporary settings. If they fail anywhere, it is in their inability to provide a coherent set of ideological positions.

Alan Lovell discusses this further regarding *Dirty Harry*: 'To identify it simply as expressing a "hard-hat" position would be to ignore important elements of the film. . . . It offers a number of meanings that lead in different ideological directions' (Lovell 1975: 44). Key to this ambiguity is the acknowledgement of the 'social existence of violence and aggression' (Lovell 1975: 44), which touches on a contradiction in modern societies, that they 'have rejected, formally at least, violence and aggression but their actual workings are decisively marked by them (economic life, war, crime, sport, etc)' (Lovell 1975: 44). The Vigilante Thrillers appealed, perhaps, because of the open acknowledgement of this contradiction. They are sceptical films that show a series of contrasts and oppositions yet fail to reconcile these relationships.

By the end of the 1970s, the anxiety surrounding these ideological issues was reconciled in several ways in popular Hollywood cinema, and the scar of Vietnam was revisioned, making the Vigilante Thriller redundant (at least as a mainstream genre). *Star Wars* (George Lucas, 1977) managed to take elements of the Western and, by placing them in a 'galaxy, far, far away' and alongside conventions from other genres such as the Swashbuckler, stripped those elements of their ideological baggage.[6] The soldiers of the Vietnam War were rehabilitated, as seen in the transformation of John Rambo from burned-out veteran in *First Blood* (Ted Kotchoff, 1982) to lone warrior freeing prisoners of war in *Rambo: First Blood Part II* (George P. Cosmatos, 1985). Ronald Reagan's Presidential Election victory in 1980, precipitating the rise of the New Right and a new militarism, is reflected in this evolution (Ryan and Kellner 1988: 10–11). The Soviet Union provided a clear other, described by Reagan in Manichean terms as an 'evil empire' and 'the focus of evil in the modern world' in a March 1983 speech to the National Association of Evangelicals (Jackson 1983).[7] Films such as *Rocky*[8] manage to deal with racial ambivalence through reversal in which the white male is cast as a working-class underdog fighting a more sophisticated Black opponent. *48 Hours* (Walter Hill, 1982), *Lethal Weapon* (Richard Donner, 1987) and other Buddy Cop Movies successfully integrate Black male characters into roles which cease to threaten the predominance of the white male. Tasker discusses this:

> In *Die Hard* (John McTiernan, 1988), as in other 1980s movies, black characters act as supportive figures for the white hero. The relationship between John McClane (Bruce Willis) and Sergeant Al Powell (Reginald Veljohnson) is central to the development of the narrative, yet Powell

---

[6]According to Kitses, 'George Lucas has been explicit in his acknowledgment that the Western's absence was a prime motivating force in the creation of his series. In his eye, the decline of the genre had created a lack, especially for the young audience, of one of the Western's traditional forms, the morality tale' (2007: 3).
[7]Of course, Reagan himself was identified with the Western by appearing in films such as *The Bad Man* (Richard Thorpe, 1941) and presenting the anthology television show *Death Valley Days* between 1964 and 1965.
[8]The success of *Rocky* at the 1977 Academy Awards is indicative of these wider ideological shifts. One of the films it beat to the Best Picture award was *Taxi Driver*.

is a marginal figure. Similarly, by the time of *Rocky III* Carl Weathers's character, Apollo Creed, has shifted from the role of Rocky's opponent, as in the first two films, to that of friend and trainer. (1993: 4)

The cultural threat represented by the Black Civil Rights movement is therefore absorbed into a system that retains white male dominance while integrating Black figures, often in roles subservient to the white hero. Similarly, women are given roles that help reorient them to a traditional role (as in *Die Hard*), become motivational tools through their deaths (*Rambo: First Blood Part II*) or are eliminated from the narrative almost completely (*Predator* (John McTiernan, 1987) and *Rambo III* (Peter MacDonald, 1988)). The emergence in the late 1980s of action films with female protagonists (*Aliens* (1986) and *Terminator 2* (1991) both directed by James Cameron and *Thelma & Louise* (Ridley Scott, 1991)) redressed this to some extent, but largely they remained an absence presence. *Rambo: First Blood Part II* and its many imitators effectively restage Vietnam, answering John Rambo's (Sylvester Stallone) question in the film; 'Do we get to win this time?' In *Magnum Force* (Ted Post, 1973) the first of the *Dirty Harry* sequels, a more extreme vigilante force (with homosexual overtones) is introduced. Callahan's personal life is shown (he flirts with a widow of a colleague and sleeps with an Asian woman), and his racial views are explored via 'his obligatory new partner at the beginning of the film [who] is an African-American man whom he treats with respect and even care' (Smith 1993: 104). Smith explains how this film 'answers' the original, clearing the ambiguities. *The French Connection II* fulfils a similar function in offering a clear resolution to the first film's narrative. Doyle's forced addiction to heroin, and then his recovery offers a rebirth from his obsessive, addictive nature, after which he shoots Charnier and atones for the accidental killing of Mulderig in the first film. *Death Wish II* (Michael Winner, 1982) simplifies Kersey's narrative, making his motive direct revenge in which he targets a gang that raped his daughter (for a second time) and his maid. Ochoa, his antagonist in the first film, is now represented as an ally (who is killed in supporting Kersey). Each sequel deliberately answers the narrative and character problems the first films raised.[9]

In the Introduction the striking resemblance between *Joe* to the earlier real-life crimes of Arville Garland was outlined. Two later crimes, those of John Hinkley Jr. and Bernard Goetz, were linked to *Taxi Driver* and *Death Wish*, respectively. No causal link between the film and each crime has conclusively made although 'Hinkley claimed to be haunted by the film *Taxi*

---

[9] A sequel to *Joe*, entitled *Citizen Joe*, was announced by Cannon Films in the 1980s but never produced (Powell and Garrett 2009: 24).

Driver and to have fallen in love with its adolescent heroine Jodie Foster' (Horsley 1999: 155) and used this as his motive for attempting to assassinate President Reagan. Goetz claimed no inspiration from *Death Wish*, but his treatment by some aspects of the media, having shot four young black men on a subway train, imitates the media reactions depicted in *Death Wish* and *Taxi Driver*: 'There seems little doubt that (like Travis) Goetz acted out of personal rage and frustration that he simply snapped and started shooting. . . . His actions were viewed not with horror or with disgust as the acts of a madman (or a fascist), but those of a brave and justifiably indignant citizen' (Horsley 1999: 157–8).[10] The desire to link these texts with the acts reinforces the dominance of the view that violent media begets violence despite a paucity of empirical evidence.

In the UK, this train of thought has continued, through the video nasty moral panic of the 1980s, to the reporting of the Jamie Bulger murder in the 1990s and the Dunblane shootings (Petley 1997). In America, shootings at educational campuses, such as Columbine High School (Ward 2001) and Sandy Hook Elementary School (Zakarin 2012), were similarly tied to video games. In 2014, Justin Borque, who murdered three and attempted to murder two more in Moncton (New Brunswick, Canada), became known as the 'Rambo Killer' (*New York Post*, 7 June 2014). The growth in popularity of video games, outstripping the Film Industry in terms of revenue by some $20 billion in 2016 (Shanley 2017), has seen the moral panic shift away from film. This has included President Donald Trump explicitly citing video games as a cause of mass-shooting in the United States stating that, in the wake of shootings in El Paso, Texas and Dayton, Ohio, that killed twenty-one people in a single weekend, 'We must stop the glorification of violence in our society. This includes the gruesome and grisly video games that are now commonplace. It is too easy today for troubled youth to surround themselves with a culture that celebrates violence' (Timm 2019). Despite this popular, and politically expedient, belief evidence of a link remains elusive, as it does with the movies. A 2020 meta-analysis of 28 studies (covering approximately 21,000 youths) concerning the supposed links between aggressive video game content and aggressive behaviour, published by the Royal Society, found that 'Overall, longitudinal studies do not appear to support substantive long-term links between aggressive game content and youth aggression. Correlations between aggressive game content and youth aggression appear better explained by methodological weaknesses and researcher expectancy effects than true effects in the real world' (Drummond et al. 2020: 1–2). Ironically, despite the increase in playing

---

[10] Whereas Hinkley was found not guilty on grounds of insanity, Goetz was found guilty of an illegal weapons charge. Later public opinion would turn on Goetz when it became less clear whether he had been threatened by the four young black men he shot (Rubin 1987).

of video games and the success of titles such as *Grand Theft Auto V* and *Fortnite*, both titles accused of glorifying and encouraging violence, crime in the United States has been consistently dropping since the 1990s. Between 1993 and 2018 violent crime (including rape, robbery and assault) has fallen between 51 per cent and 71 per cent, although the public perception of crime has grown (Gramlich 2019). Looking further back to the past we can see the work of Fredric Wertham, who, in *The Seduction of the Innocent* (1954), suggested comic books were the cause of youth violence through their promotion of sex, violence and drug use. This itself echoed nineteenth-century concerns over Penny Dreadfuls (cheap serial literature) in the United Kingdom and Dime Novels in the United States (Barker 1997: 26). This dominant discourse allied with the othering of film and audience led to a failure to recognize the complexity of the Vigilante Thrillers and the multiple pleasures they presented. More, it attempts to place the cause of a wider moral panic about crime, law and order, and social change at the films' door, rather than attempting to investigate the wider and more complex sociological factors.[11]

The Vigilante Thrillers represent a unique response to a time of great upheaval in American society. Their uniqueness lies not only in their engagement with these issues but in their willingness to complicate such issues, and the spectator's response, rather than simplifying them. The critical reaction that accompanied their release stands as much as a critique of the times and the supposed audience as of the films themselves. The accusations of fascism made are symptomatic of the political and social upheavals of the time but also grossly oversimplifies the films' meanings.

---

[11]There is, however, a single caveat. *Dirty Harry* has been reported to have had a positive impact on the sales of firearms across America (LaPell 2011).

APPENDIX

TABLE 4 *Box-Office Figures for the Vigilante Thrillers*

Film (US Release Date)	Budget	Domestic Box Office
Joe (15 July 1970)	$250,000–$300,000 (Powell and Garrett, 2014: 20)	$19,184,330 (IMDB, 2014)
The French Connection (7 October 1971)	$1,800,000 (IMDB, 2014)	$51,700,000 (Box Office Mojo, 2014)
Dirty Harry (22 December 1971)	$4,000,000 (IMDB, 2014)	$35,976,000 (IMDB, 2014)
Straw Dogs (29 December 1971)	$2,200,000 (Variety, 1973)	$8,000,000 (Variety, 1973)
Death Wish (24 July 1974)	$3,000,000 (IMDB, 2014)	$22,000,000 (Box Office Mojo, 2014)
Taxi Driver (7 February 1976)	$1,300,000 (IMDB, 2014)	$27,300,000 (Box Office Mojo, 2014)

FILMOGRAPHY

Aliens (1986), [Film] Dir. James Cameron, USA: 20th Century Fox.
All the President's Men (1976), [Film] Dir. Alan J. Pakula, USA: Warner.
The Bad Man (1941), [Film] Dir. Richard Thorpe, USA: Metro-Goldwyn-Mayer.
The Ballard of Cable Hogue (1970), [Film] Dir. Sam Peckinpah, USA: Warner Bros.
The Beguiled (1971), [Film] Dir. Don Siegel, USA: Universal Pictures.
The Big Heat (1953), [Film] Dir. Fritz Lang, USA: Columbia Pictures.
Billy Jack (1971), [Film] Dir. Tom Laughlin, USA: Warner Brothers.
Birth of a Nation (1915), [Film] Dir. D.W. Griffith, USA: Epoch Producing Co.
Blazing Saddles (1974), [Film] Dir. Mel Brooks, USA: Warner Brothers.
Bonnie and Clyde (1967), [Film] Dir. Arthur Penn, USA: Warner Bros.-Seven Arts.
The Brave One (2007), [Film] Dir. Neil Jordan, USA: Warner Bros. Pictures.
Bullitt (1968), [Film] Dir. Peter Yates, USA: Warner Bros-Seven Arts.
Chato's Land (1972), [Film] Dir. Michael Winner, USA: United Artists.
Chinatown (1974), [Film] Dir. Roman Polanski, USA: Paramount Pictures.
Cleopatra (1963), [Film] Dir. Joseph L. Mankiewicz, USA: 20th Century Fox.
A Clockwork Orange (1971), [Film] Dir. Stanley Kubrick, USA/UK: Warner Brothers.
Coogan's Bluff (1968), [Film] Dir. Don Siegel, USA: Universal Pictures.
The Deadly Companions (1961), [Film] Dir. Sam Peckinpah, USA: Pathé-America Distributing Company.
Death Valley Days (1964-6), [Television] Madison Productions.
Death Wish (1974), [Film] Dir. Michael Winner, USA: Paramount Pictures.
Death Wish (2018), [Film] Dir. Eli Roth, USA: Metro-Goldwyn-Mayer.
Death Wish II (1982), [Film] Dir. Michael Winner, USA: Cannon Films.
Death Wish V: The Face of Death (1994), [Film] Dir. Allan A. Goldstein, USA: Trimark Pictures.
Deep Throat (1972), [Film] Dir. Jerry Gerard, USA: Bryanston Distributing Company.
Deliverance (1972), [Film] Dir. John Boorman, USA: Warner Brothers.
The Detective (1968), [Film] Dir. Gordon Douglas, USA: 20th Century Fox.
Detective Story (1951), [Film] Dir. William Wyler, USA: Paramount Pictures.
Die Hard (1988), [Film] Dir. John McTiernan, USA: 20th Century Fox.
Dirty Harry (1971), [Film] Dir. Don Siegel, USA: Warner Brothers.
Django (1966), [Film] Dir. Sergio Corbucci, Italy/Spain: Euro International Film.
Dr. No (1962), [Film] Dir. Terence Young, UK/USA: United Artists.
Easy Rider (1969), [Film] Dir, Dennis Hopper, USA: Columbia Pictures.
Electra Glide in Blue (1973), [Film] Dir, James William Guercio, USA: United Artists.
The Equalizer (2014), [Film], Dir. Antoine Fuqua, USA: Sony Pictures Releasing.

The Equalizer 2 (2018), [Film], Dir. Antoine Fuqua, USA: Sony Pictures Releasing.
The Exorcist (1973), [Film], Dir. William Friedkin, USA: Warner Brothers.
The Exterminator (1980), [Film], Dir. James Glickenhaus, USA: AVCO Embassy Pictures.
First Blood (1982), [Film], Dir. Ted Kotchoff, USA: Orion Pictures.
A Fistful of Dollars (1964), [Film] Dir. Sergio Leone, Italy/West Germany/Spain: Unidis.
Five Easy Pieces (1970), [Film] Dir. Bob Rafelson, USA: Columbia Pictures.
For a Few Dollars More (1965), [Film] Dir. Sergio Leone, Italy/West Germany/Spain: Produzioni Europee Associati.
48 Hours (1982), [Film] Dir. Walter Hill, USA: Paramount Pictures.
The French Connection (1971), [Film] Dir. William Friedkin, USA: 20th Century Fox.
The French Connection II (1975), [Film] Dir. John Frankenheimer, USA: 20th Century Fox.
The Godfather Part II (1974), [Film] Dir. Francis Ford Coppola, USA: Paramount Pictures.
The Good, The Bad and The Ugly (1966), [Film] Dir. Sergio Leone, Italy: Produzioni Europee Associati/United Artists.
The Great Escape (1963), [Film] Dir. John Sturges, USA: United Artists.
The Graduate (1967), [Film] Dir. Mike Nichols, USA: Embassy Pictures.
Guess Who's Coming to Dinner (1967), [Film] Dir. Stanley Kramer, USA: Columbia Pictures.
Guns in the Afternoon (1962) [Film] Dir. Sam Peckinpah, USA: Metro-Goldwyn-Mayer.
High Noon (1952), [Film] Dir. Fred Zinnemann, USA: Stanley Kramer Productions.
The Hills Have Eyes (1977), [Film] Dir. Wes Craven, USA: Vanguard.
I Was a Communist for the FBI (1951), [Film] Dir. Gordon Douglas, USA: Warner Bros.
I Spit on Your Grave (1977), [Film] Dir. Meir Zarchi, USA: The Jerry Gross Organization.
In the Heat of the Night (1967), [Film] Dir. Norman Jewison, USA: United Artists.
Joe (1970), [Film] Dir. John G. Avildsen, USA: Cannon Films.
Kelly's Heroes (1970), [Film] Dir. Brian G. Hutton, USA/Yugoslavia: Metro-Goldwyn-Mayer.
Kiss of Death (1947), [Film] Dir. Henry Hathaway, USA: 20th Century Fox.
The Last House on the Left (1972), [Film] Dir. Wes Craven, USA: Hallmark Releasing/American International Pictures.
Law Abiding Citizen (2009), [Film] Dir. F. Gary Gray, USA: Overture Films.
Lawman (1970), [Film] Dir. Michael Winner, USA: United Artists.
The Legend of Nigger Charley (1972), [Film] Dir. Martin Gold, USA: Paramount Pictures Corp.
Lethal Weapon (1987), [Film] Dir. Richard Donner, USA: Warner Brothers.
Little Big Man (1970), [Film] Dir. Arthur Penn, USA: National General Pictures.
The Long Goodbye (1973), [Film] Dir. Robert Altman, USA: United Artists.
Love Story (1970), [Film] Dir. Arthur Hiller, USA: Paramount Pictures.
Madigan (1968), [Film] Dir. Don Siegel, USA: Universal Pictures.

The Magnificent Seven (1960), [Film] Dir. John Sturges, USA: United Artists.
Magnum Force (1973), [Film] Dir. Ted Post, USA: Warner Brothers.
Major Dundee (1965), [Film] Dir. Sam Peckinpah, USA: Columbia Pictures.
The Man Who Shot Liberty Valance (1962), [Film] Dir. John Ford, USA: Paramount Pictures.
The Man with the Golden Arm (1955), [Film] Dir. Otto Preminger, USA: United Artists.
Mean Streets (1973), [Film] Dir. Martin Scorsese, USA: Warner Brothers.
The Mechanic (1972), [Film] Dir. Michael Winner, USA: United Artists.
McCabe and Mrs Miller (1971), [Film] Dir. Robert Altman, USA: Warner Bros.
Midnight Cowboy (1969), [Film] Dir. John Schlesinger, USA: United Artists.
Monty Python's Flying Circus (1972), [TV Programme] BBC1, 30 November.
Ms. 45 (1981), [Film] Dir. Abel Ferrara, USA: Rochelle Films.
My Darling Clementine (1946), [Film] Dir. John Ford, USA: 20th Century Fox.
My Fair Lady (1964), [Film] Dir. George Cukor, USA: Warner Bros.
Night of the Living Dead (1968), [Film] Dir. George. A. Romero, USA: Continental Distributing.
Once Upon a Time in the West (1968), [Film] Dir. Sergio Leone, Italy/USA: Euro International Film/Paramount Pictures.
The Parallax View (1974), [Film] Dir. Alan J. Pakula, USA: Paramount Pictures.
Play Misty for Me (1971), [Film] Dir. Clint Eastwood, USA: Universal Pictures.
Predator (1987), [Film] Dir. John McTiernan, USA: 20th Century Fox.
Prisoners (2013), [Film] Dir. Denis Villeneuve, USA: Warner Brothers Pictures.
Psycho (1960), [Film] Dir. Alfred Hitchcock, USA: Paramount Pictures.
Rambo: First Blood Part 2 (1985), [Film] Dir. George P. Cosmatos, USA: Tristar Pictures.
Rambo III (1988), [Film] Dir. Peter MacDonald, USA: Tri-Star Pictures.
Rawhide (1959–66), [TV Programme] CBS.
Rear Window (1954), [Film] Dir. Alfred Hitchcock, USA: Paramount Pictures.
Rocky (1976), [Film] Dir. John G. Avildsen, USA: United Artists
Rocky III (1983), [Film] Dir. Sylvester Stallone, USA: United Artists.
Rolling Thunder (1977), [Film] Dir. John Flynn, USA: American International Pictures.
Rosemary's Baby (1968), [Film] Dir. Roman Polanski, USA: Paramount Pictures.
The Searchers (1956), [Film] Dir. John Ford, USA: Warner Brothers.
Shane (1953), [Film] Dir. George Stevens, USA: Paramount Pictures.
Soldier Blue (1970), [Film] Dir. Ralph Nelson, USA: Embassy Pictures.
The Sound of Music (1965), [Film] Dir. Robert Wise, USA: 20th Century Fox.
The Star Chamber (1968), [Film] Dir. Peter Hyams, USA: 20th Century Fox.
Star Wars (1977), [Film] Dir. George Lucas, USA: 20th Century Fox.
The Stone Killer (1973), [Film] Dir. Michael Winner, USA/Italy: Columbia Pictures.
Straw Dogs (1971), [Film] Dir. Sam Peckinpah, USA/UK: Cinerama Releasing Corporation/20th Century Fox.
The Strawberry Statement (1970), [Film] Dir. Stuart Hagmann, USA: Metro-Goldwyn-Mayer.
Support Your Local Sheriff! (1969), [Film] Dir. Burt Kennedy, USA: United Artists.
Targets (1967), [Film] Dir. Peter Bogdanovich, USA: Paramount Pictures.
Taxi Driver (1976), [Film] Dir. Martin Scorsese, USA: Columbia Pictures.

Terminator 2: Judgement Day (1991), [Film] Dir. James Cameron, USA: Tristar Pictures.
The Texas Chainsaw Massacre (1974), [Film] Dir. Tobe Hooper, USA: Bryanston Distributing Company.
Thelma & Louise (1991), [Film] Dir. Ridley Scott, USA: Metro-Goldwyn-Mayer.
Three Days of the Condor (1975), [Film] Dir. Sidney Pollack, USA: Paramount Pictures.
Touch of Evil (1958), [Film] Dir. Orson Welles, USA: Universal-International.
Triumph of the Will (1935), [Film] Dir. Leni Riefenstahl, Germany: UFA.
Two-Lane Blacktop (1971), [Film] Dir. Monte Hellman, USA: Universal Pictures.
Two Mules for Sister Sara (1970), [Film] Dir. Don Siegel, USA: Universal Pictures.
Vigilante Force (1976), [Film] Dir. George Armitage, USA: United Artists.
Walking Tall (1973), [Film] Dir. Phil Karlson, USA: Cinerama Releasing Corporation.
Where Eagles Dare (1968), [Film] Dir. Brian G. Hutton, UK: Metro-Goldwyn-Mayer.
Where the Sidewalk Ends (1950), [Film] Dir. Otto Preminger, USA: 20th Century Fox.
The Wild Bunch (1969), [Film] Dir. Sam Peckinpah, USA: Warner Bros.–Seven Arts.
Yojimbo (1961), [Film] Dir. Akira Kurosawa, Japan: Toho.
Z (1969), [Film] Dir. Costa-Gavras, Algeria/France: Cinema V.

BIBLIOGRAPHY

Allen, Graham (2000). *Intertextuality*. London: Routledge.
Altman, Rick (1999). *Film/Genre*. London: BFI.
Andrews, Nigel (1971). 'Joe'. *Monthly Film Bulletin*, 38 (477): 75–76.
Andrews, Nigel (1971). 'Straw Dogs'. *Monthly Film Bulletin*, 38 (455): 249–250.
ASHPD24 (2010). *Star Wars Episode IV: A New Hope (1977) Body Count Breakdown by ASHPD24*. [online] Available from http://www.allouttabubblegum.com/main/?p=6343 [Accessed 19 March 2015].
Bacon, Henry (2015). *The Fascination of Film Violence*. London: Palgrave.
Baker, Kevin (2015). 'Welcome to Fear City' – The Inside Story of New York's Civil War, 40 Years on'. *The Guardian*, 18 May [online] Available from https://www.theguardian.com/cities/2015/may/18/welcome-to-fear-city-the-inside-story-of-new-yorks-civil-war-40-years-on [Accessed 18 April 2018].
Bandura, A., Ross, D., Ross, S.A.,(1963). 'Vicarious Reinforcement & Imitative Learning'. *Journal of Abnormal and Social Psychology*, 67 (6): 601–607.
Barr, Charles (1972). 'Straw Dogs, A Clockwork Orange and the Critics'. *Screen*, 3 (2): 17–31.
Barthes, Roland (1992). *S/Z*. Translated by Richard Miller. Oxford: Blackwell Publishers.
Bazin, Andre (1976). 'The Evolution of the Western'. In: Bill Nichols (ed.), *Movies and Methods: Volume 1*. London: University of California Press.
Berger, John (1972). *Ways of Seeing*. London: Penguin.
Biskind, Peter (1998). *Easy Riders, Raging Bulls: How the Sex-drugs-and Rock 'n' Roll Generation Changed Hollywood*. London: Bloomsbury.
Blackman, Lisa and Walkerdine, Valerie (2001). *Mass Hysteria: Critical Psychology and Media Studies*. London: Wallflower.
Bliss, Michael (1993). *Justified Lives: Morality and Narrative in the Films of Sam Peckinpah*. Carbondale: Southern Illinois University Press.
Bloom, Alexander and Brienes, Wini (2003). *Takin' it to the Streets: A Sixties Reader*. Oxford: Oxford University Press.
Bourke, Joanna (2008). *Rape: A History from 1860 to the Present*. St Ives: Virago.
Box Office Mojo (2014). *The French Connection*. [online] Available from http://www.boxofficemojo.com/movies/?id=frenchconnection.htm [Accessed 11 July 2014].
Box Office Mojo (2014). *Death Wish*. [online] Available from http://www.boxofficemojo.com/movies/?id=deathwish.htm [Accessed 11 July 2014].
Box Office Mojo (2014). *Taxi Driver*. [online] Available from http://www.boxofficemojo.com/movies/?id=taxidriver.htm [Accessed 11 July 2014].

Brannigan, Edward (1992). *Narrative Comprehension and Film*. Oxford: Routledge.
Branston, Gill (2000). *Cinema and Cultural Modernity*. Buckingham: Open University Press.
Brownmiller, Susan (1975). *Against Our Will: Men, Women and Rape*. New York: Bantam Books.
Bullard, Sara (1997). *The Ku Klux Klan: A History of Racism & Violence, Fifth Edition*. Alabama: The Southern Poverty Law Centre.
Buscombe, Ed. (1988). *The BFI Companion to the Western*. London: BFI.
Buscombe, Ed. (2000). *The Searchers*. London: BFI.
Butler, Terence (1979). *Crucified Heroes: The Films of Sam Peckinpah*. London: The Gordon Fraser Gallery.
Byron, Stuart (1979). 'The Searchers: Cult Movie of the New Hollywood'. *New York Magazine*, 5 March, 44–48.
Canby, Vincent (1972). 'Has Movie Violence Gone Too Far?' *The New York Times*, 16 January, Section D, page 1.
Canby, Vincent (1974a). 'Screen: "Death Wish"' Hunts Muggers: Story of Gunman Takes Dim View of City'. *The New York Times*, 25 July, page 27.
Canby, Vincent (1974b). '"Death Wish" Exploits Fear Irresponsibly'. *The New York Times*, 4 August, page 85.
Canby, Vincent (1976a). 'Scorsese's Disturbing Taxi Driver'. *The New York Times*, 15 February, Section D, page 1.
Canby, Vincent (1976b). 'Explicit Violence Overwhelms Every Other Value On the Screen'. *The New York Times*, 17 October, 69.
Casetti, Francesco (1998). *Inside the Gaze*. Bloomington: Indiana University Press.
Cashin, F. (1972). 'The Bloodbath Is a Bore'. *The Sun*, 30 March.
Cashin, F., Coleman, J., Hibbin, N., Hinxman, M., Malcolm, D., Melly, G., Palmer, T., Plowright, M., Powell, D., Robinson, D., Russell Taylor, J., Thirkell, A. and Walker, A. (1971). 'Film Censorship'. *The Times*, 17 December.
Cawelti, John G. (1984). *The Six-Gun Mystique*. Bowling Green: Bowling Green University Press.
Cawelti, John G. (2004). *Mystery, Violence and Popular Culture*. Wisconsin: University of Wisconsin Press.
Christie, Ian (1971). 'The Message That Will Shatter You'. *The Daily Express*, 24 November.
Christie, Ian (1972). 'The French Connection'. *The Daily Express*, 18 January.
Churchwell, Sarah (2019). *Behold America: A History of America First and the American Dream*. London: Bloomsbury Publishing.
Clover, Carol J. (1992). *Men, Women and Chainsaws: Gender in the Modern Horror Film*. Princeton: Princeton University Press.
Cobley, Paul (2000). *The American Thriller: Generic Innovation and Social Change in the 1970s*. London: Palgrave.
Cohan, Steve and Park, Ena Rae (1992). *Screening the Male: Exploring Masculinities in Hollywood Cinema*. London: Routledge.
Cohen, Stanley (2002). *Folk Devils and Moral Panics: Third Edition*. Routledge: Abingdon.
Coleman, John (1975). 'Death Wish'. *The New Statesman*, 7 February.

Cook, David A. (1990). *A History of Narrative Film*. London: WW Norton & Co.
Corkin, Stanley (2011). *Starring New York: Filming the Grime and Glamour of the Long 1970s*. New York: Oxford University Press.
Costa Pinto, António (Ed.), (2011). *Rethinking the Nature of Fascism: Comparative Perspectives*. London: Palgrave Macmillan.
Creed, Barbara (1993). *The Monstrous Feminine: Film, Feminism and Psychoanalysis*. Abingdon: Routledge.
Cutler, James E. (1969) *Lynch Law: An Investigation into the History of Lynching in the United States*. New York: Negro Universties Press.
DeAngelis, Michael (2007). '1972: Movies and Confessions'. In Lester D. Friedman (ed.), *American Cinema of the 1970s: Themes and Variations*. Oxford: Berg.
Dunaway, Finnis (2015). *Seeing Green: The Use and Abuse of American Environmental Images*. Chicago: University of Chicago Press.
Durham, Michael (1970). 'Reluctant Hero of the Hardhats'. *Life*, 16 October, 69–70.
Drummond, A., Sauer J.D., Ferguson C.J. (2020). 'Do Longitudinal Studies Support Long-Term Relationships Between Aggressive Game Play and Youth Aggressive Behaviour? A Meta-Analytic Examination'. *Royal Society Open Science*, 7: 200373. [online]. Available from http://dx.doi.org/10.1098/rsos.200373 [Accessed 28 July 2020].
Drummond, Philip (1997). *High Noon*. London: BFI.
Ebert, Roger (1972). 'Dirty Harry'. *Chicago Sun Times*, 1 January, 1971. Available from http://www.rogerebert.com/reviews/dirty-harry-1971 [Accessed 3 August 2014].
Ebert, Roger (1974). 'Death Wish'. *Chicago Sun Times*, 1 January, 1974. Available from http://www.rogerebert.com/reviews/death-wish-1974 [Accessed 5 August 2014].
Eco, Umberto (1995). 'Ur-Fascism'. *The New York Review of Books*, 22 June. Available from nybooks.com/articles/1995/06/22/ur-fascism/ [Accessed 27 July 2020].
Ellis, John (1982). *Visible Fictions*. London: Routledge.
Elsaesser, Thomas (2004). 'The Pathos of Failure: American Films in the 1970s – Notes on the Unmotivated Hero [1975]'. In Thomas Elsaesser (ed.), *The Last Great American Picture Show: New Hollywood Cinema in the 1970s*. Amsterdam: Amsterdam University Press.
Epps, Gareth (1972). 'Does Popeye Doyle Teach Us How to be Fascist?'. *The New York Times*, 21 May, Section D, 15.
The Evening Standard (1971). 'No Peace for Mr Murphy'. 17 December.
Eves, Vicki (1970). 'The Effects of Violence in the Mass Media'. *Screen*, 11 (3): 31–42.
FBI (2011). 'Forcible Rape'. Available from http://www.fbi.gov/about-us/cjis/ucr/crime-in-the-u.s/2011/crime-in-the-u.s.-2011/violent-crime/forcible-rape, [Accessed 23 July 2013].
Frangioni, David and Schatz, Tom (2009). *Clint Eastwood Icon: The Ultimate Film Art Collection*. London: Titan Books.
Frayling, Christopher (1998). *Spaghetti Westerns: Cowboys and Europeans from Karl May to Sergio Leone*. London: IB Taurus.

Freemantle, Brian (1971). 'The French Connection'. *The Daily Mail*, 31 December.
Friedkin, William (2013). *The Friedkin Connection*. New York: Harper Collins.
Friedman, Lester D. (2007). 'Introduction'. In Lester D. Friedman (ed.), *American Cinema of the 1970s: Themes and Variations*. Oxford: Berg Publishers.
Fuchs, Cynthia J. (1991). '"All the Animals Come Out at Night": Vietnam Meets Noir in Taxi Driver'. In Michael Anderigg (ed.), *Inventing Vietnam: The War in Film and Television*. Philadelphia: Temple University Press.
Fuery, Patrick (2000). *New Developments in Film Theory*. London: Macmillan.
Fuery, Patrick (2004). *Madness and Cinema*. London: Palgrave MacMillan.
Gansberg, Martin (1964). 'Thirty-Eight who saw Murder Didn't Call the Police'. *New York Times*, March 27, 1.
Garfield, Brian (1974). *Death Wish*. London: Coronet.
Gershon, Livia (2016). 'Did The 1965 Watts Riots Change Anything?' *Jstor Daily*, 13 July [online] Available from https://daily.jstor.org/did-the-1965-watts-riots-change-anything/ [Accessed 26 May 2020].
Gibson, James William (1994). *Warrior Dreams: Violence and Manhood in Post-Vietnam America*. New York: Hill and Wang.
Gilbey, Ryan (2004). *It Don't Worry Me: Nashville, Jaws, Star Wars and Beyond*. London: Faber.
Gilchrist, Roderick (1975). 'Why the Yard Wants Britain to see "Death Wish"'. *The Daily Mail*. 13 January.
Gilliat, Penelope, (1974). 'Death Wish'. *New Yorker Magazine*, 26 August.
Gliserman, Marty (1975). 'Watch Out Chicago'. *Jump-Cut*, 5: 7–8.
Goldberger, Paul (1968). 'Tony Imperiale Stands Vigilant for Law and Order'. In Alexander Bloom and Wini Brienes (eds) (2003) *Takin' it to the Streets: A Sixties Reader*. Oxford: Oxford University Press.
Gow, Gordon (1976). 'Taxi Driver'. *Films and Filming*, 22 (12, 264): 30–31.
Gramlich, John (2019). '5 Facts about Crime in the U.S'. *Pew Research Centre*, 17 October [online]. Available from https://www.pewresearch.org/fact-tank/2019/10/17/facts-about-crime-in-the-u-s/ [Accessed 28 July 2020]
Greenfield, Pierre (1976). 'Dirty Dogs, Dirty Devils & Dirty Harry'. *The Velvet Light Trap*, 16: 34.
Grist, Leighton (2000). *The Films of Martin Scorsese, 1963–1977: Authorship and Context*. London: MacMillan.
Haberski Jr., Raymond J. (2001). *"It's Only a Movie": Films and Critics in American Culture*. Lexington: University Press of Kentucky.
Hall, S., Critcher, C., Jefferson, T., Clarke, J. and Roberts, B., (1978). *Policing the Crisis: Mugging, the State, and Law and Order*. Palgrave MacMillan: Houndmills.
Harding, Bill (1978). *The Films of Michael Winner*. Frederick Muller Ltd: London.
Harris, Mark (2008). *Scenes from a Revolution: The Birth of the New Hollywood*. Edinburgh: Cannongate.
Haskell, Molly (1974). *From Reverence to Rape: The Treatment of Women in the Movies*. New York: New Press.
Heath, Stephen (1976). 'Narrative Space'. *Screen*, 17 (3): 68–112.
Henderson, Brian (1985). 'The Searchers: An American Dilemma'. In Nichols, Bill (ed.), *Movies and Methods: Volume 2*. London: University of California Press.

Hill, John (1986). *Sex, Class and Realism: British Cinema 1956–1963*. London: BFI.
Hoberman, J. (2003). *The Dream Life: Movies, Media and the Mythology of the Sixties*. New York: New Press.
Hodge, Bob and Tripp, David (1986). *Children and Television*. Cambridge: Polity Press.
Horsley, Jake (1999). *The Blood Poets: A Cinema of Savagery*. Maryland: Scarecrow Press.
Hutchinson, Tom (1976). 'Taxi Driver'. *The Sunday Telegraph*, 22 August.
IMDB (2014). *Box Office/Business for Dirty Harry*. [online] Available from http://www.imdb.com/title/tt0066999/?ref_=fn_al_tt_1 [Accessed 11 July 2014].
IMDB (2014). *Box Office/Business for Death Wish*. [online] Available from http://www.imdb.com/title/tt0071402/?ref_=fn_al_tt_1 [Accessed 11 July 2014].
IMDB (2014). *Box Office/Business for The French Connection*. [online] Available from http://www.imdb.com/title/tt0067116/?ref_=nv_sr_1 [Accessed 11 July 2014].
IMDB (2014). *Box Office/Business for Joe*. [online] Available from http://www.imdb.com/title/tt0065916/business?ref_=tt_dt_bus [Accessed 11 July 2014].
IMDB (2014). *Box Office/Business for Taxi Driver*. [online] Available from http://www.imdb.com/title/tt0075314/?ref_=fn_al_tt_1 [Accessed 11 July 2014].
IMFDB (2013). *Taxi Driver* [online] Available from http://www.imfdb.org/wiki/Taxi_Driver [Accessed 25 March 2015].
Izod, John (2001). *Myth, Mind and the Screen: Understanding the Heroes of Our Time*. Cambridge: Cambridge University Press.
Jackson, Harold (1983). 'From the Archive, 9 March 1983: Reagan Calls Moscow an Evil Empire'. *The Guardian*, 9 March [online]. Available from https://www.theguardian.com/theguardian/2012/mar/09/archive-1983-reagan-russia-evil-empire [Accessed 29 July 2020].
Jet (1970). 'Joe Film Star Peter Boyle is not a Hardhat'. 10 September, 60–1.
Johnson, Paul (1997). *A History of the American People*. London: Phoenix.
KAB (2013). *KAB: A Beautiful History*. [online] Available from http://www.kab.org/site/PageServer?pagename=about_history [Accessed 11 July 2014].
Kael, Pauline (1973). *Deeper into Movies: The Essential Collection from 1969 to 1972*. London: Marion Boyars Publishers Ltd.
Keathley, Christian (2004). 'Trapped in the Affection Image: Hollywood's Post Traumatic Cycle (1970–1976)'. In Thomas Elsaesser (ed.), *The Last Great American Picture Show: New Hollywood Cinema in the 1970s*. Amsterdam: Amsterdam University Press.
Kendrick, James (2009). *Film Violence: History, Ideology, Genre*. London: Wallflower Press.
Kirshner, Jonathan (2012). *Hollywood's Last Golden Age: Politics, Society, and the Seventies Film in America*. New York: Cornell University Press.
Kistes, Jim (2007). *Horizons' West: Directing The Western from John Ford to Clint Eastwood (New Edition)*. London: BFI.
Kitses, Jim (1970). *Horizons West – Anthony Mann, Budd Boetticher, Sam Peckinpah: Studies in Authorship Within the Western*. London: Indiana University Press.
Klemesrud, Julie (1974). 'What Do They See in "Death Wish"?' *The New York Times*, 1 September, 87.

Kolker, Robert Philip (1980). *A Cinema of Loneliness: Penn, Kubrick, Spielberg, Altman*. New York: Oxford University Press.
Krämer, Peter (1999). 'A Powerful Cinema-going Force? Hollywood and Female Audiences since the 1960s'. In Melvyn Stokes and Richard Maltby (eds), *Identifying Hollywood's Audiences: Cultural Identity and the Movies*. London: BFI.
Krämer, Peter (2005). *The New Hollywood: From Bonnie and Clyde to Star Wars*. London: Wallflower Press.
Langford, Barry (2010). *Post-Classical Hollywood: Film Industry, Style and Ideology since 1945*. Edinburgh: Edinburgh University Press.
Latané, B. and Darley, J. M. (1970). *The Unresponsive Bystander: Why Doesn't He Help?* New York: Appleton–Century–Crofts.
LaPell, David (2011). 'Forty Years of Dirty Harry and His .44 Magnum'. [online] Available from http://www.guns.com/2011/04/02/forty-years-of-dirty-harry-and-his-44-magnum/ [Accessed 8 July 2015].
Lebeau, Vicky (2001). *Psychoanalysis and Cinema: The Play of Shadows*. London: Wallflower.
Leech, Michael (1975). *I Know it When I See it: Pornography, Violence and Public Sensibility*. Philadelphia: Westminster Press.
Lev, Peter (2000). *American Films of the 1970s: Conflicting Visions*. Austin: University of Texas Press.
Levesque, Christopher J. (2018). 'The Truth Behind My Lai'. *The New York Times*, 16 March. [online] Available from https://www.nytimes.com/2018/03/16/opinion/the-truth-behind-my-lai.html [Accessed 14 July 2021].
Ligensa, Annemone (2012). 'Clint Eastwood's US Audience 1964–2009: A Reception-Oriented Approach to Star Analysis'. *Celebrity Studies*, 3 (2): 232–248.
Lovell, Alan (1975). *Don Siegel: American Cinema*. London: BFI.
Lyotard, Jean-François (1984). *The Postmodern Condition: A Report on Knowledge*. Translated from the French by G. Bennington and B. Massumi. Manchester: Manchester University Press.
Mailer, Norman (1968). *Miami and the Siege of Chicago*. New York: New York Review of Books.
Malcolm, Derek (1976). 'Taxi Driver'. *The Guardian*, 19 August.
Manning, R., Levine, M. and Collins, A., (2007). 'The Kitty Genovese Murder and the Social Psychology of Helping: The Parable of the 38 Witnesses'. *American Psychologist*, 62 (6): 555–562.
Mask, Mia (2007). 'Macho Cops: The French Connection and Dirty Harry'. In Lester D. Friedman (ed.), *American Cinema of the 1970s: Themes and Variations*. Oxford: Berg Publishers.
McArthur, Colin (1975). 'Analysing the Outcry Over Death Wish'. *The Tribune*. 21 February.
McNary, Dave (2016). 'Bruce Willis' "Death Wish" Remake Sets Israeli Directing Team'. *Variety*. [online] Available from http://variety.com/2016/film/news/bruce-willis-death-wish-remake-directors-1201722814/ [Accessed 11 May 2016].
Mendik, Xavier (2002). 'Urban Legend: The 1970s Films of Michael Winner'. In Xavier Mendik (ed.), *Shocking Cinema of the Seventies*. Hereford: Noir.
Mercer, Kobena (1994). *Welcome to the Jungle: New Positions in Black Cultural Studies*. London: Routledge.

Metz, Christian (1975). 'The Imaginary Signifier'. *Screen*, 16 (2): 14–16.
Milioria, Maria T. (2004). *The Scorsese Psyche on Screen: Roots of Themes and Characters in the Films*. Jefferson: McFarland and Company.
Milne, Tom (1971). 'How Are You Going to Keep the Down on the Farm?' *The Times*, 26 November, 12.
Milne, Tom (1971). 'Straw Dogs'. *Sight and Sound*, 41 (1): 50.
Milne, Tom (1972). 'Dirty Harry'. *Sight and Sound*, 41 (2): 112.
Morris, Nigel (2007). *The Cinema of Steven Spielberg: Empire of Light*. London: Wallflower.
Mortimer, Barbera (Spring Summer 1997). 'Portraits of the Postmodern Person in Taxi Driver, Raging Bull, and The King of Comedy'. *Journal of Film and Video*, 49 (1/2): 28–38.
Moyer, Justin Wm. (2014). 'And the Zodiac Killer is…'. *The Washington Post*. [online] Available from https://www.washingtonpost.com/news/morning-mix/wp/2014/05/14/and-the-zodiac-killer-is/ [Accessed 23 May 2016].
Mulvey, Laura (1975). 'Visual Pleasure and Narrative Cinema'. *Screen*, 16 (3): 6–18.
Murdock, Graham (1997). 'Reservoirs of Dogma: An Archaeology of Popular Anxieties'. In M. Barker and J. Petley (eds), *Ill Effects: The Media/Violence Debate*. London: Routledge.
Murphy, Stephen (1971). 'Public Opinion as Film Board's Criticism'. *The Times*, 20 December.
Murray, William (2008). 'Playboy Interview: Sam Peckinpah'. In Kevin J. Hayes (ed.), *Sam Peckinpah: Interviews*. Mississippi: University Press of Mississippi.
Neale, Stephen (1990). 'Questions of Genre'. *Screen*, 31 (1): 45–66.
New York Post (2014). '"Rambo" Killer was Obsessed with Guns'. 7 June. Available from http://nypost.com/2014/06/07/rambo-cop-killer-was-obsessed-with-guns/ [Accessed 3 June 2015].
Nystrom, Derek (2009). *Hard Hats, Rednecks, and Macho Men: Class in 1970s American Cinema*. New York: Oxford University Press.
Oxford Dictionaries (2015). *Definition of Joe in English*. [online] Available from http://www.oxforddictionaries.com/definition/english/joe [Accessed 14 August 2015].
Orwell, George (1944). 'What is Fascism', *The Tribune*. [online] Available from http://orwell.ru/library/articles/As_I_Please/english/efasc [Accessed 21 May 2015].
Palmer, Jerry (1978). *Thrillers: Genesis and Structure of a Popular Genre*. London: Hodder Arnold.
Palmer, William J. (1987). *The Films of the Seventies: A Social History*. London: The Scarecrow Press.
Passmore, Kevin (2002). *Fascism: A Very Short Introduction*. Oxford: Oxford University Press.
Passmore, Kevin (2011). 'Theories of Fascism: A Critique from the Perspective of Women's and Gender History'. In António Costa Pinto (ed.), *Rethinking the Nature of Fascism: Comparative Perspectives*. London: Palgrave MacMillan.
Petley, Julian (1997). 'Us and Them'. In M. Barker and J. Petley (eds), *Ill Effects: The Media/Violence Debate*. London: Routledge.
Pirie, David (1972). 'The French Connection'. *Monthly Film Bulletin*, 39 (56): 6–7.

Powell, Dilys (1975). 'Death Wish'. *The Sunday Times*, 9 February.
Powell, Larry and Garrett, Tom (2009). *The Films of John G. Avildsen: Rocky, The Karate Kid and Other Underdogs*. North Carolina: McFarland and Company.
Prince, Stephen (1998). *Savage Cinema: Sam Peckinpah and the Rise of Ultraviolence*. Austin: Austin University Press.
Prince, Stephen (2003). *Classical Film Violence: Designing and Regulating Brutality in Hollywood Cinema 1930–1968*. New Jersey: Rutgers University Press.
Prince, Stephen (2004). 'Genre and Violence in Kurosawa and Peckinpah'. In Yvonne Tasker (ed.), *Action and Adventure Cinema*. London: Routledge.
Queally, James (2015). 'Watts Riots: Traffic Stop Was the Spark That Ignited Days of Destruction on L.A'. *Los Angeles Times*, 29 July [online]. Available from https://www.latimes.com/local/lanow/la-me-ln-watts-riots-explainer-20150715-htmlstory.html. [Accessed 26 May 2020].
Quigley Publishing (2004). *Top Ten Money Making Stars of the Past 78 Years* [online]. Available from http://www.quigleypublishing.com/MPalmanac/Top10/Top10_lists.html [Accessed 24 May 2010].
Reiner, Robert (1981). 'Keystone to Kojak: The Hollywood Cop'. In Philip Davies and Brian Neve (eds), *Cinema, Politics and Society in America*. Manchester: Manchester University Press.
Richardson, Michael (2010). *Otherness in Hollywood Cinema*. London: Continuum.
Robertson, James C. (1989). *The Hidden Cinema: British Censorship in Action, 1913–1975*. London: Routledge.
Rosen, Jane (1974). 'Film Sets off New Vigilantism'. *The Guardian*, 21 September.
Rosenthal, A.M. (1964). *Thirty Eight Witnesses*. New York: McGraw-Hill.
Ryan, Michael and Kellner, Douglas (1988). *Camera Politica: The Politics and Ideology of Contemporary Hollywood Film*. Bloomington and Indianapolis: Indianapolis University Press.
Rubin, Lillian B. (1987). *Quiet Rage: Bernie Goetz and the New York Subway Shooting*. London: Faber.
Rubin, Martin (1999). *Thrillers*. Cambridge: Cambridge University Press.
Schatz, Thomas (2004). 'Introduction'. In Stephen Jay Schneider (ed.), *New Hollywood Violence*. Manchester: Manchester University Press.
Schickel, Richard (1970). 'The Fellowship of Violence'. *Life*, 21 August, 13.
Schickel, Richard (1972). 'Don't Play it Again, Sam'. *Life*, 11 February, 14.
Schickel, Richard (1974). 'Mug Shooting'. *Time Magazine*, 19 August.
Schickel, Richard (1976). 'Potholes'. *Time Magazine*, 16 February.
"Schizothymia." *Merriam-Webster.com Dictionary*, Merriam-Webster [online], https://www.merriam-webster.com/dictionary/schizothymia [Accessed 22 April 2015].
Shanley, Patrick (2017). 'Why Aren't Video Games as Respected as Movies?'. *Hollywood Reporter* 14 December [online] Available from https://www.hollywoodreporter.com/heat-vision/why-arent-video-games-as-respected-as-movies-1067314 [Accessed 28 July 2020].
Shedlin, Michael (1972). 'Police Oscar: "The French Connection" and an Interview with William Friedkin'. *Film Quarterly*, 24 (4): 2–9.

Shiel, Mark (2006). 'American Cinema 1965-75'. In Linda Ruth Williams and Michael Hammond (eds), *Contemporary American Cinema*. Maidenhead: Open University Press.

Siegel, Don (1993). *A Siegel Film: An Autobiography*. London: Faber and Faber.

Simkin, Stevie (2006). *Early Modern Tragedy and the Cinema of Violence*. New York: Palgrave MacMillan.

Simkin, Stevie (2011). *Straw Dogs (Controversies)*. Houndmills: Palgrave MacMillan.

Slane, Andrea (2001). *A Not So Foreign Affair: Fascism, Sexuality, and the Cultural Rhetoric of American Democracy*. London: Duke University Press.

Slocum, J. David (2004). 'The "film violence" trope: New Hollywood, "the Sixties" and the Politics of History'. In Stephen Jay Schneider (ed.), *New Hollywood Violence*. Manchester: Manchester University Press.

Slotkin, Richard (1992). *Gunfighter Nation: The Myth of the Frontier in Twentieth Century America*. New York: Atheneum.

Small, Melvin (1999). *The Presidency of Richard Nixon*. Lawrence: University of Kansas Press.

Smith, Paul (1993). *Clint Eastwood: A Cultural Production*. Minneapolis: University of Minnesota Press.

Sorrento, Christopher (2011). *Death Wish (Deep Focus)*. Berkeley: Soft Skull Press.

Street, Joe (2016). *Dirty Harry's America: Clint Eastwood, Harry Callahan and the Conservative Backlash*. Gainesville: University Press of Florida.

Talbot, Paul (2006). *Bronson's Loose!: The Making of the Death Wish Films*. Nebraska: iUniverse.

Tasker, Yvonne (1993). *Spectacular Bodies: Gender, Genre and the Action Cinema*. London: Routledge.

Tasker, Yvonne (2015). *The Hollywood Action and Adventure Film*. Chichester: Wiley Blackwell.

Taubin, Amy (2000). *Taxi Driver*. London: BFI.

Thinkell, A., (1971). 'Yokel Horror is the Last Straw'. *The Daily Mirror*.

Thomas, Bill (2014). *Second Wind: Navigating the Passage to Slower, Deeper and More Connected Life*. New York: Simon and Schuster.

Thompson, David and Christie, Ian (1989). *Scorsese on Scorsese*. London: Faber and Faber.

Time (1966). 'Criminal Justice: Learning to Live with Miranda'. 5 August. Available from http://content.time.com/time/magazine/article/0,9171,836154,00.html [Accessed 2 February 2012].

Time (1968). 'Criminal Justice: Doubts About Miranda'. *Time*. 1 November 1968. Available from http://content.time.com/time/magazine/article/0,9171,839605,00.html [Accessed 2 February 2012].

Time (1970). 'Nation: The Sudden Rising of the Hard Hats'. 25 May. Available from http://content.time.com/time/magazine/article/0,9171,909247,00.html [Accessed 2 February 2012].

Time (1970). 'Crime: Joe and Arville'. *Time*. 7 December. Available from http://content.time.com/time/magazine/article/0,9171,877135,00.html [Accessed 9 September 2009].

Time (1970). 'What the Police Can – And Cannot – Do About Crime'. 13 July. Available from http://content.time.com/time/magazine/article/0,9171,909452,00.html [Accessed 7 July 2009].

Time (1972). 'Street Crime: Who's Winning? ' 23 October. Available from http://content.time.com/time/magazine/article/0,9171,878053,00.html [Accessed 7 July 2009].

Time (1975). 'The Crime Wave'. 30 June. Available from http://content.time.com/time/magazine/article/0,9171,917566,00.html [Accessed 7 July 2009].

Timm, Jane C. (2019). 'Fact Check: Trump Suggests Video Games to Blame for Mass Shootings'. *NBC News*, 6 August [online]. Available from https://www.nbcnews.com/politics/donald-trump/fact-check-trump-suggests-video-games-blame-mass-shootings-n1039411 [Accessed 28 July 2020].

Tomkins, Jane (1992). *West of Everything: The Inner Life of Westerns*. London: Oxford University Press.

Torode, John (1975). 'Winning Shot'. *The Guardian*, 18 February.

Trevelyan, John (1970). 'Film Censorship in Great Britain'. *Screen*, 11 (3): 19–30.

Variety (1969). 'Review: Joe'. 31 December. Available from http://variety.com/1969/film/reviews/joe-1200422205/ [Accessed July 7 2014].

Variety (1971). 'Review: Straw Dogs'. 31 December. Available from http://variety.com/1970/film/reviews/straw-dogs-2-1200422432/ [Accessed 8 March 2010].

Variety (1973). 'ABC's 5 Years of Film Production Profits and Losses'. 31 May, 3. Cited in http://en.wikipedia.org/wiki/Straw_Dogs_(1971_film) [Accessed 11 July 2014].

Virtue, Graeme (2017). 'Death Wish: Is the Bruce Willis Remake an Alt-Right Fantasy?'. [online] *The Guardian*. Available from https://www.theguardian.com/film/filmblog/2017/aug/08/eli-roth-death-wish-remake-alt-right-film-bruce-willis [Accessed 27 October 2017].

Walker, Alexander (1971). 'After This, Anything Goes...' *The Evening Standard*, 25 November.

Walker, Alexander (1975). 'Dead Simple, Dead Wrong'. *The Evening Standard*, 6 February.

Ward, Mark (2001). 'Columbine Families Sue Computer Games Makers'. *BBC News* [online] Available from http://news.bbc.co.uk/1/hi/sci/tech/1295920.stm [Accessed 3 June 2015].

Webb, Lawrence (2014). *The Cinema of Urban Crisis: Seventies Films and the Reinvention of the City*. Amsterdam: Amsterdam University Press.

Weber, Eugen (1964). *Varieties of Fascism*. London: D. Van Nostrand Company.

Weddle, David (1996). *Sam Peckinpah: If They Move... Kill 'Em!* London: Faber and Faber.

Wertham, Fredric (1954). *The Seduction of the Innocent*. New York: Rinehart & Company.

Whipple, Amy C. (2010). 'Speaking for Whom? The 1971 Festival of Light and the Search for the "Silent Majority"'. *Contemporary British History*, 24 (3): 319–339.

Williams, Gordon (2003). *Straw Dogs: Formerly Published as Siege at Trencher's Farm*. London: Bloomsbury Publishing.

Williams, Linda Ruth (1995). 'Women Can Only Misbehave – Peckinpah, "Straw Dogs", Feminism and Violence'. *Sight and Sound,* 5 (2): 26–7.

Williams, Linda Ruth and Hammond, Michael (2006). *Contemporary American Cinema*. Maidenhead: Open University Press.
Williams, Tony (1996). *Hearths of Darkness: The Family in the American Horror Film*. Cranbury: Associated University Press.
Wills, Garry (1997). *John Wayne: The Politics of Celebrity*. London: Faber & Faber.
Wilson, Cecil, (1971). 'Hoffman Horror in our Wild West'. *The Daily Mail*, 24 November.
Wilson, Cecil (1972). 'The Trouble with Harry....'. *The Daily Mail*, 29 March.
Wood, Robin (2003). *Hollywood from Vietnam to Reagan and Beyond*. New York: Colombia University.
Worland, Rick and Countryman, Edward (1998). 'The New Western American Historiography and the Emergence of the New American Western'. In Ed Buscombe and Robert E. Pearson (eds), *Back in the Saddle Again: New Essays on the Western*. London: BFI.
Wright, Will (1975). *Six-Guns and Society: A Structural Study of the Western*. Berkley: University of California Press.
Zakarin, Jordan (2012). 'Sandy Hook Shooter Linked to Violent 'Call of Duty' Games, Sparking Debate'. *The Hollywood Reporter*, [online] Available from http://www.hollywoodreporter.com/news/sandy-hook-shooter-linked-violent-404576 [Accessed 3 June 2015].
Žižek, Slavoj (2008). *Violence*. London: Profile Books Ltd.

INDEX

abject 23
abortion debate 52
alignment 12, 20, 21, 30, 57, 116, 123, 134, 138–9, 142–4, 158–60, 163, 166–7, 171, 174–6, 178–9, 181–2, 185
allegiance 21, 166, 174–5, 178–9, 209
Allen, Graham 25, 26
Altman, Rick 12, 78, 96
Andrews, Nigel 13, 48, 49, 89
angst, anxiety 3, 5, 16, 23, 50, 68, 80, 107, 125, 166, 192, 193, 195, 197, 207–8, 212
Ardrey, Robert 169
auteur debate 10, 32
Avildsen, John G. 1

Bandura, Albert 78, 209
Barr, Charles 49, 129, 136, 138
Bazin, Andre 113–14
BBFC, *see* British Board of Film Classification
Berger, John 22, 169
Big Heat, The 86–7
Birth of a Nation, The 206
Biskind, Peter 9, 17, 57, 113
Blackman, Lisa and Walkerdine, Valerie 125, 209
Blazing Saddles 5, 96
Bliss, Michael 10, 14, 138, 157
Bonnie and Clyde 4, 9, 10, 34, 74, 78
Bourke, Joanna 16, 17, 33, 61–3, 67–8
Boyle, Peter 32, 43, 47

as Joe Curran in *Joe* 1–2, 30, 43, 56, 81, 104, 107, 110, 129, 135, 152, 163, 192–4, 203, 207
as Wizard in *Taxi Driver* 152
Brannigan, Edward 20, 124, 174
Branston, Gill 21, 124
Bravo, Enrique 79
Bremer, Arthur 16
British Board of Film Classification (BBFC) 13, 49, 76
Bronson, Charles 32, 38, 95, 99, 147, 148, 150, 183, 207
as Paul Kersey in *Death Wish* 15, 37–9, 47, 51, 84, 85, 92–3, 99, 101, 104–8, 146–9, 152, 160, 162, 182–6, 189, 192–5, 197, 201, 203, 204, 213
Brownmiller, Susan 16, 60–2, 137
Bullard, Sara 17, 206
Bullitt 12, 81, 86–8
Buscombe, Ed 11, 93, 95, 98, 99, 114–15
Butler, Terence 10, 98
Byron, Stuart 100, 114
bystander effect, the 58

Callan, K. 164
as Mary Lou Curran in *Joe* 164–6
Canby, Vincent 41, 44–6, 48
CARA, *see* The Code and Ratings Administration
Casetti, Francesco 19–20, 124, 154
Cashin, Fergus 49, 50
castration 23, 90, 175, 178
Cawelti, John G.
generic transformation 12, 78, 82

on the Western 11, 27, 79, 95–6, 100–1, 106–8, 116, 118, 146
Chato's Land 99, 207
Chinatown 67, 78, 80
Christie, Ian 14, 48, 50
Churchwell, Sarah 17, 24, 67, 126, 206
civilization 8, 12, 89, 92, 99–104, 106, 114, 116, 120, 176, 191, 196, 201
Civil Rights movement 8, 17, 26, 54–5, 71, 85, 113, 190, 207, 213
A Clockwork Orange 49, 85, 123, 136
Clover, Carol 13, 22, 91–3, 167, 173
Cobley, Paul 11, 12, 78, 80, 82–5, 97, 147
Code and Ratings Administration, The (CARA) 75–6
Coleman, John 50
Columbine School Shootings 214
conspiracy, conspiracy thriller 11, 45, 80–2, 84–5
Coogan's Bluff 11, 12, 81, 87–8, 93, 97, 99, 103
Cook, David A. 11, 12, 95
Corkin, Stanley 14
Cornwall 5, 48, 93, 191, 201
Costa Pinto, António 7, 24, 126
Creed, Barbera 23, 90–1
crime 5, 7, 16–17, 38, 42, 51, 53–63
crime rates 16, 53–6
Crist, Judith 41
Crowther, Bosley 4

Daily Mail, The 42, 49–51
Death Wish 2–3, 9, 14–15, 23, 60, 63, 64, 67, 70, 74, 79–85, 90, 92, 200, 204, 207, 213–14
  critical reaction to 43–5, 47–8, 50–1
  and fascism 207
  and the gaze 160, 162, 182–6
  and madness 195, 197
  marketing of 37–9
  and otherness 200–1
  and rape 195, 197, 200

  and violence 122, 128, 129, 146–9
  and the Western 98, 99, 101, 104–8, 115
Death Wish (2018) 3
Death Wish II 213
Death Wish V: The Face of Death 3
Deliverance 86, 92, 173
De Niro, Robert 39, 40, 51, 145, 150
  as Travis Bickle in *Taxi Driver* 39, 40, 46, 57, 63, 68, 79, 81, 83–5, 90, 103–8, 115, 150–2, 161, 186–8, 192–5, 197, 200–4
Die Hard 212, 213
Dirty Harry 2, 9, 12, 15, 17, 23, 80–5, 87–8, 90, 195, 197, 200, 207, 210–11
  critical reaction to 42, 44–5, 48, 50, 57, 60
  and fascism 44–5, 83, 210–11
  and the gaze 159, 162, 179–82
  and madness 195, 197
  marketing of 35–7
  and otherness 201–2
  and race 10, 67, 92
  and rape 60, 63, 107, 115
  and violence 22, 127–9, 142–6
  and the Western 75, 93, 98–9, 101, 105–8, 113, 115
Django 116
Dr. No 75
Drummond, Philip 113, 115
Dunblane school shooting 214

Eastwood, Clint 5, 23, 35–7, 75, 87, 93, 99, 103, 118, 145, 150, 159, 179
  as Harry Callahan in *Dirty Harry* 35–7, 64, 83, 99, 101–6, 108, 111, 113, 115, 128, 142–6, 159–60, 179–82, 192–4, 197, 201, 203, 207, 211
Easy Rider 9, 57, 74, 97
Ebert, Roger 45, 48
Egan, Eddie 141
  as Simonson in *The French Connection* 142
Electra Glide in Blue 97
Ellis, John 26, 29

Elsaesser, Thomas 23
Epps, Gareth 43, 45
Equalizer, The 3
Equalizer 2, The 3
Eves, Vicki 77, 125, 209
Exorcist, The 37
Exterminator, The 3

fascism 2, 6–8, 19, 23, 24, 42–5, 50–2, 70, 74, 83, 126, 205–8, 210–11, 214, 215
FBI, *see* Federal Bureau of Investigation
Federal Bureau of Investigation (FBI) 55, 60–1, 111
film noir 78, 86, 87
First Blood 212, 213
Fistful of Dollars, A 37, 75, 118
Five Easy Pieces 74
focalization 20, 158, 160, 162, 174–5, 182, 186, 198
Folk Devils and Moral Panics (Cohen et al.) 16, 27, 59
For a Few Dollars More 37, 75
formalism 11, 27, 95, 100–11, 117
Foster, Jodie 3, 63, 214
  as Iris in *Taxi Driver* 63, 103, 105, 107, 150–2, 197
Foucault, Michel 52, 205
Frayling, Christopher 12, 117
French Connection, The 15, 17, 79–81, 84, 86–8, 90, 194, 195, 207
  critical reaction to 43, 45–6, 50, 70
  and fascism 207
  and the gaze 159, 162, 173–8
  and madness 194–5
  marketing of 34–5, 38
  and otherness 201, 203
  and race 67, 70, 92
  and violence 50, 51, 129, 140–2, 150
  and the Western 100, 106–8, 116
French Connection II, The 32 n.4, 179 n.3, 213
Freud, Sigmund 8, 18, 90, 124, 192, 193, 195, 209

Friedkin, William 15, 45, 140–1, 194
Friedman, Lester D. 17, 26, 55
Frontier Myth, the 94, 97, 148
Fuchs, Cynthia J. 14, 151, 200
Fuery, Patrick 6, 21, 124, 189–98, 202, 205, 211

gangster film 78, 150
Gardenia, Vincent 39
  as Lt. Ochoa 39, 195, 201, 213
Garfield, Brian 15, 148, 160
Garland, Arville 1, 213
gaze, the 123–4, 138, 143–4, 153–5, 157–63, 165–73, 175–83, 185–7, 189, 193, 196, 201, 211
generic innovation 11, 82–4
generic transformation 78–9, 82
Genovese, Kitty 17, 27, 56, 58–60, 63, 146, 210
genre 5, 7, 11–13, 27, 38, 45, 49–51, 75, 79–86, 89, 94–101, 106, 111, 113–14, 116–20, 129, 145, 149, 175, 200, 204, 211–12
George, Susan 13, 33, 49
  as Amy Sumner in *Straw Dogs* 13, 33, 50, 76, 110, 115, 139, 158, 167, 170
Gilbey, Ryan 9
Gilchrist, Roderick 51
Gilliat, Penelope 41, 48
Gillis, Judge Joseph A. 1
Gliserman, Marty 15, 195
Godfather Part II, The 150
Goetz, Bernard 122, 205, 213–14
Goldberger, Paul 17, 68
Good, The Bad and The Ugly, The 75
Gow, Gordon 51
Graduate, The 9, 32, 72, 88
grand narratives/metanarratives 23, 203, 208, 211
Great Escape, The 147
Greenfield, Pierre 139
Grist, Leighton 14
Guardian, The 42, 49, 50
Guess Who's Coming to Dinner 74

INDEX

Haberski Jr., Raymond J. 4, 29, 40–1
Hackman, Gene 32, 34, 140
   as 'Popeye' Doyle in *The French Connection* 34–5, 43, 50, 87, 103, 104, 106–8, 111, 141–2, 159, 173–9, 192–5, 197, 200–1, 203, 207, 213
Hall, Stuart 16, 27, 60
Hard-Boiled Detective thriller 79
Harris, Leonard 85
   as Charles Palantine 85, 103, 108, 187, 192
Harris, Mark 32, 36
Haskell, Molly 12, 22, 81, 85–6, 88
Henderson, Brian 115
Henney, Del 63
   as Charlie Venner 63, 138, 139, 158, 167, 169
hermeneutic code 31, 33, 156, 163
High Noon 95, 99, 113–16, 127, 196
Hills Have Eyes, The 90, 173
Hinkley Jr., John 205, 213–14
hippy counterculture 1, 30–1, 57, 84, 97, 103, 107, 155–7, 163, 165–6, 192, 196
Hoberman, J. 65
Hodge, Bob and Tripp, David 22, 123, 128
Hoffman, Dustin 5, 32–3, 37, 39, 49, 98, 139, 140, 150, 157, 158, 207
   as David Sumner in *Straw Dogs* 5, 32–4, 45, 70, 76, 81, 93, 103, 105, 137–9, 157–8, 166–73, 191–4, 196–7, 201, 203
homology 208
horror genre 13, 38, 49, 69, 89–93, 97, 161, 173
Horsley, Jake 144, 145, 214
hyphenate groups 63, 206
hysteria 6, 21, 24, 124, 190, 195–7

ideal law 115, 195
identification, process of 6, 14, 19–22, 44–5, 121–4, 128, 139, 141, 154–7, 159–88, 199–200, 202, 208, 210
In the Heat of the Night 6, 12, 72, 87
interpellation 99, 125, 154–5

intertextuality 27, 30, 54, 99, 150–1
I Spit on Your Grave 91, 173
Izod, John 23, 125, 200

Jet 43
Joe 1–2, 9, 14–15, 55–6, 70, 80–1, 84, 90
   critical reception of 43, 47–8
   and fascism 207
   and the gaze 155–6, 162–6
   and madness 194–6
   marketing of 30–1
   and otherness 200–3
   and violence 129–35
   and the Western 92, 99, 101, 104, 106–8, 110–11, 116
Johnson, Lyndon B. 63, 115
Johnson, Paul 16, 54–6
Jung, Carl 23
Jungian archetypes 125, 200

KAB, *see* Keep America Beautiful
Kael, Pauline 4–5, 26, 41
   on *Dirty Harry* 44, 45
   on *The French Connection* 45–7, 124
   and *Straw Dogs* 42, 44, 137
   and *Taxi Driver* 43, 46
Keathley, Christian 9, 24, 70, 74
Keep America Beautiful (KAB) 30, 72, 120
Keitel, Harvey 103
   as Sport in *Taxi Driver* 103, 150–1, 192, 200
Kendrick, James 21, 146
Kennedy, John F. 36, 61, 73, 94, 115, 211
keying 21, 166
Kirschner, Jonathan 58, 61
Kiss of Death 87
Kitses, Jim 11–12, 27, 95, 100–6, 108, 116
KKK, *see* Ku Klux Klan
Klemersrud, Julie 47–8
Kolker, Robert Philip 14, 150, 161
Korean War 81, 152
Krämer, Peter 10, 88, 125
Kristeva, Julia 23
Ku Klux Klan, The 17, 206

INDEX

Lacan, Jacques 18, 193, 194
  mirror stage 124, 174, 189, 202, 208
  on psychosis 190, 194, 198
Langford, Barry 9
Last House on the Left, The 13, 90
Law Abiding Citizen 3
law and order 2, 3, 5, 7–8, 17, 26, 42, 53–71, 80, 82, 85, 192, 207, 215
Lebeau, Vicky 18
Le Bon, Gustave 8, 209
Leech, Michael 13, 73
Leone, Sergio 12, 37, 75, 99, 116–18, 211
Lethal Weapon 212
Lev, Peter 1, 9, 15, 26, 35, 47, 80, 84, 201
libido 115, 195
Life Magazine 38
Little Big Man 12, 96, 98
Lovell, Alan 22, 128, 153, 211–12
Love Story 74
lynching 66–8, 146
Lyotard, Jean-François 23, 203

McArthur, Colin 51
McCabe and Mrs Miller 74
McDermott, Patrick 31
  as Frank Russo in *Joe* 31, 84, 100, 107, 115, 128, 134–5, 156–7, 163, 165–6, 196, 200
McKenna, T.P. 85
  as Major John Scott in *Straw Dogs* 34, 85, 98, 110, 139, 173
Madigan 12, 87–8
madness 7, 40, 105, 124–5, 150, 189–98, 202, 205, 211
Magnificent Seven, The 99, 147, 207
Magnum Force 213
Mailer, Norman 65
Malcolm, Derek 51
Manifest Destiny 15, 94, 211
Mann, Anthony 101, 104–5
Manning, R., Levine, M., and Collins, A. 58–9
Manson Family 17, 56–7

Man Who Shot Liberty Valance, The 24, 96
Man with the Golden Arm, The 75
Marseilles 141, 159
Mask, Mia 15, 100, 140
Mean Streets 114, 150
Mechanic, The 38, 147
Mendik, Xavier 15, 84
Mercer, Kobena 23, 125, 202
metanarrative, *see* grand narrative
Metz, Christian 18–19, 96, 121, 124, 174, 187, 189
Midnight Cowboy 32, 74
Milioria, Maria T. 14
Milne, Tom 49, 50
Miranda, Ernesto 17
Miranda Rights 17, 26, 63–4, 81, 102
mirror stage, *see* Lacan
modality 7, 22, 35, 37, 123, 128, 129, 135, 140–2, 145, 147, 152, 162, 173–4, 179
Moore, Robin 15, 35, 141
moral panic 5, 7, 16, 24, 27, 38, 51, 58, 59, 214–15
Morris, Nigel 118
Mortimer, Barbera 203
Motion Picture Association of America (MPAA) 4, 75
Motion Picture Production Code 4, 13, 75
MPAA, *see* Motion Picture Association of America
Ms .45 3
Mulvey, Laura 18, 19, 22, 124, 166, 175, 189
Murphy, Stephen 49, 76
Murray, William 44, 135
My Darling Clementine 87
My Lai Massacre 47, 69–70, 83, 97

narrative image 7, 14, 22, 26, 29, 40, 128, 139–41, 145, 147, 150, 155–6, 163–6, 173–5, 183
narrative structure 99–101, 108, 111, 122, 150, 156–7, 159, 161–4, 173, 175, 179, 182, 186, 189, 196, 200, 210–11, 213

narratology   118–19, 123
nationalism   7, 52, 205
Native Americans   23, 30, 71, 72, 96, 118, 120, 148, 200, 207, 211
Nazism   42, 52, 85, 205, 206, 208, 211
neuroses   124, 190–3, 202
New Hollywood   2, 9, 21, 26, 78
New York   14, 17, 34, 38, 40, 47, 50, 56, 58–9, 61–2, 93, 99, 101, 103–4, 111, 147–8, 150–2, 159–60, 183, 188, 201, 210
New York Times, The   58–9
Nietzsche, Friedrich   45
Night of the Living Dead   90
Nixon, Richard   5, 17, 54–6, 70
Nordicism   206–7
Nystrom, Derek   9, 210

objectification   138, 160, 162, 187, 201
Oedipal complex/Theory   18, 124, 196
Once Upon a Time in the West   99, 117
Orwell, George   51, 52, 126, 205
Oswald, Lee Harvey   73, 75
other, the/otherness   6, 23, 70–2, 83, 85, 91, 93, 100, 101, 111, 114, 120, 122, 125, 199–203, 208–10, 215

Palmer, Jerry   11, 79–85
Parallax View, The   74, 80
paratextuality   26, 27, 40, 42, 154
Passmore, Kevin   126, 205–8
Patrick, Dennis   1
  as Bill Compton in *Joe*   1, 31, 81, 84, 104, 107, 110, 115, 128, 134, 156, 194, 203
Peckinpah, Sam   10, 13, 22, 32, 44, 70, 75, 98, 105–6, 135–6, 138–40, 157, 169
Petley, Julian   210, 214
phallic anxiety   166
phallic imagery   138
Pirie, David   50
Play Misty for Me   38, 145

point of view techniques   134, 138, 143–4, 148, 152, 157–61, 165, 167, 170–2, 175, 180–2, 187
Police, the   15, 17, 26, 35, 38, 44, 51, 53, 58–65, 70–1, 80–1, 84, 87, 99, 103, 109, 113, 141–2, 173, 179, 183, 192, 194, 201, 207
Police Procedural   151, 173
Police thriller   11–13, 27, 81, 86–7, 97–8
postcolonialism   208
postmodernism   79, 203
Powell, Dilys   51
Powell, Larry and Garrett, Tom   4, 30, 31
Predator   213
Prince, Stephen   10, 13, 21, 22, 70, 75–6, 78, 117, 123, 127–8, 136, 138–9, 169
Prisoners   3
Psycho   138, 140
psychopathy   6, 46, 124, 197
psychosis   101, 106, 190, 194–5, 198
Puritan Captivity Narrative   89, 93, 99, 103, 107, 115

Quigley Publishing   32 n.4, 150 n.5

race/racism   7, 9, 11, 45–6, 50, 66–8, 70–1, 83, 96, 114, 165, 174, 197, 207
Rambo: First Blood Part II   212, 213
Rambo III   213
rape   15–16, 22, 33, 44–5, 49–50, 55, 60–4, 66–8, 76, 90–1, 93, 104, 107, 115, 137–9, 145–8, 166–7, 169, 170, 172, 182, 197
Rawhide   99
Reagan, Ronald   122, 212, 214
Rear Window   175
Reiner, Robert   12, 87
Rey, Fernando   103
  as Charnier in *The French Connection*   103, 108, 142, 175–9, 194, 203
Richardson, Michael   125, 199
Riefenstahl, Leni   42, 45
road movie, the   97, 161

Robertson, James C. 13, 76
Robinson, Andrew 35
    as Scorpio in *Dirty Harry* 35, 36, 57, 69, 83, 85, 102, 104–7, 115, 127, 142–6, 159, 179–82, 197, 200, 201, 203
Rocky 212
Rocky III 213
Roizman, Owen 141
Rolling Thunder 3
Rosemary's Baby 38
Rosen, Jane 50
Rubin, Martin 11, 86–7, 97–8
Ruby, Jack 73, 75
Ryan, Michael and Kellner, Douglas 10, 200, 212

Sandy Hook Elementary School 214
San Francisco 99, 102, 104, 142, 145, 179, 182
Santoni, Reni 132
    as Chico Gonzalez in *Dirty Harry* 144, 180
Sarandon, Susan 1
    as Melissa Compton in *Joe* 31, 84, 101, 104, 107, 110, 115, 134–5, 155–6, 162, 163, 166, 196, 203
Sarris, Andrew 26, 41
Scheider, Roy 108
    as 'Cloudy' Russo 108, 141, 142, 159, 174–5, 197
Schickel, Richard 41, 43, 46, 47
schizothymia 191
Schrader, Paul 3, 40, 100, 114
scopophilia 19, 144, 158, 166, 169, 171, 192
Scorsese, Martin 2, 4, 14, 40, 51, 114, 151, 161, 162, 186
Searchers, The 95, 100, 113–16, 150, 190–1, 195
Shane 95, 113–16
Shedlin, Michael 15, 45, 141
Shepherd, Cybil 103
    as Betsy in *Taxi Driver* 103–5, 107, 115, 151, 186–8, 194–5, 197, 200
Siege at Trencher's Farm 15
Siegel, Don 2, 4, 22, 88, 99, 181
Simkin, Stevie 14, 32, 50, 76

Slane, Andrea 24, 52, 208
Slocum, David J. 122
Slotkin, Richard 11, 17, 66–7, 89, 94, 97, 115, 119, 148–50, 211
Small, Melvin 16
Smith, Murray 21
Smith, Paul 12, 23, 44, 52, 66, 94, 99, 117, 118, 210–11, 213
Soldier Blue 12, 96
Sorrento, Christopher 15
Sound of Music, The 74, 88
Spaghetti Western 12, 95, 116–18
Speck, Richard 17, 56–7
spectatorship 2, 6–8, 18–19, 21, 22, 25, 121, 123–4, 128, 140, 193, 197–8
    active 19, 166, 176, 184–5, 190
    passive 19, 51, 52, 165, 176, 189, 194
Star Chamber, The 3
Star Wars 10, 114, 118, 129, 212
Stone Killer, The 37, 38, 147
Straw Dogs 2, 13–15
    critical reaction to 10, 13, 42, 44–6, 48–9
    and fascism 5, 42, 207–8
    and the gaze 157, 159, 162, 166–74
    and the horror genre 89–91, 93
    marketing of 32–4
    and otherness 200, 202
    and rape 60, 63, 137–9, 169–70
    and the thriller genre 80, 81, 84, 85
    and violence 10, 22–3, 44–6, 48–9, 70, 76, 123, 135–40, 146, 148, 200
    and the Western genre 98, 103, 105–8, 110–11, 116
Street, Joe 15, 16, 68, 144, 181
structuralism 108
subjectivity 20–2, 138–40, 142–4, 148, 159–62, 166, 169–71, 173–4, 180–1, 186–7
subject positions 2, 20, 142, 154–5, 159, 162
Support Your Local Sheriff! 96
Symbolic Order 190, 198

Talbot, Paul 15, 99, 205
Targets 57

INDEX

Tasker, Yvonne   11, 15, 23, 96, 145, 212–13
Taubin, Amy   151, 161
Taxi Driver   2–3, 10, 14, 16, 214
   critical reaction to   46, 51
   and fascism   15
   and the gaze   161–2, 186–8
   and the horror genre   90, 92
   and madness   193, 197, 198
   marketing of   39–40
   and otherness   6, 200–4
   and the thriller genre   80–5
   and violence   63, 67–8, 70, 128–9, 149–52
   and the Western   94, 95, 100, 103–6, 108, 114–16, 118
Terminator 2: Judgement Day   213
Texas Chainsaw Massacre, The   13, 89, 90, 149, 173
Thelma & Louise   213
Thinkell, A.   48
Thomas, Bill   1
Thompson, David and Christie, Ian   14, 153, 162
Thomsett, Sally   85
   as Janice Heddon in *Straw Dogs*   85, 139, 158, 169, 171–2
Three Days of the Condor   80
Timm, Jane C.   214
Todorov, Tzvetan   100, 118, 123, 191
Tomkins, Jane   12, 95, 111–13
Torode, John   50
Touch of Evil   86, 87
Trevelyan, John   13, 76–7
Triumph of the Will   42, 205, 211
Trump, Donald   214
Two-Lane Blacktop   97
Two Mules for Sister Sara   99

ultraviolence   123

Vaughan, Peter   92
   as Tom Heddon in *Straw Dogs*   92, 139, 173
video games   214–15
Vietcong   72, 94
Vietnam War   8, 9, 11, 13, 17, 26, 35, 53–4, 68–72, 74, 89–90, 92–4, 96, 101, 104, 113–15, 120, 152, 207, 211–13
vigilantism   3, 17, 26, 53, 56, 66–9, 92, 211

Walker, Alexander   49, 51
Walking Tall   3
Wallace, George   16, 56, 165, 207
Warner, David   84
   as Henry Niles in *Straw Dogs*   84, 110, 139, 169, 172–3
Watergate scandal   4, 53, 82
Watts Riots   64–5
Wayne, John   5, 35, 99, 113, 191
Webb, Lawrence   17, 79
Weber, Eugen   7, 24, 126, 205
Weddle, David   14, 98, 137
Wertham, Dr Fredric   77, 209, 215
Western, the   5–8, 11–12, 23, 27, 33, 39, 51, 68, 72, 75, 78–9, 87, 93–120, 139, 146–50, 170, 179, 191, 194–6, 199–201, 203–4, 211–12
Whitehouse, Mary   77, 209
Whitman, Charles Joseph   17, 56–7
Wild Bunch, The   86, 96, 98, 153
wilderness   8, 12, 71, 88, 89, 100, 101, 103–4, 106–8, 114, 116, 118, 119, 170, 176, 196, 200–1
Williams, Linda Ruth   9, 137
Williams, Linda Ruth and Hammond, Michael   9
Williams, Tony   13, 17, 69, 89–90, 92, 93
Wills, Garry   35
Wilson, Cecil   49, 50
Winner, Michael   38–9, 51, 99, 147, 148
Wood, Robin   3, 10, 74
Worland, Rick and Countryman, Edward   11, 96
World War Two   35, 70, 90, 129, 152
Wright, Will   27, 95, 108, 110, 113, 116

Z   45
Žižek, Slavoj   125, 199, 202
Zodiac killer, the   15–16